TALLIES AND TRENDS

For the priceless
Gordy, Kay, Josh, Jesse, and Pam

TALLIES AND TRENDS

THE LATE BABYLONIAN COMMODITY PRICE LISTS

by
Alice Louise Slotsky
and
Ronald Wallenfels

CDL Press
Bethesda, Maryland
2009

LIBRARY OF CONGRESS CATALOGING-IN-PUBLICATION DATA

Slotsky, Alice Louise.
Tallies and trends : the late Babylonian commodity price lists / by Alice Louise Slotsky and Ronald Wallenfels.
p. cm.
ISBN 978-1-934309-23-0
1. Prices—Iraq—Babylon (Extinct city)--History. 2. Babylon (Extinct city)--Commerce--History. I. Wallenfels, Ronald. II. Title.

HB221.S52 2009
935--dc22 2009044178

Published by CDL Press, P.O. Box 34454, Bethesda, MD 20827;
E-Mail: cdlpress@erols.com; website: www.cdlpress.com; Fax: 253-484-5542

ISBN 978-1934309-230

TABLE OF CONTENTS

TABLES

SELECTED BIBLIOGRAPHIC AND OTHER ABBREVIATIONS

Cuneiform texts are cited according to the abbreviations of *The Chicago Assyrian Dictionary* (CAD). In addition, the following abbreviations are used:

AD I — A. J. Sachs and H. Hunger, *Astronomical Diaries and Related Texts from Babylonia. I: Diaries from 652 B.C. to 262 B.C.* Österreichische Akademie der Wissenschaften. Philosophisch-Historische Klasse, Denkenschriften 185. Wien: Österreichischen Akademie der Wissenschaften, 1988.

AD II — A. J. Sachs and H. Hunger, *Astronomical Diaries and Related Texts from Babylonia. II: Diaries from 261 B.C. to 165 B.C.* Österreichische Akademie der Wissenschaften. Philosophisch-Historische Klasse, Denkenschriften 210. Wien: Österreichischen Akademie der Wissenschaften, 1989.

AD III — A.J. Sachs and H. Hunger, *Astronomical Diaries and Related Texts from Babylonia. III: Diaries from 164 B.C. to 61 B.C.* Österreichische Akademie der Wissenschaften. Philosophisch-Historische Klasse, Denkenschriften 247. Wien: Österreichischen Akademie der Wissenschaften, 1996.

AD V — H. Hunger, *Astronomical Diaries and Related Texts from Babylonia. V: Lunar and Planetary Texts.* Österreichische Akademie der Wissenschaften. Philosophisch-Historische Klasse, Denkenschriften 299. Wien: Österreichischen Akademie der Wissenschaften, 2001.

AHw — W. von Soden, *Akkadisches Handwörterbuch.* Wiesbaden: Otto Harrassowitz, 1965–

CAD — *The Assyrian Dictionary of the Oriental Institute of the University of Chicago.* Chicago/Glükstadt, 1956–

Finkel and van der Spek BCHP — I. Finkel and R. J. van der Spek, "Babylonian Chronicles of the Hellenistic Period." *Livius: Articles on Ancient History.* http://www.livius.org/cg-cm/chronicles/chron00.html

FGrHist — F. Jacoby, *Die Fragmente der griechischen Historiker.* Fifteen volumes. Leiden: Brill, 1999.

Jursa Fest. Walker
: M. Jursa, "*Florilegium babyloniacum*" in Cornelia Wunsch, ed., *Mining the Archives: Festschrift for Christopher Walker on the Occasion of his 60th Birthday*. Babylonische Archive 1. Dresden: Islet, 2002, pp. 107–30.

RIAA^2
: T. Boiy, "RIAA^2 293-300. Hellenistic Legal Documents from Uruk in the 'Royal Museums of Art and History' (Brussels)," *Akkadica* 124 (2003): 19-64.

OTHER ABBREVIATIONS AND SYMBOLS

A.E.	Arsacid Era
AR	silver
B.C.E.	Before the Common Era
bl	blank
BM	sigla of tablets in the collections of the British Museum
ca.	circa
C.E.	Common Era
cf.	compare
col(s).	column(s)
l(l).	line(s)
Le.E.	left edge
Lo.E.	lower edge
MN	month name
m	unknown month
n.d.	no date
nn	numeral
no.	(unknown) number
o(bv).	obverse
p(p).	page(s)
pq	poor quality (NU.DÙ.MEŠ)
r.	reigned
R.E.	right edge
r(ev).	reverse
Rm	sigla of tablets in the collections of the British Museum (Rassam)
RN	royal name
S.E.	Seleucid Era
Sp	sigla of tablets in the collections of the British Museum (Spartali)
stA	staters of Arsaces
stD	staters of Demetrius
U.E.	upper edge

var.	variant
x	undecipherable sign
y	unknown year
@b	at the beginning of the month (AŠ SAG ITU)
@m	in the middle of the month (AŠ $MURUB_4$ ITU)
@e	at the end of the month (AŠ TIL ITU)
(nn)→m	(from day nn) to the middle of the month (TA nn EN $MURUB_4$ ITU)
(nn)→e	(from day nn) to the end of the month (TA nn EN TIL ITU)
+	marks join
=	marks duplicate tablet
< >	marks scribal omission
{ }	marks scribal plus
[ ]	marks break (and restoration)
( )	marks interpolation
⌜ ⌝	marks partially preserved sign
!	marks corrected reading
*	marks reconstructed/unattested form
?	uncertain

N.B. Numbers in the market quotations and date formulas are kept in sexagesimal form; market values are given as commodity amounts per shekel(s) of silver; calendar dates, in the form day/month/year RN, are days in the Babylonian month as recorded on the tablets.

ACKNOWLEDGMENTS

This volume grew out of a collaborative study of the eighteen mostly unpublished Late Babylonian commodity price-only tablets in the British Museum. The purpose of this project was two-fold. First, we wanted to prepare text editions of all the preserved tablets in the corpus. Second, we wanted to pursue the perplexing matter of if and/or how these tablets and their market values were related to the prodigious arsenal of ostensibly similar price quotations in the Astronomical Diaries.

We especially want to thank Hermann Hunger, who greatly honored us by putting this project into our hands and who provided a seemingly endless reservoir of both encouragement and concrete assistance over the years. He unstintingly relinquished all pioneering materials left by the legendary Abe Sachs. He defined for us the scope of the available corpus; and by adding and subtracting texts from the list throughout the years, he made our search for additional price tablets minimal. He answered our countless questions with precision and speed. He patiently awaited the long overdue completion of our work without a nagging word.

We are truly indebted also to the late Abraham Sachs, whose neat and elegant worksheets were an inspiration, as well as the groundwork of this study. His polished lines of transliterations for many of the tablets gave us an immediate advantage in copying and translating all eighteen. His annotative remarks in the margins were both endearing and on the mark.

We had another giant head start from Donald J. Wiseman, whose article (Wiseman, 1988), in the Sachs Festschrift, "A Note on Some Prices in Late Babylonian Astronomical Diaries," presented seven of the price tablets in copies and identified other possible additions to the corpus. Also invaluable were the Pinches copies, the Strassmaier copies, and photographs taken by The British Museum.

Christopher Walker has our gratitude for so many things: finding price lists of which we had no knowledge; recognizing those tablets that turned out to be something else; advising us on the readings of signs; identifying the scribal peculiarities; and supplying Museum Acquisition numbers. His many tablet joins condensed the original list of texts considerably. In addition, Jonathan Taylor, at our request, collated several tablet fragments permitting us to suggest a new join. We thank the British Museum for its hospitality and the Trustees for permission to publish the texts and photos.

Text 3A was first brought to our attention in January 2009 by Paola Corò, who most graciously relinquished her rights to publish this tablet so that it might more appropriately be included in the present study. Christopher Walker and Irving Finkel most kindly provided additional collations for this poorly preserved fragment known to us only from digital photographs.

The late David Pingree read an early version of the manuscript with scrutiny and considered every statement and inference with conscientious care. It is to his substantive criticism that we owe the integrity of this work, for he not only contributed crucial information and corrected errors but pointed out examples of indulgent speculation and downright flights of fancy.

We above all thank those patient and supportive members of our respective families who endured our absences while we worked at the British Museum and our preoccupation with the project when at home. Finally, we thank each other for an amiable and fruitful collaboration.

For all the merits of this volume, we are sincerely grateful to all of you.

Alice Louise Slotsky
Yale University

Ronald Wallenfels
New York University
Monmouth University

INTRODUCTION

When Abraham J. Sachs first scavenged the basement of the British Museum in the 1950s in search of unpublished astronomical cuneiform material, one of the collections of tablets that caught his eye was a small group of commodity price lists. Together with some newly rediscovered Pinches hand copies,[1] they intrigued him because of their likeness to the monthly summaries of market quotations in the Astronomical Diaries (Sachs and Hunger 1988–96; Slotsky 1997). Although he could not fathom their purpose or source, he was struck by the choice of commodities, their fixed order, and the metrology, all of which had the ring of Diary reports. Always curious about cases in which specific classes of data appear to have been abstracted from the Astronomical Diaries or from mutual sources available for such data, he began to prepare copies, transliterations, and translations, making pithy notes in the margins of his otherwise elegant worksheets. Unfortunately, he did not get to finish the edition of the tablets or publish any conclusions because of his untimely death. In 1988, Donald J. Wiseman, as a tribute to his colleague, published hand copies of seven of the tablets[2] in his contribution to the volume, *A Scientific Humanist* (Wiseman 1988), honoring Sachs' memory, and he challenged Assyriologists to complete Sachs' pioneering work

At the time, a dozen price-only tablets had been identified. Since then, the number in the corpus has been both supplemented by new finds in the British Museum's stores and shrunk by misidentifications and joins. There are now eighteen texts, almost all fragmentary. We can date the contents of eleven, but the remaining seven remain problematic. We are lucky to be that fortunate. Typically, the data in these tablets were dated by month within a regnal year with the year name written at the very beginning (the top) of the tablet and/or

---

1 Text 1; BM 35089 in Text 5; BM 35123 in Text 6; Text 7; BM 34686 in Text 9.

2 Text 2 (individual copies of BM 36847 and 37353 before join); Texts 4 (two separate copies); 13; 14; 15; BM 37054 in Text 16.

at the end (frequently the bottom). The edges are the most vulnerable parts of any tablet, and these broken texts only rarely retain a top and/or bottom. By relying on the presence of any intact written dates, we can say only that the prices in these tablets span 186 regnal years at the least. They yield commodity prices intermittently from I/23 S.E. to II/209 S.E. (289 to 103 BCE), although one undatable tablet is likely Achaemenid. All attempts to securely date the contents of the remaining six tablets by comparison with data in the Astronomical Diaries are suggestive at best.

The existence of these commodity-price tablets has been mentioned in a number of publications about Babylonian prices since Wiseman's paper appeared. The unanimous consensus, reached without knowing anything about them other than that they occupied space in the British Museum, was that these lists of prices were connected to the Astronomical Diaries and, moreover, that one was the source of the other (Wiseman 1988, 365; Sachs and Hunger 1988-96, I: 34; Slotsky 1997, 8; Vargyas 1997, 352, note 1). This judgment seemed logical at the time, given the number of similarities between the two groups of price lists first noted by Sachs. As we worked with the details of the market quotations, however, we began to be struck by dramatic differences that were not obvious at first glance, dissimilarities that now seem so consequential that they call into question any such link. Preliminary conclusions now appear to have been overly simplistic and need to be re-examined. At the same time, these deviations raise a larger question about the inner workings and goals of Late Babylonian scholarship.

In spite of the magnitude, complexity, and sophistication of the work of the Late Babylonian scribes, many modern scholars try to understand the scholarship of this period in just one cultural dimension, one in which all intellectual scribal activity was ultimately connected and related in a single, integrated, and continuous system of fixed or standardized major genres of work. How, then, does one account for activity that is decidedly outside of such a grand scheme, being either separate from, unrelated to, or parallel to, yet independent of, any such major work. For example, within the body of astronomical omens, an extraneous series of so-called *aḫû* omens existed alongside the main series of omens, *Enūma Anu Enlil*. The *aḫû* omens were quoted and used, copied, and considered as valid as the omens in the major collection, although they could be quite different, even in phraseology and content (Rochberg-Halton 1987; Hunger and Pingree 1999, 21). The *aḫû* omens were not omens that were excluded from *Enūma Anu Enlil* but, rather, a supplementary source of additional material (Rochberg-Halton 1987, 327–37; Lieberman 1990, 308). In fact, most *Enūma Anu Enlil* tablets are not canonical; their contents are often compilations from other sources. Another case is provided by some of the nominal "atypical" astronomical texts of the Achaemenid period in which scribes tried simultaneous but different approaches of no seemingly uniform character, some not preserved in the later stream of tradition, to create mathematical prediction schemes for astronomical phenomena (Neugebauer and Sachs 1967, 183–214; idem 1969, 92–111;

Neugebauer 1975 I: 541).[3] Even as far as astronomical observation itself is concerned, tablets show that observing and recording independent of any major body of work co-existed with that carried out for the main projects: the Astronomical Diaries, Ephemerides, Almanacs, and Goal Year texts. Representative of these would be those texts containing observed dates and names of nearest Normal stars for planetary phenomena that either deviate from normal recording procedures or contain unusual material, making it doubtful that these tablets were written in the service of the principal enterprises (Hunger and Pingree 1999, 174, 178). In fact, not all astronomical activity for the major projects was inveterate. Ephemerides based on a variety of mathematical models of System A have many variants; the contents of System B tables differ; some Diaries are unlike others in content; and planetary tables for the same function are disparate. As much as modern scholarship can attempt to group things, there was no one universally followed system. Babylonian scientific investigation was carried out both within and without a fixed tradition, and the intellectual activity that fell outside the main stream of traditional scholarship resulted in an expanded body of authoritative knowledge regardless of its independent nature.

A priori, one might easily suppose that the tablets presented here were connected in some fashion to the Astronomical Diaries. There are so many unmistakable similarities. It is the number of significant departures from Diary practice, however, that are suspect, and these are fundamental to any valid conclusion. It is necessary to consider whether the deviations are mere anomalies or whether they are grave enough to undercut any thought of a direct link to the Diaries. If the latter is true, it is likely that one list of prices did not come from the other. In that case, instead of drawing a link between the two sources, one could speculate that the discrepancies demonstrate that the tablets of prices were a separate but parallel set of price records compiled independently of the Diaries. The implication would then be that the price tablets, like the *aḫû* omens, the "atypical" texts, and the independent astronomical texts, are one more indication of scribal scholarship outside the traditional repertoire. In the following pages, these issues will be examined as we explore both corpora individually and in juxtaposition with each other.

3 "Atypical" texts, which continue into the Seleucid period, certainly go back to the seventh century. Some can be grouped together, but we have no "corpus," because no archive of these texts has been found.

INVENTORY OF TEXTS

Price equivalences in units of silver (AR) for barley (b), dates (d), mustard (m), cress (c), sesame (s), and wool (w).

BY PUBLICATION NUMBER

No.	*Museum No.* (BM)	*Date*	*Contents*	*Equivalence* (AR)
1	34712	11–15 (RN?)	b d m c s w	1 mina
2	36847 (+) 37353	23–26? S.E.	b d m [...]	1 mina
3	32937b	46–48 S.E.	b	1 shekel
3A	95313	58–[...] S.E.	b d m c [...]	1(?) shekel
4	36730	69?(71!)–71[*sic*] S.E.	b d	1 shekel
5	35089 + 45724	... 142–143 S.E.	b d m c s w	2 shekels
6	34073 + 35123	173–175 S.E.	b d m c s w	2 shekels
7	34598	Month VIII, 178–185 S.E.	[d]	2 shekels
8	33479 + 33639	184–190 S.E.	b d	2 shekels
9	34686 + 35604	186–187 S.E.	b d s	2 shekels
10	55535	194?–195? S.E.	d	?
11	35710	11/XII/208–II/209 S.E.	b	1 shekel
12	33023 + 33027 (+) 46161	n.d. (Arsacid?)	b d m c s w	2 shekels
13	36960	n.d. (Seleucid?)	b d	2(?) shekels
14	36989	n.d. (Seleucid?)	[b] d	?
15	37034	n.d. (Seleucid?)	[... d?] m c s w	1 shekel
16	37054 + 40100	n.d. (Seleucid?)	[... d?] s	1(?) shekel
17	46138	n.d. (Arsacid?)	b d s	?

BY MUSEUM NUMBER

Museum No. (BM)	*Acquisition No.*	*Text No.*
32937b	78-5-31,26b	3
33023	78-10-15,4	12
33027	78-10-15,8	12
33479	Rm IV 33	8
33639	Rm IV 195	8
34073	Sp 169 + Sp II 653	6
34598	Sp II 72	7

34686	Sp II 173 + Sp II 956	9
34712	Sp II 201 + Sp II 785	1
35089	Sp II 627	5
35123	Sp II 666	6
35604	Sp III 114	9
35710	Sp III 229	11
36730	80-6-17,463	4
36847	80-6-17,587	2
36960	80-6-17,701	13
36989	80-6-17,733	14
37034	80-6-17,778	15
37054	80-6-17,798	16
37353	80-6-17,1110	2
40100	81-2-1,65	16
45724	81-7-6,131	5
46138	81-7-6,593	17
46161	81-7-6,622	12
55535	82-7-4,118	10
95313	1901-10-12,966	3A

BY ACQUISITION NUMBER

Acquisition No.	*Museum No.* (BM)	*Text No.*
Rm IV 33	33479	8
Rm IV 195	33639	8
Sp 169 (+ Sp II 653)	34073	6
Sp II 72	34598	7
Sp II 173 (+ Sp II 956)	34686	9
Sp II 201 (+ Sp II 785)	34712	1
Sp II 627	35089	5
Sp II 653 (+ Sp 169)	34073	6
Sp II 666	35123	6
Sp II 785 (+ Sp II 201)	34712	1
Sp II 956 (+ Sp II 173)	34686	9
Sp III 114	35604	9
Sp III 229	35710	11
78-5-31,26b	32937b	3
78-10-15,4	33023	12
78-10-15,8	33027	12

80-6-17,463	36730	4
80-6-17,587	36847	2
80-6-17,701	36960	13
80-6-17,733	36989	14
80-6-17,778	37034	15
80-6-17,798	37054	16
80-6-17,1110	37353	2
81-2-1,65	40100	16
81-7-6,131	45724	5
81-7-6,593	46138	17
81-7-6,622	46161	12
82-7-4,118	55535	10
1901-10-12,966	95313	3A

1. The Price Tablets and Their Market Quotations

1.1 — The Price Tablets

Many of the eighteen tablets presented here first came to light in the early 1950s when Abraham Sachs toiled at the British Museum, identifying and translating astronomical cuneiform texts long buried away in the museum's tablet rooms. Among some tens of thousands of tablets and fragments of an astronomical and mathematical nature, he discovered tablets, termed here (commodity) price tablets, that exclusively listed commodity price equivalents, one quotation after another, typically month after month, year after year.

Being intermingled with the scientific texts, almost all of which are believed to have come from that still unlocated astronomical archive in Babylon (Neugebauer 1975, I: 352; Slotsky 1997, 2), these commodity-price tablets likely did, too, but this is merely an educated guess. On the basis of their acquisition and/or museum numbers, it can be surmised that just nine of the twenty-nine originally acquired fragments—now joined into the eighteen discrete tablets—were actually the products of controlled excavations, these by Rassam, ca. 1879–1880.[4] The balance of the fragments apparently had been dug up previously and all but one purchased during the period of Rassam's excavations.[5]

4 Text 8 (33479 + 33639)—Rm IV collection arrived in the British Museum on 24 Dec. 1879 from Babylon (Reade 1986, pp. xxix–xxx); Texts 2 (36847 + 37353), 4 (36730), 13 (36960), 14 (36989), 15 (37034), and 16 (37054)—80-6-17 collection, mainly from Babylon, excavated between October 1879 and January 1880 (Reade 1986, p. xxx).

5 Text 6 (34073 [Sp. 169])—Sp collection purchased in 1879 (arrived in London 1878); Texts 1 (34712), 5 (35089), 6 (34073 [Sp II 653] + 35123), 7 (34598), and 9 (34686)—Sp II

Most of the eighteen tablets, despite the numerous joins, are rather fragmentary, each composed of from one to three of the twenty-nine original fragments; only one (Text 11) is substantially complete. Where the shapes of the tablets can be determined, all but two (Texts 11 and 13) are longer than wide. One tablet (Text 5) of indeterminate form has two columns of text on its one surviving face; the remainder all appear to have been single-column tablets. The smallest complete tablet (Text 11), approximately 5 cm long, has just 13 lines of text written with large widely spaced signs. The largest fragment (Text 6), almost 17 cm long, still bears eighty-eight lines of minute, tightly cramped script. Several exemplars are written variously in the typical Late Babylonian vulgar diagonal tablet cursive.

Despite the fact that the tablets display no generic physical form to speak of, their signature concentration of quotations of variant price levels for from one to six commodities identifies them as a distinct, coherent class of texts. Furthermore, although we can say with certainty only that the earliest dateable data presented in the tablets are of Seleucid date (Text 2), there are grounds for inferring that these records go back to the Achaemenid period (Text 1), if not earlier. In any case, the history of the commodity price lists now spans at least one hundred eighty-six years, I/23 S.E. to II/209 S.E. (289 to 103 BCE). Whether or not the two probable Arsacid texts, Texts 12 and 17, extend this range cannot be known. The remaining tablets whose dates still cannot be established, Texts 13-16, appear to be Seleucid. Three tablets, Texts 7, 8, and 9, overlap in time. Text 7 shares a single datum point with Text 8—the commodity dates in VIII/185 S.E.—although the specific value is not preserved in the latter text; Texts 8 and 9, in turn, each in its own way, cover barley and date price equivalents from I/186 S.E. through XII/187 S.E.

It should be pointed out that only the dates of the market quotations themselves may be determined; the dates of the compositions of the tablets themselves are not known. It may be added trivially that the *terminus a quo* for the composition of any given tablet is established by its latest datable quotation. Also note that whereas there is preserved on the lower and left edges of Text 9 a docket not unlike those found on the Astronomical Diaries summarizing the contents of the tablets, Text 11, which is substantially complete, shows no evidence of such a docket. Lastly, there is no evidence to suggest that the price tablets, unlike the Astronomical Diaries, ever bore colophons identifying the

---

collection purchased in 1879; Texts 9 (35604) and 11 (35710)—Sp III collection purchased in 1880; Text 16 (40100)—81-2-1 collection purchased in 1881 (arrived in London November 1880); Texts 5 (45724), 12 (46161), and 17 (46138)—81-7-6 collection probably acquired in 1879, but not accessioned until 1881; and Text 10 (55535)—82-7-4 collection purchased 1882 (Reade 1986, xv). Text 3A (95313), presumably a stray from the same original Babylonian archive, was part of a large collection purchased from the Paris dealer I. E. Gejou, and accessioned by the Museum in 1901 (courtesy Christopher Walker).

scribes by name (see Slotsky 1997, 99–100) or catchlines at the beginning of the text identifying its contents or at the end of the text identifying the first line of the next tablet in the series.

1.2 — The Market Quotations

Technically, the market quotations are not stated as prices *per se,* that is the number of shekels of silver for which a certain amount of a commodity is offered for sale, but rather as equivalences of amounts of commodities that a certain stated amount of silver will buy. If one wanted to turn a given quotation of, for example, so-and-so many *qa* per shekel of silver into a price, it would only require taking its reciprocal (1 divided by the number of *qa* per shekel). The use of either, equivalence or price, is valid, and both can easily be graphed with modern software, with the absolute values of their slopes being identical. In practice, the use of calculated prices has drawbacks. It entails generating the given quantities into prices and then dealing with the decimal amounts of a shekel rounded to an appropriate number of significant digits. This may results in lost accuracy and potentially misleading results. Further, one must endure the difficulty of working with very small fractions of a shekel. To choose an admittedly extreme but nonetheless real example, if one shekel of silver would buy exactly 6 kor of mustard (see Slotsky 1997, 50 [Table 2]), then one kor of mustard would cost ⅙ or approximately $0.1\overline{6}$ (i.e., an infinitely repeating decimal) shekel of silver. Since 1 kor = 180 *qa*, one *qa* of said mustard would bear the infinitesimal price of $^{1}/_{1080}$ or approximately $0.0009\overline{259}$ shekel of silver. In comparison, the quoted 6 kor (= 1080 *qa*) of mustard per shekel of silver is precise, free from secondary error, and certainly easier to use. If we add to this the merit and elegance of using primary evidence—those actual market values as their native copyists understood them—then the use of equivalences stands out as the best approach.

The market quotations are not uniform and display a wide-ranging variation. In fact, it is difficult to speculate about the model of a standard market quotation, or even if there was such a thing, because of the few quotations with their statements of equivalency intact, the variety of forms that are used in those that are preserved, and the fact that all full-scale examples that we can date are late, certainly not before 178 S.E. Common elements crop up, such as the price-equivalency declarations, but few are worded exactly alike; furthermore, they might be in the catch-line at the beginning of the text, or they might appear within the quotations, in a docket on an edge, or in all these spots, sometimes with different wording.

When commodity values are introduced at the beginning of the text, the statement might take several forms. Although the equivalency of amounts of commodities to silver, written KI.LAM (*maḫīru*), the "price equivalent" or "market rate," is the main point of listing market quotations, the term KI.LAM might or might not be written. In fact, the writing KI.LAM is preserved on only four tablets, twice as part of the beginning statement of equivalency in the first line (Texts 4 and 9), in a cuneiform graffito written over an erasure (Text 4), once in a unique tablet title (Text 2), and once in the context of noting the possible suspension of commodity sales (Text 14); the term does not appear in any preserved docket. In Texts 1, 3, 5, 6, 8, 10, 12, and 17, price equivalents simply follow the year and month with no introductory statement.

In Text 9, KI.LAM launches the listing of market values immediately following the year date in the first line: [MU.1 ME 1,26.KÁ]M ITU.BAR KI.LAM ŠE.IM, "[Year 186]. Month I, the market rate: barley." In subsequent months, ITU.MN KI.LAM ŠE.IM, "Month MN, the market rate: barley," precedes each month's quotations. Text 4 is similar: KI.LAM was written in the next line following the year date. It presents the first quotation of the year: BAR KI.LAM ŠE.IM, "Month I, the market rate: barley." In the preserved months thereafter, KI.MIN, "ditto," substitutes for KI.LAM, as in MN KI.MIN, "Month MN, ditto" for "Month MN, the market rate: barley." Text 7's initial line is damaged, and it might or might not have had a KI.LAM in the missing portion: [...] TA MU.1 ME 1,18 KÁM [EN MU.1 ME 1],25.KÁM *šá ana* 2 GÍN KÙ.BABBAR, "[...] from year 178 [to year 1]85 (the market rate), which is for 2 shekels of silver." Finally, Text 11 introduces the first record of year 209 not with KI.LAM but with *nadān*, translated here as "sale" or "delivery": MU.2 ME 9.KÁM *na-da*[*n*] *šá* ITU BAR, "Year 209. Delivery for month I." Text 15 might have originally had an introductory equivalency statement, but all that remains is an *ana* 1 GÍN KÙ.BABBAR, "for one shekel of silver," after each month's data.

There are several formulaic statements of equivalency in catch-lines at the beginning of the text and dockets on the tablet edges stating the tablet's contents. These usually contain year dates and the silver unit used in the quotations. Although the first line of Text 9 has an introductory KI.LAM statement, as mentioned above, it is the dockets that give the silver unit used in the quotations. It does not contain KI.LAM but, rather, *nadān*: [... *n*]*a-dan šá ana* 2 GÍN KÙ.BABBAR *ina* KUR SUM, "[... s]ale that was paid in the land for two shekels of silver." This price list also has two dockets. In the one on the left edge, [ŠE.IM (*u*) ZÚ.LU]M *u* ŠE.GIŠ.Ì *šá* MU.1 ME 1,26 [KÁM ...], "[barley (and) dat]es and sesame for year 186...," one would expect KI.LAM before ŠE.IM, but we cannot be sure that it was actually written there. The docket on the upper edge of the tablet, however, again gives the unit of silver to which the commodity amounts correspond, and this time we have no doubt that KI.LAM is eliminated from the formula: [...MU.1] ME 1,26.KÁM *u* MU.1 ME 1,27 KÁM *šá ana* 2 GÍN [KÙ.BABBAR], "[…year 1]86 and year 187, (the market rate) which is for 2 shekels of silver." Text 11 is a similar case, *na-da*[*n*] *šá* ITU BAR, "Delivery for month I," but it has a closing statement with the equivalency rate: *šá ana* 1 GÍN [K]Ù.BABBAR *šá ina* KUR SUM, "which was sold in the land for one shekel of silver." Text 15, although badly broken, repeats after each month's data: *a-na* 1 GÍN KÙ.BABBAR.

KI.LAM, besides being used in the equivalency statements, appears in the beginning line of Text 2 as a tablet name, EN.NUN *šá* KI.LAM (*maṣṣartu ša maḫīri*), "watch of price equivalent," or "market watch." This is the only case within the corpus, unless we restore the first part of Text 7's initial line to [EN.NUN *šá* KI.LAM] TA MU.... It is easy to imagine that this was the name given to this class of texts much as the Astronomical Diaries were given the title, EN.NUN *šá ginê* (*maṣṣartu ša ginê*), "regular watch." KI.LAM might also appear in another context in Text 14: we are tempted to restore the end of its third line to read: ZÚ.LUM KI.L[AM KUD$^{?}$- *is*$^{?}$]: "dates: the sa[le was cut off(?)]" (see Text 14 Comments).

Given the variety of formulas used in the price lists, it is not surprising that the form of a complete and fixed quotation cannot be determined. Nowhere is there a preserved quotation that would express in its entirety all the elements found in the statements of equivalency, nor do we know that one set expression ever existed. One might surmise that a standard quotation, or at least the semblance of one, might take either the form: *ITU MN KI.LAM x *šá ana* y GÍN KÙ.BABBAR *šá ina* KUR SUM, "month MN, the market rate x (i.e., x amount of a commodity), which was paid in the land that was for y shekels of silver," or **na-dan šá ana* y GÍN KÙ.BABBAR *šá ina* KUR SUM: "delivery/sale that was paid in the land that was for y shekels of silver."

Whatever the form of the quotation, however, it was the equivalency of amounts of commodities to silver that was of primary interest. Certainly four tablets, and perhaps six altogether, give market rates based on one shekel of silver; six, possibly seven, equate amounts of commodities to two shekels of silver; and two use one mina (60 shekels) of silver as the standard of value. The equivalency rates are either specifically stated on the tablets or are readily assumed upon comparison with the data for the same period in the Diaries, which are almost without exception at the rate of one shekel of silver.[6] The silver unit on the remaining six tablets is not clear, but it appears to be either one or two shekels of silver. Whereas the tablets offering the equivalency of one shekel occur throughout the corpus, the two tablets at one mina equivalency are the earliest, while the tablets at two shekels equivalency are dated towards the end of the Seleucid and throughout the Arsacid periods, including all three of the chronologically overlapping Texts, 7, 8, and 9. Table 1 gives the market rate for each text, along with the date range of its quotations.

6 Note AD I -418A (5 Darius II), which was "excerpted for reading" (r.15'), twice specifies a price equivalence of 1⅛ shekel (1 GÍN *bit-qa*), once for cress in month I (o.4), and a second time for barley at the end of month II (o.8-o.9).

TABLE 1
MARKET RATES ON PRICE TABLETS

	Equivalent (silver)			
Text	*1 shekel*	*2 shekels*	*60 shekels (1 mina)*	*unknown*
1			11–15 (RN?)	
2			23–26? S.E.	
3	46–48 S.E.			
3A				58–[…] S.E. 1(?) shekel
4	69?(71!)–71[*sic*] S.E.			
5		…142–143 S.E.		
6		173–175 S.E.		
7		178–185 S.E.		
8		184–190 S.E.		
9		186–187 S.E.		
10				194?–195? S.E.
11	11/XII/208–II/209 S.E.			
12		n.d. (Arsacid?)		
13				n.d. (Seleucid?) 2(?) shekels
14				n.d. (Seleucid?)
15	n.d. (Seleucid?)			
16				n.d. (Seleucid?) 1(?) shekel
17				n.d. (Arsacid?)

Although the Diaries and the price tablets self-evidently reflect the purchasing power of (coined) silver at any given moment, it remains less clear what fraction of any given Babylonian household's monthly income one shekel of silver, for example, might represent and what fraction of that household's needs that shekel's worth of a given commodity might provide. In some preliminary remarks on these topics, van der Spek (1998a, 246–53) has estimated that 50 *qa* of barley might not be an unreasonable estimate for an average individual's monthly dietary needs. The data for wages for workers remains anecdotal and sparse while the data for estimating the size of the household a given worker supported is virtually nonexistent; nonetheless note, e.g., that in 218 S.E. low-level temple employees (porters and cleaners) might earn on average about 1 shekel per month, while a parchment scribe might earn twice that (van der Spek 1998a, 252).

Ordinarily in these texts, and in direct contrast to the contemporary archival texts, the specie of payment is not specified. According to Wallenfels (2001, 220–22), the term, "staters of Alexander in good condition" replaced "minas of refined silver" previously evidenced in Achaemenid and early Hellenistic Uruk archival texts dated through ca. 295 BCE. Thereafter, staters of the ruling king became the stated standard unit of payment, except for 68 to 71 S.E., the time of the Third Syrian (Laodikean) War, when Seleucus II, although nominally the ruler, was supplanted temporarily by Ptolemy III.[7] During the Arsacid period, the designation "Arsaces" prevailed regardless of the personal name of the king. Uniquely, however, in Text 6, alongside market quotations elsewhere throughout this text valued simply at two shekels of silver, the worth of barley just for month III/175 S.E. is given in both Seleucid and Arsacid coinage. Specifically, for the amounts of barley that month we read: (r.12) … *ina* KÙ.BABBAR *bab-b*[*a-né-é-tú*] (r.13') [… *i*]*s-ta-ter-ra-an-na šá* [m]*de-met-ri-*[*su*] (r.14') ... 2(p) 2(b) ⸢*ù*⸣ AŠ *is-ta-ter-ra-an-na* (r.15') [... m*ar-šá-ka*]*-a* LUGAL 2 PI …: "in silver in good condition … staters of Demetrius (II) … 2 pān 2 sūt and in staters of Arsaces, the king, 2 pān" (see further Text 6 Comments).

The market quotations contain other unique aberrations scattered among the eighteen tablets. Only one text uses fractions, that of ¼ written 4 -ʾ-*ú* (Text 11). We can pose two hypothetical explanations, one being that this was a late innovation for the price tablets, since this tablet's equivalents date to 208–209 S.E. On the other hand, this text listed data for only three months, and in clusters of days at that, so it is easy to imagine that the scribe required more precision than usual. Another tablet, Text 1, undated but most likely Achaemenid, has anomalies (see further Text 1 Comments), possibly reflecting Achaemenid habits or a stage in the development of price lists before forms became more fixed. Next, Text 4 has the only instance of KI.MIN, used as "ditto" for KI.LAM. Finally, only five tablets use the ITU sign as a determinative for month (Texts 3A, 9, 10, 11, and 17).

1.3 — The Six Commodities

The commodities listed in the price tablets number between one and six, but we can assign clear-cut identifications to only three. These are the same six commodities that appear in the concluding monthly summaries of the Astronomical Diaries, and they are arranged in the same established order known in the Diaries from the middle of the fifth century BCE (Slotsky 1997, 14-15). The first commodity listed is barley; then dates; next, the inexplicable *kasû*, conventionally translated as "mustard"; next, *saḫlû*, so-called cress; next,

7 Also note the absence of a royal name in the designation of the payment in an unpublished Uruk archival tablet in the Princeton Theological Seminary (PTS 2178) copied by the late A. Goetze and slated to be published as YOS 15 9 (forthcoming); several features of this tablet suggest that this land sale may have been concluded quite close to the period of the transition of Uruk from Seleucid to Arsacid rule, ca. 166 S.E.

šamaššammū, presumably "sesame"; and, finally, wool. As in the Diaries, only the market values of these six commodities are quoted.[8]

The definitions of the three yet-to-be definitively identified commodities, *kasû*, *saḫlû*, and *šamaššammū* are problematic.[9] Geller (2000, 409–12) is certainly right when he challenges identifications made in the past, for these were assumptions based on philological or other grounds that cannot be confirmed by solid physical evidence. The truth is that we cannot yet identify *kasû*, *saḫlû*, or *šamaššammū* unequivocally. What, then, to call these dubious commodities? We find it expedient, although by no means faultless, to revert to the conventional nomenclature, respectively "mustard," "cress," and "sesame" used in the translations of the published Astronomical Diaries and much of the Diary literature.

There are not many changes over time in the written form of the commodities, as the following table (Table 2) of dated tablets, arranged chronologically, shows. Barley, conventionally normalized *še'u*,[10] could be written ŠE.BAR or ŠE.IM or abbreviated simply ŠE. Apparently ŠE.BAR was merely one more interchangeable alternative and had no special significance here, unlike in the Diaries, where it may have been used as a special term for barley that came to the market after a suspension of sales (Slotsky 1997, 27). Dates, *suluppū* are never written syllabically, but always appear as the logogram ZÚ.LUM, usually abbreviated ZÚ; ZÚ.LUM.MA, seen rarely and only from 50 S.E. on in the Diaries does not occur here. Mustard, *kasû*, is consistently designated by *kàs*, except for three consecutive monthly examples of *ka-si*, which quickly change to *kàs*, on an undated but most likely Achaemenid tablet (Text 1). In the Diaries, it was consistently written *ka-si* through at least 11 S.E., and then, after some ten years, mostly *kàs*. Cress, *saḫlû*, takes three forms, *saḫ*, *saḫ-le*$_{10}$, and *saḫ-le*$_{x}$ (peculiar to Text 6); ZÀ, seen in the Diaries, does not appear in these price tablets. Sesame, *šamaššammū*, is written ŠE.GIŠ and ŠE.GIŠ.Ì. Finally, wool, *šīpātu*, is always written with the logograms SÍG or SÍG.ḪÁ.

---

8 Other foods are mentioned in the Diaries on very rare occasions, but no market values are given (see Slotsky 1997, 16).

9 See the discussions and references at the end of the respective entries in the CAD: K, s.v. *kasû;* S, s.v. *saḫlû*; cf. Š/1, s.v. *šamaššammū* ("probably flax").

10 For the reading *û*(*m*), or the like, see Cavigneaux 1989; Vanstiphout 1989; Livingstone 1997. Also note ŠE.BAR = *uṭṭatu* "Getreide, Gerste; Korn" (AHw, *s.v.*).

TABLE 2

WRITINGS FOR COMMODITIES ON DATED PRICE TABLETS ARRANGED CHRONOLOGICALLY

Date S.E.	*Text*	*Barley*	*Dates*	*Mustard*	*Cress*	*Sesame*	*Wool*
23–26?	2	ŠE.BAR	ZÚ, ZÚ.LUM[a]	*kàs*	[...]	[...]	[...]
46–48	3	ŠE, ŠE.IM					
58 – [...]	3A	ŠE.BAR	ZÚ	*kas*$_x$	*saḫ*[...]	[...]	[...]
69?(71!)–71[*sic*]	4	ŠE, ŠE.IM	ZÚ				
...142–143	5	ŠE.BAR	ZÚ	*kàs*	*saḫ*, *saḫ-le*$_{10}$[b]	ŠE.GIŠ, ŠE.GIŠ.Ì[c]	SÍG, SÍG.ḪÁ
173–175	6	ŠE.BAR	ZÚ	*kàs*	*saḫ-le*$_x$	ŠE.GIŠ.Ì	SÍG.ḪÁ
178–185	7		[...]				
184–190	8	ŠE, ŠE.IM	ZÚ				
186–187	9	ŠE.IM	ZÚ.LUM			ŠE.GIŠ, ŠE.GIŠ.Ì[d]	
194?–195?	10		ZÚ.LUM				
11/XII/208–II/209	11	ŠE.IM					

[a] Written ZÚ.LUM only once (o.16).
[b] Written *saḫ-le*$_{10}$ only once (o.i':16').
[c] Written ŠE.GIŠ.Ì only once (o.i':16').
[d] Written ŠE.GIŠ.Ì only twice (o.5; Le.E.).

The variability noted here may be a reflection of the sources from which the scribes were copying, or may represent nothing more than idiosyncrasies of a particular scribe at any given moment. Only in a single case on a tablet that cannot be securely dated (see Table 3) does a particular writing for mustard—*ka-si* in Text 1—potentially have chronological significance (see Text 1 Comments).

TABLE 3

WRITINGS FOR COMMODITIES ON UNDATED PRICE TABLETS ARRANGED BY TEXT NUMBER

Text	*Date*	*Barley*	*Dates*	*Mustard*	*Cress*	*Sesame*	*Wool*
1	11–15 (RN?) (Achaemenid?)	ŠE.BAR	ZÚ	*ka-si*, *kàs*[a]	*saḫ*	ŠE.GIŠ	SÍG
12	n.d. (Arsacid?)	ŠE.BAR	ZÚ	*kàs*	*saḫ-le*$_{10}$	ŠE.GIŠ.Ì	SÍG.ḪÁ
13	n.d. (Seleucid?)	ŠE, ŠE.BAR[b]	ZÚ				
14	n.d. (Seleucid?)	[...]	ZÚ.LUM				
15	n.d. (Seleucid?)	[...]	[...]	*kàs*	*saḫ-le*$_{10}$	ŠE.GIŠ, ŠE.GIŠ.Ì	SÍG.ḪÁ
16	n.d. (Seleucid?)	[...]	[...]			ŠE.GIŠ, ŠE.GIŠ.Ì[c]	
17	n.d. (Arsacid?)	ŠE.IM	ZÚ.LUM			ŠE.GIŠ	

[a] Written *ka-si* through V/12 S.E. and *kàs* throughout thereafter.
[b] Written ŠE.BAR only once (o.4').
[c] Written ŠE.GIŠ.Ì in first two occurrences only (1, 2).

One, two, three, or six commodities might be recorded on any one tablet. None of the tablets has four or five, perhaps the result of accidents of preservation and excavation rather than of scribal policy. Four tablets, possibly seven, list all 6 commodities, while four list one (two texts for barley only, two for dates only). Four tablets concern two commodities, barley and dates, and two lists, perhaps three, have three: barley, dates, and sesame. Barley and dates are the commodities most consistently recorded.

TABLE 4

NUMBER OF COMMODITIES LISTED ON PRICE TABLETS

Number of Commodities	*Commodity*[a]	*Text*
1	b	3, 11
1	d	7, 10
2	b, d	4, 8, 13, 14
3	b, d, s	9, 16(?), 17
6	b, d, m, c, s, w,	1, 2(?), 3A(?), 5, 6, 12, 15(?)

[a] (b) barley, (d) dates, (m) mustard, (c) cress, (s) sesame, (w) wool.

The first five commodities in the price lists, as far as we understand them, are harvested crops in their natural unprocessed state that have appeared in the marketplace. Dates and barley and, only once, sesame, are occasionally differentiated by quality. The following three qualifying adjectives are used: GIBIL/GIBIL.MEŠ, "new," in the sense of fresh, newly harvested products just delivered to the market; SUMUN/SUMUN.MEŠ, "old," signifying commodities left over from the last harvest; and NU.DÙ.MEŠ, "of poor quality," perhaps products newly picked but defective or improperly handled, or old, stale, or spoiled crops. (Produce designated by the term *babbanētu*, written syllabically or DÙ-*tú*, "of very good quality," although in evidence in the Diaries, is not found in the price tablets.) According to evidence in the Astronomical Diaries, the likely months for a barley harvest are I, II, and III; for dates, VI, VII, VIII; and for sesame II, III, VII, and VIII (Slotsky 1997, 25–38)—the apparent variability in the time of the harvest is of course largely due to the drift of the Babylonian lunar calendar against the more fixed celestially determined seasonal background. In the price lists, commodities described as new, old, or of poor quality conform perfectly to these time frames.

TABLE 5
PRICE TABLETS WITH COMMODITIES DIFFERENTIATED BY QUALITY

	GIBIL(.MEŠ) "new"		SUMUN(.MEŠ) "old"		NU.DÙ(.MEŠ) "poor quality"		
Month	*barley*	*dates*	*barley*	*dates*	*barley*	*dates*	*sesame*
I					12	12	
II	9, 12				11		
III				6	12		
IV			17	6	6		
V							
VI							
VI_2							
VII		9, 17					
VIII		5					
IX					6,12		
X							6
XI							
XII					6,9		
XII_2					6		

1.4 — Format and Structure of the Quotations

Although the contents of each tablet are at all times sequences of market rates, the price lists are by no means uniform. Some tablets contain simple runs of market rates, one per month, month after month. Text 14, with its one quotation a month each for barley and dates for (probably) two years, Text 15, for probably all six commodities for two-plus years, and Text 8, barley and dates for seven years, are examples of this type. The market values are mostly listed in running lines, one or more months or commodities per line of text, but uniquely there is one tablet that appears to be a two-column text (Text 5). Some tablets cite market values at the beginning, middle, and end of the month (Texts 7 and 10)[11]; or almost daily (Texts 9 and 11). Still others use various combinations of quotations with market rates for once a month for some commodities; beginning, middle, and end of month for others; and day-by-day or groups of days for still others (Texts 2, 5, 6, 12). Market rates might be tabulated monthly for a period of years (Text 8); for one particular month year by year (Text 7); for specific consecutive months, such as month VII to the end of the year, for 2 successive years (Text 10); or, in one case, 3 consecutive months bridging two successive years (Text 11). Single monthly values might not always be recorded at the same date each month (Text 8). As was shown in the foregoing discussion, market values might be recorded for one or more commodities; most favored were barley and dates.

The scribes who compiled these lists are a mystery to us. No scribe's name is found, so besides not knowing who they were, we have no idea where they worked, what outside tasks they might have performed, and if or how they were associated with the major bodies of work, e.g., the Astronomical Diaries, Ephemerides, Almanacs, and Goal Year Texts. Further, there is no indication of when these tablets were actually written; thus we do not know if their contents were of relatively current or of long-term historical interest to whoever might have commissioned them. We notice, however, a suspiciously large number of scribal irregularities and blunders on twelve of the eighteen tablets. Some of these errors, both of omission and commission, perhaps indicate a general level of inexperience on the part of the scribes given their sizable number. Just as likely, however, the copyists may have been copying the data from older tablets, and these may have been broken, damaged, poorly preserved, or otherwise unreadable, although the term *ḫe-pi*, "broken," indicative of copying from defective sources and certainly in evidence in the Astronomical Diaries, is not seen in this corpus.

---

11 The precise meaning of the terms "mịddle" and "end" of the month in the light of their usage here and in the Diaries is somewhat vague: note in Text 9:o.22 the price equivalent for dates "to the middle of the month" (EN MURUB$_4$ ITU) is followed by the statement "at the middle of the month" (AŠ MURUB$_4$ ITU); in Text 12:27' the equivalent for dates "at the end of the month" (AŠ TIL ITU) is followed by a value for days 28–29; and in AD III -123A:o.16' the equivalent for barley "until the end of the month" is followed by a value for days 27–29.

Whether the results of scribal error or poor copy material, the slips of the stylus, corrected or not by the ancient scribes, are numerous. Erasures of from one to a few signs in a given line are to be found in Texts 7:8, 9, 14, 17; 11 (beneath l. 13); and 16:10–11, 17, 22. In Text 3, the scribe omitted all mention of months X, XI, XII, and XII$_2$/47 S.E.; after IX/47 S.E., he continued on the same line with <MU>.48 ŠE.IM; in four of five middle-of-the-month quotations, he abbreviated AŠ MURUB$_4$ ITU to simply AŠ MURUB$_4$ (ll.o.4', o.5', r.7', r.9'), perhaps a form of haplography given the similarity of the MURUB$_4$ and ITU signs in the Late Babylonian ductus; and for AŠ or EN MURUB$_4$ ITU, he wrote TA (o.1'). In Text 8 the scribe wrote MU.2 ME 28 for the intended MU.1 ME 1,28; he repeated the end of r.7 at the beginning of r.8; he started a new year with month VI$_2$ in r.10, leaving out months I–VI, although all other years have these; and he may have written ŠE for the intended month I logogram (BAR) in o.13'. The scribe of Text 9 repeated EN twice in TA {EN} 17 EN 25 in r.16' and wrote EN for TA in r.27'. In Text 7 there are three erasures: one, in o.8, is a legitimate correction of an error that the scribe caught and changed, because the tablet amount is consistent with the comparable Diary amount; the erasure in o.9 looks as if the scribe had started to write "beginning" (or "middle" or "end") of the month (since all other quotations here have all 3 values) but realized he had only one quotation, saw his mistake, erased, and put in one value for the whole month; and there is another erasure in r.17 where 2 GUR, which occurs in both the previous and following lines, may originally have been written. In Text 17, ITU is missing in AŠ MURUB$_4$ ITU in o.3', and in AŠ TIL ITU in o.7'; and AŠ is omitted in AŠ SAG ITU in r.5'. In Text 10, the scribe left out the writing of ZÚ.LUM twice, o.4 and o.5. Text 12 has only one problem: ITU is missing in EN MURUB$_4$ <ITU> in 22'. In Text 1 the copyist mistakenly wrote 3(b) for the no doubt intended 3(g) of cress in o.6'; he left out ZÚ in o.7' but gave a quantity for it; he omitted *kàs* but gave a quantity for it (r.6'); he wrote AŠ TIL ITU NE: "at the end of *this* month" for the usual AŠ TIL ITU: "at the end of *the* month"; and he left out data for one of the first four months of year 12. Finally, Text 4 contains perhaps the most striking breaches of judgment of all: the scribe erased everything except the initial signs for the month names in each of twelve consecutive lines (12'–23') spanning the full calendar year identified on the tablet as 70 S.E; further, the price equivalents listed for the previous year (date lost), presumably 69 S.E., are completely incongruent with the corresponding data from the Diaries for that year but can be correlated with the Diary data from 71 S.E.—just what equivalents (now lost) he did copy into the section actually labeled 71 S.E. (24' ff.) cannot be determined. Texts 2, 3A, 5, 11, 13, 14, 15, and 17 appear to be free of serious errors, but, with the exception of Text 11, these tablets are not well preserved.

Even as we wonder about competence of the tablets' scribes, we feel that we are on firm ground in our judgment of the observational nature of all of the market quotations, regardless of the stated equivalence rate. Like the entries in the Astronomical Diaries, these are too random and too detailed when market rates were volatile to have been computed. The matches of the data in both sources are mostly on the mark, although there are notable exceptions (see §2.2

The Market Quotations of the Price Tablets and the Astronomical Diaries in Juxtaposition, below). A perfect example is the data on the three chronologically overlapping tablets Texts 7 (VIII/178 to VIII/185 S.E.), 8 (XII/184 to VI/190 S.E.), and 9 (I/186 to XII/187 S.E.). Text 9 does not match Text 7, but Text 7 agrees with the Diaries. Text 9 matches best to mid-month Diary values. Texts 8 and 9 sometimes match exactly, sometimes merely closely; when they agree with each other, they also agree with the Diaries (see further Comparanda for Text 7, 8, and 9, respectively, below). We strongly suspect that the single monthly values in Text 8 were not recorded at the same date each month, which might explain some of the discrepancy. Texts 1 and 2, however, are outliers, as they value commodities at one mina of silver. Also, the quotations in Text 1 at least, with three possible exceptions, seem to have been computed from original values in multiples of one or one-half *qa*/shekel.

Just as distinctions may be drawn between texts within the corpus of commodity-price tablets, so may these texts be measured against the corresponding market quotations in the summaries of the Astronomical Diaries.

2. MARKET QUOTATIONS: THE TABLETS VS. THE ASTRONOMICAL DIARIES

2.1 — The Market Quotations of the Astronomical Diaries

The vast body of month-by-month Late Babylonian market values reported in regular summaries in the Astronomical Diaries[12] (Slotsky 1993; idem 1997) is a prodigious, albeit broken, record of market rates scattered across almost half a millennium of Babylonian history. It is our largest source of Late Babylonian economic data, and it is fair to say that it is unmatched by all other existing ancient economic archives in its sheer size, continuity, detail, and kind of information. And because it comes from mostly astronomical cuneiform texts with a long well-established tradition, it provides reliable, accurately dated, homogeneous raw price data (Slotsky 1997, 104).

These records were named "(Astronomical) Diaries" in modern times because of their day-by-day scheme of reporting (Sachs 1948, 285), but the Babylonians called them *maṣṣartu* (EN.NUN) *ša ginê*, "regular watch." With the exception of one or two, they were composed in Babylon[13] and consist of almost daily accounts of celestial and terrestrial phenomena within a given month. They have a long and continuous history. The consensus of opinion is that, in the light of *Ptolemy's Royal Canon* (see Depuydt 1995), the composition of these texts began in 747 BCE, the first year of the reign of the Babylonian king Nabonassar. Berossos (writing ca. 280 BCE) tells us that Nabonassar "collected together and destroyed the records of the kings before him in order that the list

12 Published in Sachs and Hunger 1988-96; Hunger and van der Spek 2006.

13 One, possibly two, were written in Uruk (-463, -99C).

of Chaldean kings might begin with him."[14] However, the earliest preserved dated Diary was composed in the 16th regnal year of Šamaš-šum-ukīn (652 BCE). One reason for the absence of earlier Diaries, beside the vicissitudes of preservation and recovery, might be the result of the ferocity of the destruction of Babylon in 689 BCE claimed by Šamaš-šum-ukīn's grandfather, Sennacherib.[15] On the other hand it should be noted that Šamaš-šum-ukīn's brother, Aššurbanipal, was the greatest collector of omen tablets—including the canonical version of the celestial omen series *Enūma Anu Enlil*—which formed the bulk of his famed library at Nineveh.[16] Aššurbanipal, even more so than his father before him, held a powerful interest in better understanding the will of the gods, given that the three previous kings of Assyria died in ways that can only be described as inauspicious: his father, Esarhaddon, who himself frequently consulted diviners and ecstatics, unexpectedly died on campaign in Egypt; his grandfather, Sennacherib, was murdered in his palace in Nineveh by his own son(s), and his great-grandfather, Sargon II, was killed in battle against Cimmerians; also note Šalmaneser V's brief reign and the less-than-clear mechanism of Sargon's succession. Thus, Šamaš-šum-ukīn may well have brought similar concerns and interests with him to Babylon, the home of celestial divination, when he took the throne there in 667 BCE, and the expression of those interests, as formulated by the Babylonian scribes in the light of their own interests, was the Diaries themselves in an early if not their earliest form. The latest Diary yet found is dated 61 BCE, year 251 of the Seleucid Era, although Diaries may well have been written up until the very end of the cuneiform writing tradition in the mid-first century CE, if not later.[17] If so, Astronomical Diaries might have been compiled throughout some eight centuries, although, as Table 6 demonstrates, the distribution of the published Diaries is far from homogeneous. With data representing just 212 different years, in whole or in part, scattered across seven centuries, fully 97% are concentrated in the last four centuries, and of these 40% fall within just the second century, during which Babylonia was eventually wrested from the Seleucids by the Parthians.

14 Burstein 1978, 22 [5.1]. On the modern interpretation of this statement, see Hallo 1988, 186–90.

15 OIP 2 83–84, cf. ibid., 137–38; see additionally Brinkman 1984, 67–70.

16 Oppenheim 1977, 15–18.

17 On the possible survival of the cuneiform tradition into the third century CE, see Geller 1997, idem 2008; cf. Westenholz 2007.

TABLE 6

DISTRIBUTION OF ASTRONOMICAL DIARIES (AD I–III) BY CENTURY

Century (BCE)	*Number of Different Years Represented*
7th	1[a]
6th	1[b]
5th	4[c]
4th	37[d]
3rd	63[e]
2nd	82[f]
1st	24[g]

[a] -651.

[b] -567.

[c] -463, -453, -440, -418.

[d] -391, -384, -382 – -378, -375, -373, -372, -370 – -368, -366, -362,* -361, -357, -346, -343, -342, -338, -333, -332, -330 – -328, -324, -322, -321, -309 – -307, -304, -302 – -300.

[e] -299, -294, -293, -291, -289 – -286, -284, -283, -281, -278 – -276, -273, -270, -266, -264 – -259, -257 – -253, -251, -249 – -245, -242 – -237, -234, -232, -230, -229, -227 – -225, -222, -221, -218, -214 – -207, -204 – -200.

[f] -199 – -197, -195 – -175, -173, -171 – -160, -158 – -151, -149, -148, -146, -144 – -140, -137 – -129, -126 – -117, -112 –-103.

[g] -99, -97 – -93, -90, -88 – -85, -83, -82, -80 – -75, -73, -72, -63, -62, -60.

*Published in Hunger and van der Spek 2006.

During those centuries successive generations of Diary scribes saw Babylon savagely destroyed by the Assyrian king Sennacherib in 689 BCE, then restored as a political and commercial center by his son Esarhaddon. The city was rebuilt a century later to its fullest magnificence by the greatest king of the last native dynasty, Nebuchadrezzar II, only to fall forevermore into the hands of foreign conquerors, first the Persians (538 BCE), then the Macedonians (331 BCE) and their Seleucid Successors (by 301 BCE), and finally the Parthians (by 127 BCE). Perhaps of greatest significance to those Diary scribes was that with the coming of the Persians, whose kings were surrounded by their own advisors, *magi* (Briant 2002, 245–46), the native scholars likely lost their access to the king, which once would have seemed to both king and scholars alike unthinkable. The Babylonian scholars may have enjoyed a brief period of influence again when Alexander took up residence in Babylon toward the end of his life. Shortly before his death, Alexander apparently quite willingly participated in the ancient ritual of the Substitute King in response to what must have been a series of dire omens.[18] Berossos, a Babylonian priest in the Seleucid court who wrote

18 See conveniently Parpola 1983, xxix–xxx [15, 15a-b].

in Greek a complete history of Babylonia, the *Babylonaica*, for the instruction of Antiochus I, may have hoped that by implicitly linking there Antiochus and his father Seleucus I with Nebuchadrezzar II and his father Nabopolassar, some luster might be restored to Babylon. Nonetheless, with the loss of the sitting king's ear, Babylonian scholars, no longer consumed with the need to keep the king constantly abreast of what the celestial omens portended—as the earlier correspondence from Nineveh between the scholars and Esarhaddon and Aššurbanipal make clear was once the case (Parpola 1993)—turned their attention more fully to examining in greater detail the voluminous body of observations at their disposal. In fact, it has been suggested that it was in the competitive environment engendered by the Late Assyrian court that "the invention of predictive astronomy" (Brown 2003) occurred when scholars began to realize that ominous celestial events were predictable (cf. Rochberg-Halton 1990). That such events, at least initially, remained ominous despite their predictability is evidenced by the performance at Larsa of apotropaic rituals in year 8 Cyrus II (531 BCE) in anticipation of an expected lunar eclipse that in fact was not observed (Beaulieu and Britton 1994). Late texts from Seleucid Uruk describing apotropaic rituals to be performed in part by the king at the time of a lunar eclipse are also known but whether these were merely formal scribal exercises or actually reflected ongoing cultic practices for which there exists no other evidence is unknown.[19]

The archetypal Diary covered a period of half a year, spanning either the first or last half of a Babylonian year. It would have six sections, seven in an intercalary year, each detailing phenomena in one lunar month. Those shorter records spanning no more than a single month may have been short-term compilations drawn from the daily observations perhaps recorded on wax writing boards that would later be consolidated into the standard half-year Diaries. Each monthly unit would be filled with observations and computations of an astronomical and meteorological character with major emphasis on the behavior of the moon. It would begin with what was considered to be the beginning of the new month: the sight of the first thin crescent of the new moon in the western sky towards sunset, when the new Babylonian day began. This served to define the length of the preceding month, whether 29 or 30 days long. It would continue with the monthly progress of the moon among the stars and planets, citing the planets' first and last appearances, stationary points, oppositions for the superior planets, as well as their positions relative to the "normal stars." Then it would report time intervals of various phenomena that would help predict the date on which the next month would begin. Mixed in were detailed local weather conditions, when unfavorable, by night and day, in part, no doubt, because these had an impact on the visibility of the phenomena being sought. Eclipses would be dated and described; equinoxes and solstices

---

19 Linssen 2004, 109–17.

were recorded; the seasonal rising and setting of the bright star Sirius were noted; meteors and comets, rainbows and haloes, and "falls" of fire were mentioned; and various terrestrial events, such as outbreaks of locusts, anomalous births, the appearance of wild animals in the city, and earthquakes were listed. At the end of the daily reports, there would be a final statement about the moon's last appearance and a measurement of the interval between moonrise and sunrise. Then came a recapitulation of planetary positions at the end of the month with respect to the zodiac, a list of the market values of six commodities (see Slotsky 1997), and precise measurements of the changes in the water level of the Euphrates (see Brown 2002). Often, but not always, there were some historical anecdotes that might be of local or national import.[20]

Because of the continuous attention to the changing position of the moon in the course of each month, as well as the other astronomical content, it is possible, in the absence of a preserved year date, to date most Diary texts confidently to the very day, if they can be dated at all. This means that any evidence extracted from these texts—astronomical, meteorological, economic, or historical—can also be dated with certainty. This makes it possible for us to date securely the Diary's market quotations, even on broken tablets with missing dates.

These summaries of the variant market rates of six commodities during each month in a regnal year[21] were framed in running lists of fixed commodity quotations that were expressed in an identical way throughout the history of Diary-writing. These quotations of market values were stated as equivalencies, written KI.LAM, Akk. *maḫīru*, "equivalent" or "market rate," of amounts x of commodities that one shekel (approximately 8⅓ grams) of silver could buy: ITU BI KI.LAM x *ana* 1 GÍN KÙ.BABBAR, "That month, the market rate for one shekel of silver was some quantity x of such-and-such commodity." The only

20 Del Monte (1997) has conveniently compiled all the historical anecdotes in AD I–III for the Hellenistic period; for case studies drawn from the corpus as a whole, see, e.g., van der Spek 1993, idem 1997/98, idem 1998b, Joannès 2000, Hunger and van der Spek 2006. Rochberg-Halton 1991 (330–31) has collected from AD I a sampling of diary observations with possible correspondences with protases from *Enūma Anu Enlil* and *Šumma izbu*.

21 The scribes of the Astronomical Diaries dated their records using Babylonian months and regnal years of the named king or, later, beginning in 281 BCE, years of the Seleucid Era (Hallo 1984-85, 144-47). From 141 BCE on, Diaries double dated in years of the Seleucid and Arsacid eras can also be found. The modern editors named each Diary by the Julian year in which all or most of the Diary falls (Sachs and Hunger 1988, I: 37) and used astronomical dating whereby year -nn = year nn+1 BCE. For example, the Diary of 45 S.E. is called the Dairy of -266 (267 BCE) because most of the months of this Seleucid year (in this case, almost 10 out of 13) are in -266 (267 BCE); 45 S.E. began in the spring of -266 on 27 March and ran until the following spring on 14 April -265 (266 BCE) after an intercalary month XII_2. In cases in which a Diary text covers two regnal years, the Diary name might contain two Julian years (Slotsky, 1997, 44).

variations of this standard formula were that (1) the writings *an*, *ana*, or *a-na*, might be used to express "for" in "for one shekel of silver"; (2) occasionally the form of the quotation was shortened by the elimination of the phrase "for one shekel of silver"; and (3) rarely, in fact in less than two dozen cases among the preserved Diaries, the phrase written *šá ina* KUR SUM/*innadnu*, "which was paid in the land" was added. A quotation was never stated as a true price, since it reported a quantity of a particular commodity that could be purchased for a standard unit of one shekel of silver rather than the number of shekels of silver for some specified amount of a commodity.

Market values of the same six commodities were listed each month, and in a set order sometime after the Diary of 454 BCE (-453): barley, dates, "mustard," "cress," "sesame," and wool (cf. §1.3 The Six Commodities, above). Barley (*še'u*/*û*, or the like) was written ŠE, ŠE.IM, and, twice only, ŠE.BAR. The logograms ZÚ, ZÚ.LUM, and ZÚ.LUM.MA were used for writing *suluppū*, dates. Mustard, *kasû*, was consistently written *ka-si* through at least 11 S.E.; then, some ten years later, *kàs*, with very few exceptions, became the norm. Cress, *saḫlû*, could have any of three forms, *sa*, *saḫ-le*$_{10}$, and ZÀ. Sesame, *šamaššamū*, was written ŠE.GIŠ and ŠE.GIŠ.Ì. Finally, *šīpātu*, wool, was always designated by the logograms SÍG, SÍG.ḪI or SÍG.ḪÁ. Occasionally, commodities were distinguished by quality. They might be new or fresh, *eššu*, written GIBIL or BÍL; or old or leftover, *labēru*, written SUMUN or *ina labēri*. Either DÙ-*tú* or *babbanētu* designated very good or excellent produce; and NU.DÙ, NU.DÙ-*tú* signified yield that was newly harvested but of poor quality or old and rotting.

As written evidence for Late Babylonian commodity values, the data of the Astronomical Diaries are unbiased, uncorrupted (save for the occasional scribal lapse or break in the original manuscript being copied), and thus seemingly trustworthy. With regard to the monthly summary of commodity values, Wiseman reasoned that, "[s]ince the prices are given in precise measure, with variations within a month or several days given, they were the result of actual observation."[22] In support of that statement, Slotsky observed that the quotations could not possibly have been calculated. First of all, the values were too irregular to have been computed according to some abstract principal. Second, they were far too minutely detailed when market rates were changing, even being recorded in ranges of days when they were fluctuating rapidly (and in one case, during the course of a day). Last but not least, the reports of specific interruptions of commodity sales incorporated into the market summaries had to come from observation (Slotsky 1997, 20–22).[23] Peter Temin, an economist at MIT, agreed, after having tested the data for random movement and variation over time by time series techniques (Temin 2002). He concluded that prices that varied this randomly in response to changing conditions, "like the random

---

22 Wiseman 1988, 365.

23 Sales of barley stopped: -324 II; -164 XII; -107 IX; -82 I; -62 I. Sales of dates stopped: -253 VII; -82 VII.

walk of modern prices," (ibid., 59) could not be non-market administered prices and could only be real market values.[24] Even though we now know that the Diaries contain more predicted astronomical phenomena than was first realized, it is beyond doubt that the market quotations themselves were observed phenomena, with large-scale fluctuations often occurring in concert with significant political events (Grainger 1999; Aperghis 2004, 78–86).

The reason for the inclusion of observed market values in the Astronomical Diaries has long been a topic of speculation. As for the Diaries themselves, Hallo (1988, 188) was certain that they "represented a deliberate effort to assemble a 'data base' on which to build a new astrological omen corpus, with astronomical or meteorological phenomena in the protases and terrestrial events in the apodoses."[25] In response, Rochberg-Halton (1991, 330) noted that the relationship of the diaries to celestial divination "seems particularly convincing," but adds that "there is no evidence that the intent was to produce a new compendium of celestial omens based on the updated observations of phenomena." Swerdlow (1998, 22–23) has suggested "that the Diaries were intended as an empirical, scientific record of ominous celestial phenomena...and the fortunes...of kingdoms, with the object of investigating whatever correlations could be found and reducing the interpretation of the omens to an empirical science...." On the other hand, others have proposed reasons why the Diaries could not have been written for the purpose of providing material for omens (Hunger and Pingree 1999, 139–44, elaborating on Slotsky 1997, 16–20). Nonetheless, a celestial omen from Uruk, datable to the fifth or fourth century BCE, unequivocally links the general rise and fall of the price equivalent for barley with specific celestial activity:

> If you want to make a prognosis concerning the market price of barley—break—you scrutinize the movement of the planets; you observe (first) visibility, (last) visibility, stationary point, conjunction...the faintness and brilliance of the planets and *lumāšu*-star, maximum positive latitude and maximum negative latitude...then you can make a prognostication for the coming year; it will be propitious.[26]

---

[24] Unfortunately, the virtually complete absence of comparative data among the contemporary archival documents suggests that sales of these six staple commodities were not as a general rule recorded on cuneiform tablets. Nonetheless, note the disbursement in Babylon of 6 shekels of silver for the purchase of 3 kor barley (ŠE.BAR) as millers' rations for each of two successive month-long periods, 12/XI – 11/XII/218 S.E. (CT 49 150: 8–9) and 12/XII – 11/XII$_2$/218 S.E. (BRM I 99: 5–7). Although the Diaries do not preserve data for these specific periods, the computed price equivalent of 90 *qa* barley per 1 shekel of silver for the millers' monthly rations compares favorably with price equivalents in the Diaries of a half-year earlier: 102 *qa*/shekel in IV/218 S.E. and 108 *qa*/shekel at the end of V/218 S.E. (AD III -93A: r.9, r.21, respectively) (van der Spek 1998a, 247).

[25] Similarly, Aaboe 1991, 278; van Driel 1992, 39; Britton and Walker 1996, 50.

[26] Hunger Uruk 94: 1–4; the text was copied by the scribe Iqīša, son of Ištar-šum-eriš, a

Regardless, what the Diaries do reflect is the Babylonian belief in an ordered universe. They are, as Hunger and Pingree note, an "explicit expression of the view that celestial motions are periodic in this ordered universe." They conclude that the astronomical observations and computations entered into the Diaries were intended from the beginning to be "the basis of a mathematical, predictive system" (Hunger and Pingree 1999, 139–44).

The compilers of the Diaries may have regarded the economic summaries (as well as the records of the water level of the Euphrates) as potentially periodic as the astronomical phenomena, and it is for this reason that the market values of six special commodities were included in the Diary observations. In their thinking, commodity records, like astronomical reports, might lend themselves to predictive schemes. They were observing and quantifying what they considered to be the important periodic elements in their ordered universe. The Late Babylonian Astronomical Diaries may, therefore, be looked upon as records of phenomena, carefully chosen from the realms of the celestial, the atmospheric, and the terrestrial, whose purpose was to define their periodicity and provide an observational basis for prediction.

2.2 — The Market Quotations of the Price Tablets and the Astronomical Diaries in Juxtaposition

In stark contrast to the Astronomical Diaries, the price tablets are few. Whereas in the Diaries we have a representative sample of what would have been all the Diaries' economic data had all Diaries been recovered, we have no idea how many price tablets were written, when they began to be compiled or when they ceased, and whether or not eighteen is a small or large fraction of them. The limitations of comparing a group of eighteen price tablets spanning, at the least, 186 years to the corpus of Diary texts, which number some 420, including duplicates, and span almost 600 years, are obvious.

As a preliminary step, however, we can look at how the two contemporary sources of raw price data match when there are counterpart records. Since both sets of data contain real market rates that were observed, we would expect a general level of agreement. In fact, there are eight tablets (Texts 2, 4, 5, 6, 7, 8, 9, and 10) in which the Astronomical Diaries and the price tablets yield complementary quotations, and in the majority of cases, the two corpora

---

descendant of Ekur-zakir, active during the Early Macedonian and early Seleucid periods (Oelsner 2000; de Breucker 2003, 21-23), from an older tablet; because of the references to zodiacal signs, the original cannot date to earlier than ca. 500 BCE (see van der Waerden 1952-53). Also note the texts TCL 6 19 and 20 (for editions, see Hunger 1976, 246ff., and 237ff., respectively), also from Seleucid Uruk, in which the levels of rainfall and the seasonal flooding of the rivers are specifically related to planetary positions; twice in TCL 6 19 (o.35-o.37) anticipated improvements in the commodity market as a whole are also mentioned.

present the same market rates for the same specific times. In other instances, the market quotations are well within range, especially allowing for observation at different times of the month. Still, there are a number of cases in which market values observed on the same day do not match (e.g., Text 9, the observation for 2/ I/186 S.E.) and where the tablet and Diary market values widely diverge (e.g., Text 6, II/174 S.E.). Sometimes the tablet market rates best match Diary mid-month (or other days of the month) amounts as in Text 8, whose one market rate each for barley and dates each month do not appear to have been measured on the same date each month. Even Text 6, which once values barley both in shekels of silver and silver staters, corresponds well with the Diaries (despite the errant II/174 S.E. entry mentioned above). Sometimes the match is exact, at other times close; at times, the price tablet market rate matches one Diary variant and not another. In the case of Text 10, there is a large and systematic lack of congruence, perhaps the result of a lapse of the stylus on the part of the ancient scribe (see Text 10 Comments).

The significance of the observation that there are a number of cases in which the market rates themselves and/or the specified time periods for which they are quoted are conspicuously different in the two corpora, even taking into account possible scribal irregularities or actual errors, must be considered, in part, in the light of the fact that there is a qualitatively similar variability in the data in what are ostensibly duplicates within the corpus of Astronomical Diaries itself. We suspect, but are by no means certain, that the variations within and between the two sources might be due in part to the way in which the respective scribes treated their source material, which included cuneiform clay tablets, wax writing boards, and perhaps even Aramaic leather documents. It is also very likely that some of the data in the sources from which they were copying were damaged and/or entirely missing. At the same time, we cannot discount the possibility that the market rates in the Diaries and the tablets did not come from the same source or that the price tablet scribes made their own observations.

If the data of both sources do show a certain degree of compatibility, there are also other characteristics of their price records that underscore even more their commonality. Both price tablets and Diaries use identical metrology; they quote monthly variant market values for the same six commodities, which are ordered in the same way and are dated in the same way by month and regnal year; they both express market rates, called KI.LAM, as amounts of commodities that could be bought for a certain amount of silver. They quote these monthly values for consecutive months in the same variety of ways: one quotation for the month; variant market rates during the month, such as beginning and end of the month, or beginning, middle, and end; or market rates by days when they were changing rapidly. The day dates on the price tablets mostly conform to or are in range of the Diary dates of quotations. Many of the same expressions are used, such as qualifying adjectives for the commodities (GIBIL, SUMUN, NU.DÙ), and commodities are mostly written with the same logographic and syllabic values. Both sources have similar names that classify them as a class or category of work. Just as the Astronomical Diaries were distinguished by the title *maṣṣartu ša ginê* (EN.NUN *šá gi-né-e)*, "regular watch," so the price lists seem to have been labeled *maṣṣartu ša maḫīri* (EN.NUN *šá* KI.LAM), "market watch."

Nevertheless, alongside these common features, stunning contradictions defy the apparent homogeneity of the two corpora. We noticed that, out of eighteen price tablets, only four texts (Texts 1, 5, 6, 12), and probably three others (Texts 2, 3A, 15), followed the Diary practice of recording data for all six staple commodities in each and every monthly record. Otherwise, the tablet scribes expanded their repertoire to include observation of one commodity by itself or two or three in combination. Two tablets list market rates for barley only (Texts 3, 11), two for just dates (Texts 7, 10), four for only barley and dates (Texts 4, 8, 13, 14), and two or three (Texts 9, 17 and probably 16) for only barley, dates, and sesame.

Moreover, in the archetypal Astronomical Diary, market values were recorded for six or seven months of half a given regnal year or twelve or thirteen months in the case of a one-year Diary. Whereas only three Diaries span more than one regnal year, only one or two price tablets, Texts 13 and 15(?), do not. The price tablets might present data for as many as eight years (Text 7), and, in fact, the period covered could vary widely. Texts 1, 2, 3, 3A, 4, 6, 7, 8, 9, 10, 12, 15(?), and 16, and also probably 5 and 14, report two or more years of market values.[27] Text 10 gives quotations for only the commodity dates in the last halves of two consecutive years, Text 11 gives data for barley for just three consecutive months spanning the end of one calendar year and the beginning of the next, and Text 7 reports values for just month VIII and only for the commodity dates for eight consecutive years.

The remaining inconsistencies between the two sources are of much greater consequence. They center on three defining issues: (1) the silver equivalencies to which amounts of commodities are valued; (2) vocabulary; and (3) methodology.

(1) *Silver Equivalences*

In the Diaries, the market rate, KI.LAM, for a given commodity is at all times quoted at the rate of so-and-so many measures per one shekel of silver. In centuries of Diary-writing, there is only one exception to this custom of quoting quantities of commodities as an equivalency to one shekel of silver, and that is in a Diary of year 5 Darius I (AD I -418A), a Diary filled with anomalies,[28] where one and one-eighth shekels of silver is twice stated to be the standard.[29] During

---

27 Three months: Text 11; one year: Texts 13, 15(?), 17(?); two years: Texts 3A(?), 9, 10; three years: Texts 3, 4, 5(?), 6, 12, 14(?), 16(?); four years: Text 2(?); five years: Text 1; seven years, Text 8; eight years: Text 7.

28 Among them a market quotation, unparalleled elsewhere in the Diaries, for 3 *sūt* minus 1 *qa* (-418: o.9 ... ZÚ.LUM 3(b)[?] 1 *qa* LAL ...) instead of the normal 2 *sūt* 5 *qa*.

29 1 GÍN *bit-qa* (-418A:o.4, o.9); for *bitqu*, "one-eighth of a shekel," see CAD B, 228, s.v. *bitqu* [6].

these same centuries as seen in the contemporary archival texts, the form taken by silver to be weighed out in payment shifted from pieces of scrap metal, rings, and cut pieces of ingots to the first introduction and tentative use of regularly minted coins towards the end of the Achaemenid period (Powell 1996; Vargyas 2000; Aperghis 2004, 214–16); beginning in the Early Macedonian period, silver staters or coins are regularly denoted for payment.[30]

Within the corpus of commodity price tablets, the price equivalency may, as in the Diaries, be expressed in terms of the buying power of one shekel of silver, but just as often it is expressed per two shekels of silver, or even, in two cases, of one mina, i.e., sixty shekels of silver;[31] only once, in Text 6, is barley described relative to the specific species of payment, whether Seleucid or Arsacid coinage.

Furthermore, not only are the silver equivalency rates in the price tablets variable and at odds with Diary custom, but so are the stated market quotations themselves. Even as both sources use common elements in their statements of value, the literal expressions of market values in the price tablets are not static as they are in the Diaries, and they stray from the rigid Diary formula. In fact, there is no one stock quotation for the price tablets as there is for the Diaries. All kinds of forms and arrangements are seen, whether in the running lists of changing market values or statements of content in the catch-lines or dockets. KI.LAM is not ubiquitous, as it is in the Diaries; in fact, it appears on only three tablets, and the price tablets' KI.MIN as "ditto" for KI.LAM is never seen in the Diaries' quotations. Expressions differ not only from tablet to tablet but on the same tablet. Most significant is the addition of a *šá* before *ana* and the silver unit (*šá ana* 2 GÍN KÙ.BABBAR); this phrase, as it appears in the price lists, cannot be found in the Diaries. Even the AŠ/EN TIL ITU BI of the diaries is abbreviated to AŠ TIL ITU in the price tablets, except for one case of AŠ/EN TIL ITU NE. To be sure, the sense of what is recorded, changing market values, is the same, but the formulas of statement prove to be different.

(2) *Vocabulary*

Although the same six commodities, identically ordered, appear in both sources, the stock expressions of these goods, as well as their adjectival attributes, might differ. One striking deviation is the interchangeable use of ŠE, ŠE.BAR, and ŠE.IM for barley in the price lists, with two different writings sometimes appearing on the same tablet (see Tables 2 and 3, above). Although ŠE.BAR is seen in other kinds of texts, and is especially frequent in incantations and rituals, it is conspicuously absent in the Diaries, preserved in only two

30 The earliest reference in a Babylonian text to payment in coined silver appears to be Jursa Fest. Walker 120 8:1 ⅓ MA.NA KÙ.BABBAR KI.LÁ 10 ⸢*is-ta-ter*⸣*-ra*.MEŠ "one-third mina of silver in the form of 10 staters" (2 Philip III).

31 See Inventory of Texts and §1.2. The tablets whose market rate could not be determined were valuing goods at either one or two shekels of silver.

instances, once in the Diary of II/-324 and another in that of I/-82. Even considering the gaps in data due to missing and broken Diaries, this rarity of the writing ŠE.BAR potentially underscores its significance. In both Diary cases, it is used in the same context and only at times when the sale of commodities was suspended, and new supplies were brought in from elsewhere. A reasonable explanation might be that ŠE.BAR was meant to signify barley that came to the market after the sale of barley was stopped, i.e., barley brought in "from the outside" (BAR). Reinforcing this solution is the fact that the barley whose sale was interrupted was called ŠE or ŠE.IM, and the barley sold after the stoppage was called ŠE.BAR. In addition, this ŠE.BAR was described as *ina mālak*,[32] "barley en route," "barley on the way." This infers that ŠE.BAR was not used in the Diary commodity lists as a simple alternative logogram for barley as in the price tablets, but rather as a special term for some kind of "reserve barley" (Slotsky 1997, 27).

Other commodity writings also show some variation in the two sources. ZÚ.LUM.MA, a writing for the commodity dates in the Diaries, is never seen on the price tablets, nor is ZÀ for cress. Moreover, the qualifying adjectives for commodities in the price lists are limited to GIBIL/ GIBIL.MEŠ; SUMUN/ SUMUN.MEŠ; and NU.DÙ.MEŠ. The Diaries' BÍL and *eššu* "new," *labāri* "old," and *babbanētu* "very good," are not seen.

(3) *Methodology*

The commodity summaries of the Diaries show, for the most part, a certain unity over time,[33] and because every price tablet contains line after line of monthly market rates, the tablets might too initially appear to be also of a comparatively fixed character. However, there are not only many variations within the group but also several different kinds of texts. Some have simple runs of variant market rates; others record continuous sequences according to a particular theme, such as successive quotations of only one commodity, or only two or three, rather than all six. Some texts report one commodity value a month for each commodity, whereas others record varying market rates during the month with either beginning/middle/end of month quotes or

32 CAD M/1, 158a, s.v. *mālaku* A: (1) march, marching, advance; (2) course of a river or canal, watercourse; (3) passage, course of a procession; (1) march, marching, path, advance; (2) river or watercourse; (3) passage, course; (4) distance. John Steele (2003, 269–89) translates *ina mālak* "on the path" when the term is found in astronomical texts (see Slotsky 1997, 27–28).

33 Only varying by different writings of commodities and the preposition "for" (as in "for" one shekel of silver), and the inclusion or elimination of the two phrases, "for one shekel of silver" and "which was paid in the land." Although the commodity sections of the Astronomical Diaries show only these minute changes, Diaries as a whole were by no means rigidly unchanging or static. Close inspection of Diary texts shows that there are differences, especially in content. See Hunger and Pingree 1999, throughout for numerous examples.

values for clusters of days. Some report market rates month by month for a series of years, others for only a few consecutive months, and one for only one and the same month for a series of years.

It is not difficult to conjecture that there was a rationale for the development of these varied schemes and, further, to wonder if they were, in fact, deliberate attempts to investigate and tally trends of market rates in general and, in particular, before, during, and after harvest time, sometimes at critical periods of Babylonian history. The simple fact that the kind of data they contain was a regular component of the Astronomical Diaries, themselves devoted to the recording of much of what the scribes already knew to be cyclical phenomena, suggests that the tablet scribes might have been seeking to identify short- and/or long-term behavior in the market rates themselves. There are more than enough grounds to support this hypothesis in those texts that suggest a particular and narrow interest on the part of the scribe. Those include, first of all, those tablets that list market rates for one commodity only (and perhaps those dealing with only two or three); second, those texts that plainly intend to track a particular harvest (for example, quotations for only those few consecutive months around harvest time); and last, but not least, those tablets that appear to keep track of harvest output by year (records for only one particular month for a series of years).

Four of the eighteen tablets limit themselves to quotations for one commodity only: Text 3, barley; Text 7, dates; Text 10, dates; Text 11, barley. These are by far the best evidence we have to show that the motive behind these texts was to tally and track market values over time in search of trends, and they will be discussed individually in the respective text editions below. However, even with only four examples so far, we can begin to make a strong case that among the six commodities the scribes appeared to be mostly interested in the market rates of barley and dates. In fact, only barley and dates appear again and again in all remaining fourteen texts.

Four tablets list the market values of two commodities, always barley and dates: Texts 4, 8, 13, and 14. Two, and probably three, tablets record market rates for three commodities. Texts 9 and 17 monitor barley, dates, and sesame, and it is likely that Text 16 does too. Whatever the purpose of these schemes, whether to simply record market values for two or three commodities at once, to investigate relative variations in market rates, to spot trends, or to judge the correlation of political change with commodity values, we can only guess.

We are on firmer ground with tablets like Text 11, when we speculate about an economic motive on the part of the scribes. This text contains quotations only for barley and only for 3 successive months, XII/208, I/209, and II/209 S.E. We know that barley is harvested in the spring, and, according to the Diaries, that the delivery date of the harvested barley into Babylon could fall in any of the first three months of the year (Slotsky 1997, 25). It could not be more significant, then, to have a record of market values for this commodity in months XII, I, and II, the month prior to, and the first two months of, the harvest season. Month XII is watched in groups of days; month I in just two observations, one from days 1–22 and the other, the 24th to the end of the month; month II gives two quantities, one being ordinary barley for the whole month and the other, poor quality barley, also for the entire month. The facts that (1) the scribes chose what they thought were the three most important months to watch before and at harvest time; (2) market rates were tallied for two of these months in clusters of days until the end of the month; and (3) fractions of amounts are used for the first and only time in the corpus, implies a conscious intent to tally market values and track possible trends in minute detail during one year's harvest of barley.

The date harvest is the focus of Text 10, which tallies market values only for the latter halves, beginning in month VII, of two consecutive years. Dates were usually harvested in the fall, in months VI, VII, and VIII in the data of the Astronomical Diaries (Slotsky 1997, 29), so the last half of a year from harvest time to year's end would have been the critical time for the observation of harvest effects and also for the comparison of harvest output from one year to the next.

Year by year market values of dates seem to be the aim of Text 7. Here the scribe concentrated on one particular month and recorded date values for the beginning, middle, and end of only month VIII for eight successive years. Fresh dates would normally have reached the market by this time, so this was an appropriate month in which to tally date harvest values over time. More significantly, the years 178 to 185 S.E. might have also been an apt time to undertake such a project. The market quotations of the Astronomical Diaries show that, beginning about 107 S.E., supplies of dates began to rise rapidly, i.e., market prices were falling. However, beginning about 193, and especially after 200 S.E., market rates once again dropped off and market prices were on the rise (Slotsky 1997, 59). The data presented in our price tablet show that the drop in the market rate was, in fact, quite precipitous, with 183 S.E. being the critical year. The contemporary political situation could very well have roiled the market (see Text 7 Comments). Not only were dates of interest to the scribes in this period, but the two contemporary Texts, 8 and 9, show that other market values were also tracked. Text 8 concentrates on barley and dates, Text 9 on barley, dates, and sesame. Similarly, Text 3 intended to track monthly barley values over a three-year period, 46–48 S.E. recording beginning, middle, and end-of month quotations as well as market rates in shorter periods during politically changing times (see Text 3 Comments). Text 3A, though fragmentary, appears to have charted price equivalents for all six commodities during a period in which the sale of dates at the market in Babylon was suspended (VII/59 S.E.).

It is difficult to fathom the purpose of those texts that equate enormous quantities of commodities to one mina of silver. One, Text 2, covers I/23 to XII_2/26 S.E. and lists monthly quantities of barley, dates, and mustard. The other, Text 1, likely Achaemenid in date, is similar and records market rates of all six commodities. With two such examples among the eighteen tablets, it is easy to imagine that there was some motive for this scheme, but we are at a loss to adequately explain it. Is it possible that each is a copy of another tablet with amounts equivalent to one or two shekels of silver converted into equivalencies per mina of silver? Or are they inventory texts of a storage house, an accounting of exports to a neighboring country, or a projected prediction?

We suspect multiple motives and purposes at work as the scribes expanded their repertoire from the simple listing of monthly observations to selective tallies and identification of trends. Plainly, in the composition of all these very different kinds of price-only tablets, something other than the observation and recording of variant market values was going on, and the scribes turned their attentions to the investigation of trends of market values during the course of the year, over a span of years, and especially at harvest time. Even as they tracked all six commodities, they underscored the importance of barley and dates above all by tallying trends mostly for these two commodities.

2.3 — Conclusions

Speculation on the relationship between the body of a mere eighteen price lists and the vast data from the Astronomical Diaries would be reckless were it not for conspicuous and momentous differences. Even with such a small sample, we are left with little doubt that the corpus of price tablets and the economic observations in the Astronomical Diaries were not directly linked, neither in the sense that one derived from the other nor that one was composed in the service of the other.

Although the data in both sources are contemporary, and the few matches that could be made were, for the most part, perfect or near-perfect (for some conspicuous exceptions, see §2.2), and despite the fact that both record variant market rates for the same six commodities, the market quotations in each corpora differ radically. They do not use the same statements of equivalency, and the price lists equate commodities to various units of silver instead of the Astronomical Diary's standard one shekel. There are differences in vocabulary and grammar. Most importantly, the Diaries merely record market values, while the price lists particularize and dissect them. Their purpose we suggest was to tally commodity values in order to watch for and track trends in market rates, both short and long term, especially in troubled political times. So distinctive was this enterprise that the price tablets they composed were identified as a separate and specific group of texts and given their own name.

This evidence leads us to believe that the commodity price tablets were a separate but parallel set of price records compiled independently of the Diaries. Like other extraneous scholarly activity, such as the *aḫû* omens, the atypical texts, and the independent astronomical texts, they provide one more indication of scribal scholarship outside what we in our prejudgment regard as the traditional organized repertoire.[34] We want to propose further that, in the belief

34 In September 2008, Christopher Walker informed us of the existence of the cuneiform tablet BM 34117 (Sp 218) for which he most kindly provided photographs and a

that market values were regarded as potentially periodic and, therefore, possibly amenable to predictive schemes, the scribes of the price tablets were also tallying trends in the hope of eventually being able to predict them.

3. THE TEXTS

Reader's Note

In the following text editions, the texts are ordered chronologically when the dates can be determined (Texts 1–11); for the remainder (Texts 12–17) the texts are ordered by their Museum numbers. Tablet dimensions (height × width × thickness) are given in centimeters. For each text a hand copy (life-sized), trans-

---

preliminary transliteration. BM 34117 is a fragment (3.1 × 7.0 × 2.0 cm) of the top left corner of a very well written tablet, with flat squared edges. The tablet was a part of the Sp collection dug up illicitly prior to Rassam's excavations, and was acquired by the British Museum in 1879 (Reade 1986, xv). On the obverse the first five lines are nearly fully preserved with no more than a handful of signs missing along the right margin. On the reverse, portions of the last three lines are less well preserved, followed by a blank space that could have accommodated up to three additional lines of script. The text on the obverse commences with price equivalents for the first five of the six standard commodities in their standard order—barley, dates, mustard, cress, and sesame—and it may be fairly assumed that the price equivalent for wool would have followed at the end of line o.5 or the beginning of line o.6, now largely lost. No year is given, only the month name, APIN (o.1: month VIII), followed immediately by the listing of price equivalents (note similarly Text 11).

Obv.

o.1. ITU.APIN KI.LAM ŠE.IM AŠ SAG ITU 3(b) TA U$_4$.⸢4⸣?(+)[ ]

o.2. TA 11 EN 25 2(b) 3½ *qa* 26 2(b) 4½ *qa* 27 2(b) 4 *qa* x [ZÚ.LUM]

o.3. U$_4$.1 2(p) 3(b) TA U$_4$.2 EN U$_4$.8 2(p) 4(b) 5 *qa* TA U$_4$.9 EN U$_4$.⸢10+⸣[nn]

o.4. 14 2(p) 2(b) 15 2(p) 1(b) 3 *qa* TA 16 EN 21 2(p) 1(b) T[A 22 EN]

o.5. ⸢TA 23+nn EN TIL ITU⸣ 2(p) 1(b) ⸢*kàs*⸣ 1 GUR 2(p) 3(b) *saḫ-le*$_{10}$ 4 *qa* ŠE.G[IŠ]

o.6. [ ] x [ ]

(remainder lost)

Rev.

r.1'. [x x x x 2 SISKUR+DIŠ SISKUR+DIŠ x x [ ]

r.2'. x-*sa-raq-qu-ú* 25 26 SISKUR+DIŠ *šá* É.SA.B[AD?]

r.3'. EN TIL ITU ba ši me[š? ITU] ⸢BI⸣ nam.meš ^{lú}⸢*ar*⸣-[*ba-a-a*(?)]

(*3 lines left blank*)

However, because the text on the reverse, despite its poor condition, appears in part to report (sheep) offerings (SISKUR+DIŠ), which are commonly mentioned in the historical anecdotes in the later Astronomical Diaries where such anecdotes typically conclude the data for any given month, it is self-evident that this tablet stands outside the norms of the Diaries as well as the present corpus. Further speculation as to the purpose of this tablet and the nature of its relationship to the price-only tablets and the Astronomical Diaries is best left for another occasion.

literation, and translation are offered. These are followed, when warranted, by textual notes, comparanda with price equivalents listed for the same time periods in the Astronomical Diaries and/or other price equivalency tablets within the present corpus, and comments. There follows a summary of the price equivalences, reduced uniformly to units of *qa*[35] per 1 shekel[36] of silver for the commodities barley, dates, mustard, cress, and sesame, and of mina[37] per 1 shekel of silver for wool. Babylonian dates are converted into their Julian equivalents following the conventions of Parker and Dubberstein 1956 (cf. Sachs and Hunger 1988, 15). Life-sized photographs of the tablets are collected in the plates.

For many of the tablets in this corpus there exist older hand copies and transliterations by Pinches, Sachs, and/or Wiseman, which, when available to and consulted by the authors, are appropriately cited in the editions below. These older studies, with the exception of Wiseman's copies (Wiseman 1988, 367-73), are unpublished and in most cases obviously preliminary editions by the copyists never intended for publication. Nonetheless, when compared with the newly prepared editions in the present volume the effects on the tablets of handling and storage over the past one and a quarter centuries are often manifest, especially along the margins of the tablet fragments where individual or even whole groups of signs are no longer legible or even evident. Where the older copies lend themselves to improved readings, these have been included in the restorations in the editions and duly referenced in the notes.

35 About 0.84 liter (~ 1 US quart).

36 About 8⅓ grams, or approximately the weight of the current U.S. Sacagawea dollar coin (8.1 g).

37 60 shekels, or about 0.5 kilogram (~ 1 pound).

TEXT EDITIONS

TEXT 1

BM 34712 (Sp II 201 + Sp II 785)
Dimensions: 13.5 x 10.5 x 3.5
Date: years 11 – 15 (RN?)
Commodities: barley, dates, mustard, cress, sesame, wool
Equivalence: 1 mina silver
Unpublished Pinches hand copy (Sp II 201 + Sp II 785)
Photo: Plates I–II

obv.

o.1' [ ] x ⸢3(b)⸣ [ ]

o.2' [*ka-si*] ⸢1⸣,30 GUR [ ]

---

o.3' [MU.12 ZÚ](+) ⸢5(g)⸣ *ka-si* 1,⸢30⸣ [GUR]

o.4' [ ] *ka-si* 1,30 GUR *sa*[*ḫ*]

o.5' [ ] *ka-si* 1,30 GUR *saḫ* 3(g) Š[E.GIŠ]

o.6' ⸢NE⸣ ŠE.BAR 10 GUR ZÚ [nn(g)] ⸢*kàs*⸣ 1,30 GUR *saḫ* 3(g)! ŠE.GIŠ ⸢3(g)⸣ [ ]

o.7' KIN ŠE.BAR 11 GUR <ZÚ> 15(g) *kà*[*s*] ⸢1⸣,30 GUR *saḫ* 2(g) 1(p) 4(b) ŠE.GI[Š]

o.8' DU$_6$ ŠE.BAR 7(g) 2(p) 3(b) ZÚ 14(g) *k*[*às*] ⸢1,10(+)⸣ [GUR *sa*]*ḫ* ⸢3(g) ŠE.GIŠ⸣ [ ]

o.9' ⸢APIN ŠE⸣.BAR 7(g) 1(p) 4(b) ZÚ 12(g) *kàs* ⸢1,30⸣ [GUR]

o.10' [GA]N ŠE.BAR 7(g) 1(p) 4(b) ZÚ 10 GUR *kàs* 1,30 [GUR *sa*]*ḫ* 2(g) 2(p) 3(b) ŠE.GIŠ 2(g) SÍG 2½ G[UN]

o.11' [A]B ŠE.BAR 6(g) 3(p) ⸢1(b)⸣ ZÚ 10 ⸢GUR⸣ *kàs* 1,20 GUR *saḫ* 2(g) 3(p) 2(b) Š[E.GI]Š 2(g) SÍG 3 G[UN]

o.12' ZÍZ ŠE.BAR 7(g) ZÚ 10 GUR *kàs* 1,10 GUR *saḫ* 2(g) 1(p) 4(b) ⸢ŠE.GIŠ nn(g) SÍG nn GUN⸣

o.13' ŠE ŠE.BAR 6(g) ZÚ 8(g) *kàs* 1,20 GUR *saḫ* 2(g) 1(p) 4(b) ˹ŠE.GIŠ 3(g)˺ SÍG 3 G[UN]

---

o.14' MU.13 BAR ŠE.BAR [ ](+)2(p) 3(b) ZÚ 8(g) 2(p) 3(b) ˹*kàs*˺ 1,20 GUR *saḫ* 2(g) 2(p) 3(b) ˹ŠE.GIŠ 3(g) 1(p) 2(+)(b)˺ SÍG 3 [GUN]

o.15' [G]U$_4$ ŠE.BAR 5 ˹GUR˺ ZÚ 8(g) 2(p) 3(b) *kàs* 1,20 GUR *saḫ* 2(g) $1^?$(p) $3^?$(b) ˹ŠE.GIŠ˺ nn(g) 1(b) SÍG 3 [GUN]

o.16' SIG ŠE.BAR 11(g) ZÚ 8(g) *kàs* 1+*šu* GUR *s*[*aḫ*] ŠE.GIŠ 2(g) SÍG [ ] x [ ]

o.17' [Š]U Š[E.BAR] nn GUR 3(p) 2(b) ZÚ 9(g) ˹*kàs*˺ 1+*šu*(g) *saḫ* 5(g) ŠE.GIŠ 4(g) x [ ]

o.18' [NE] ˹ŠE˺.[BAR] 10(+)[ ] x ZÚ 9(g) *kàs* 1,20(g) *saḫ* 5(g) ŠE.GIŠ [ ]

o.19' [KIN] x ˹*kàs*˺ 1,30(g) ˹*saḫ*˺ 5(g) ŠE.GIŠ [ ]

o.20' [DU$_6$] ˹ŠE.GIŠ˺ [ ]

(*remainder lost*)

rev.

r.1' [ ] x x x x x x x [ ]

r.2' [ ] x x x x (bl)

r.3' [KIN ŠE.BAR] 21(g) ZÚ 12 (g) *kàs* 50(g) *saḫ* 8(g) ŠE.GIŠ 2(g) SÍG 2½ [GUN]

r.4' [DU$_6$ ŠE.BAR] 20 GUR ZÚ 12(g) AŠ TIL ITU NE 20 GUR *kàs* 40 GUR

r.5' (bl) *saḫ* 8(g) ŠE.GIŠ 3(g) SÍG 2 GUN

r.6' [APIN ŠE.BAR](+)˹1˺8(g) ZÚ 20 GUR <*kàs*> 30 [G]UR *saḫ* 7(g) ŠE.GIŠ [nn SÍG]

r.6a' (bl) 1½ G[U]N

r.7' [GAN ŠE.BAR](+)5(g) ZÚ 20 GUR *kàs* 10 GUR *saḫ* x ŠE.GIŠ

r.8' (bl) 1(g) 1(p) 4(b) SÍG 2½ G[UN]

r.9' A[B ŠE.BAR](+)2(g) ZÚ 20(g) ˹*kàs*˺ 6(g) *saḫ* 7(g) ŠE.GIŠ 2(g) 1(p) ˹4(b)˺ [SÍG]

r.10' ZÍ[Z] Š[E.BAR](+)2(g) ZÚ 1˹4(+) GUR *kàs*˺ <nn> *saḫ* 10 GUR ŠE.˹GIŠ 2(g) 1(p) 4(b)˺ SÍG x

r.11' ˹ŠE ŠE˺.BAR ˹40(g)˺ [ ] x ˹ZÚ 20 GUR *kàs*˺ 8(g) *saḫ* 10(g) ŠE.GIŠ [ ]

r.12' ˹MU˺.[15] BAR Š[E.BAR]+6(g) ZÚ 20(+)(g) x x ˹*kàs* 7(g)˺ [ ]

r.13' [GU$_4$ ŠE].BAR ˹40(g)˺ [Z]Ú 30(g) ˹*kàs*˺ [*sa*]*ḫ* 12(g) ˹ŠE.GIŠ˺ [ ]

r.14' [SIG ŠE].BAR 40(g) [ ] x [*kàs* nn]˹+1(g)˺ *saḫ* 16(g) ŠE.GIŠ [ ]

r.15' [ŠU *kàs*] 40(g) *saḫ* 16(g) ŠE.GIŠ [ ]

r.16' [NE] x ˹*kàs*˺ 40(g) *saḫ* 16(g) ŠE.GI[Š]

r.17' [KIN] *kàs* 1+*šu*(g) *saḫ* 16(g) Š[E.GIŠ]

r.18' [DU$_6$] *kàs* 1,15(g) *s*[*aḫ*]

(*remainder lost*)

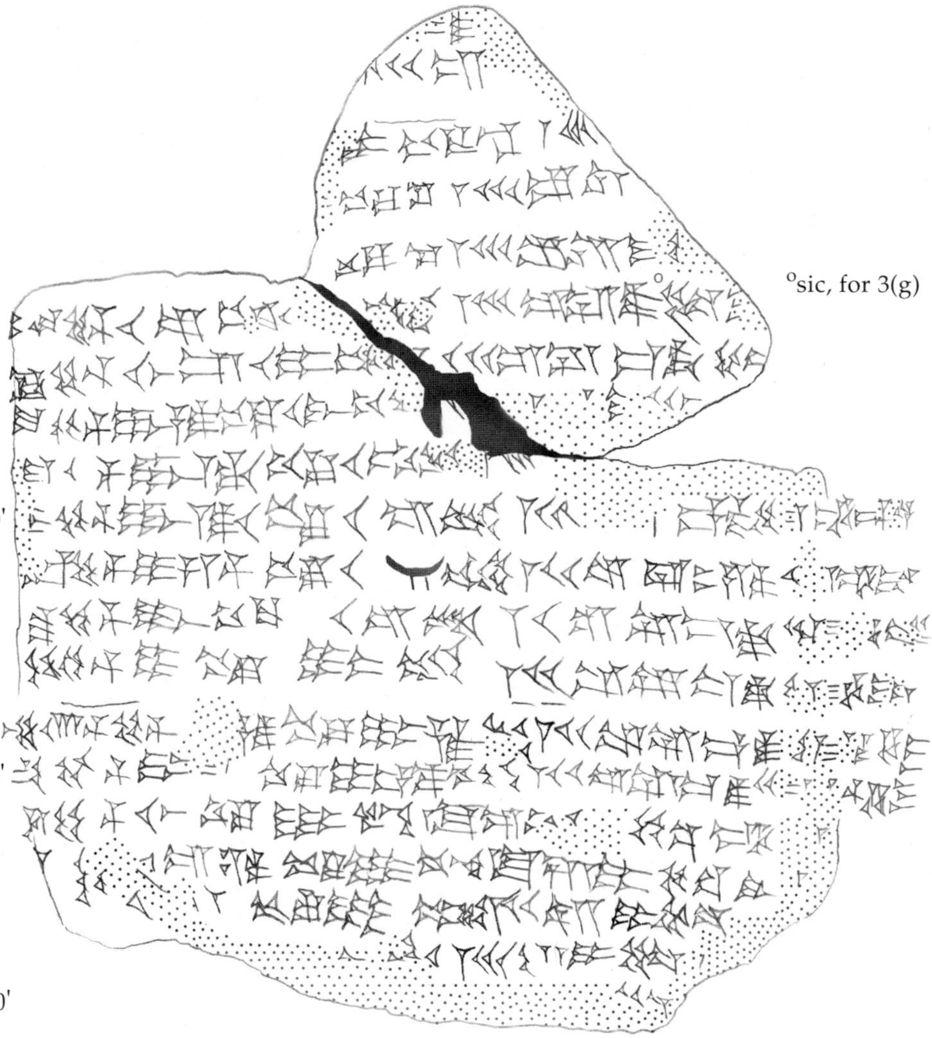

°sic, for 3(g)

BM 34712 obverse

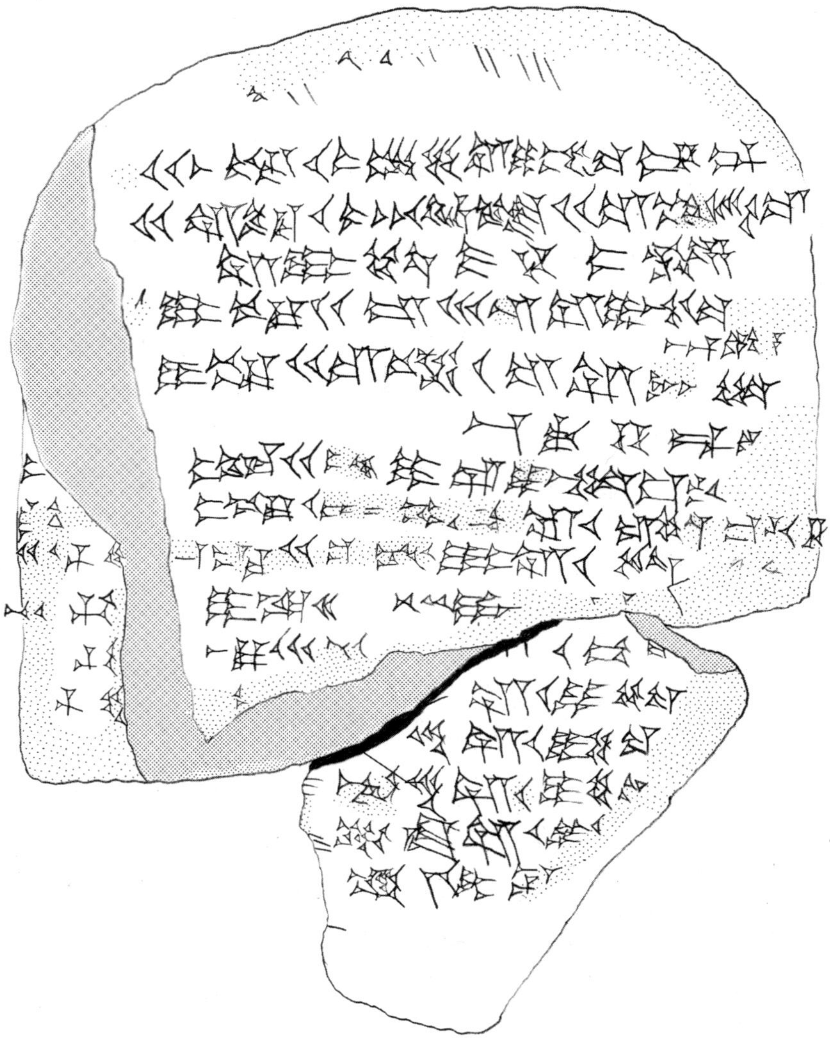

BM 34712 reverse

TRANSLATION

o.1' [...] ... 3 sūt [...].

o.2' [(Year 11) (month $m_{1'}$) ... ; mustard] 1,30 kur [...].

---

o.3' [Year 12 (month $m_{1''}$) ... ; dates](+) 5 kur; mustard 1,30 [kur ...].

o.4' [(month $m_{2''}$) ...]; mustard 1,30 kur; cre[ss ...].

o.5' [(month $m_{3''}$) ...]; mustard 1,30 kur; cress 3 kur; s[esame ...].

o.6' Month V: barley 10 kur; dates [nn] kur; mustard 1,30 kur; cress 3 kur$^{!}$; sesame 3 kur [...].

o.7' Month VI: barley 11 kur; <dates> 15 kur; must[ard] 1,30 kur; cress 2 kur 1 pān 4 sūt; sesa[me ...].

o.8' Month VII: barley 7 kur 2 pān 3 sūt; dates 14 kur; mu[stard] 1,10(+) [kur; cre]ss 3 kur; sesame [...].

o.9' Month VIII: barley 7 kur 1 pān 4 sūt; dates 12 kur; mustard 1,30 [kur ...].

o.10' [Month] IX: barley 7 kur 1 pān 4 sūt; dates 10 kur; mustard 1,30 [kur; cre]ss 2 kur 2 pān 3 sūt; sesame 2 kur; wool 2½ ta[lent].

o.11' [Mon]th X: barley 6 kur 3 pān 1 sūt; dates 10 kur; mustard 1,20 kur; cress 2 kur 3 pān 2 sūt; s[esam]e 2 kur; wool 3 ta[lent].

o.12' Month XI: barley 7 kur; dates 10 kur; mustard 1,10 kur; cress 2 kur 1 pān 4 sūt; sesame nn kur; wool nn talent.

o.13' Month XII: barley 6 kur; dates 8 kur; mustard 1,20 kur; cress 2 kur 1 pān 4 sūt; sesame 3 kur; wool 3 ta[lent].

---

o.14' Year 13. Month I: barley [...](+)2 pān 3 sūt; dates 8 kur 2 pān 3 sūt; mustard 1,20 kur; cress 2 kur 2 pān 3 sūt; sesame 3 kur 1 pān 2(+) sūt; wool 3 [talent].

o.15' [Mon]th II: barley 5 kur; dates 8 kur 2 pān 3 sūt; mustard 1,20 kur; cress 2 kur 1$^{?}$ pān 3$^{?}$ sūt; sesame nn kur 1 sūt; wool 3 [talent].

o.16' Month III: barley 11 kur; dates 8 kur; mustard 1,0 kur; cr[ess ...]; sesame 2 kur; wool [...] ... [...].

o.17' [Month] IV: ba[rley] nn kur 3 pān 2 sūt; dates 9 kur; mustard 1,0 kur; cress 5 kur; sesame 4 kur ... [...].

o.18' [Month V] ba[rley] 10(+)[...] ... ; dates 9 kur; mustard 1,20 kur; cress 5 kur; sesame [...].

o.19' [Month VI ...] ... ; mustard 1,30 kur; cress 5 kur; sesame [...].

o.20' [Month VII ...]; sesame [...]. (*remainder lost*)

r.1' [...] ... [...].

r.2' [...] ... .

r.3' [(Year 14.) Month VI: barley] 21 kur; dates 12 kur; mustard 50 kur; cress 8 kur; sesame 2 kur; wool 2½ [talent].

r.4' [Month VII: barley] 20 kur; dates 12 kur, at the end of this month 20 kur; mustard 40 kur

r.5' cress 8 kur; sesame 3 kur; wool 2 talent.

r.6' [Month VIII: barley nn](+)18 kur; dates 20 kur; <mustard> 30 [k]ur; cress 7 kur; sesame [... ; wool]

r.6a' 1½ ta[len]t.

r.7' [Month IX: barley nn](+)5 kur; dates 20 kur; mustard 10 kur; cress ... ; sesame

r.8' 1 kur 1 pān 4 sūt; wool 2½ ta[lent].

r.9' Mon[th X barley nn](+)2 kur; dates 20 kur; mustard 6 kur; cress 7 kur; sesame 2 kur 1 pān 4 sūt; [wool ...].

r.10' Month [XI]: b[arley nn](+)2 kur; dates 14(+) kur; mustard <nn>; cress 10 kur; sesame 1 kur 1 pān 4 sūt; wool ... .

r.11' Month XII: barley 40 kur [...]; dates 20 kur; mustard 8 kur; cress 10 kur; sesame [...].

r.12' Year [15]. Month I: b[arley nn](+)6 kur; dates 20(+) kur; mustard 7 kur [...].

r.13' [Month II: bar]ley 40 [kur; da]tes 30 kur; mustard [... ; cres]s 12 kur; sesame [...].

r.14' [Month III: bar]ley 40 kur [...] ... [... ; mustard nn](+)1 kur; cress 16 kur; sesame [...].

r.15' [Month IV ... ; mustard] 40 kur; cress 16 kur; sesame [...].

r.16' [Month V ...] ... ; mustard 40 kur; cress 16 kur; sesa[me ...].

r.17' [Month VI ...]; mustard 1,0 kur; cress 16 kur; s[esame ...].

r.18' [Month VII ...]; mustard 1,15 kur; cr[ess ...].

(*remainder lost*)

NOTES

o.6' The text shows 3(b) for the no doubt intended 3(g).

o.11' Perhaps the value for barley is to be read 6(g) 3(p) ⸢2(b)⸣ (= 20 qa/shekel); see further Comments, below.

o.14' Perhaps the value for sesame is to be read 3(g) 1(p) ⸢4(b)⸣ (= 10 qa/shekel); see further Comments, below.

o. 15' The evident reading for cress 2(g) 1(p) 3(b) may be an error for either 2(g) 1(p) 4(b) (= 7 qa/shekel) or 2(g) 2(p) 3(b) (= 7½ qa/shekel); see further Comments, below.

COMMENTS

Text 1 is preserved on two joined fragments of a larger tablet from which are missing perhaps as many as ten lines above and probably six lines below. Portions of the left and right edges are preserved; the last few signs of ll. o.10'–o.15' are written on the right edge. The text records, with a single exception, individual monthly price equivalents for each of the six standard commodities for a period of five or more (consecutive?) years. A second quote for the price equivalent for dates at the end of the month is added for what is presumed to be month VII of year 14 (l. r.4'); the formula used here, AŠ TIL ITU NE "at the end of this month," is unique and differs from that used in comparable situations throughout the remainder of this corpus as well as throughout the Astronomical Diaries by the addition of NE "this."[38]

[38] Contrast ITU BI "that month" in the introductory formula to the commodity price equivalents section in the typical Astronomical Diary.

The price equivalent, although nowhere explicitly stated, is per 1 mina (60 shekels) of silver (cf. Text 2). In addition to the obviously huge quantities expressed by the price equivalents themselves for most commodities, note that wool is expressly (ll. o.10'–o.13') measured in units of *biltu* (GUN) "talent," or 60 mina. Furthermore, the appearance of the values suggests that they were in fact calculated from original measurements in multiples of 1 or ½ qa/shekel. Of the three apparent exceptions, the readings for barley in l. o.11' and sesame in l. o.14' are questionable because of the condition of the tablet surface, and the value for cress in l. o.15' may simply be a scribal error (see Notes, above).

The obverse appears to have contained data for at least three years, each separated from the next by a ruled line; the third year is identified as year 13 (l. o.14'), written without an associated royal name. On the reverse, partial data for two successive years are preserved, presumably years 14 and 15. The regular distribution of the data on the preserved portions of the tablet strongly suggests that each line of the tablet obverse recorded data for a single month. However, if this is in fact the case, then there is only data for three of the first four months of year 12.[39] On the reverse, the data for three successive months (VII – IX) were each completed on a second half line offset toward the right edge (ll. r.4'–r.5', r.6'–r.6a', r.7'–r.8').

The absence of a royal name in the date formula, written simply MU.13 (o.14') and MU.[15] (l. r.12'), prevents the tablet from being securely dated. The year prior to year 13, presumably year 12, ends with month XII (l. o.13') rather than intercalary month XII_2, as would be expected for year 12 of the Seleucid Era (Parker and Dubberstein 1956, 37). Several orthographic practices characteristic of the pre-Seleucid Astronomical Diaries suggest that this tablet should be dated prior to the Seleucid period: mustard is written both as *ka-si* (ll. o.3'–o.5') and *kàs* (ll. o.6'ff.)[40]; and wool is written throughout simply as SÍG.[41] Among the Late Babylonian rulers who enjoyed reigns of at least 15 years and whose 12th regnal year did not contain an intercalary month VI_2 and whose 12th and 14th regnal years did not contain an intercalary month XII_2, Darius I, Artaxerxes I, Darius II, Artaxerxes II, and Artaxerxes III may be considered.[42] Although the evidence from the Astronomical Diaries from the reigns of these rulers is scant,

---

39 Compare Text 3 where data for months X to XII_2/48 S.E. were accidentally or otherwise omitted; see further Text 8.

40 *ka-si* is evidenced consistently in Astronomical Diaries with preserved market prices from year 37 Nebuchadrezzar II through 11 S.E. and only exceptionally thereafter; *kàs* is first evidenced in 20 Artaxerxes II but only becomes the norm after 20 S.E. (Slotsky 1997, 34).

41 SÍG is found exclusively in Astronomical Diaries prior to 3 Darius III, when SÍG.ḪÁ is first seen; thereafter both appear although the latter more frequently (Slotsky 1997, 41).

42 No intercalary month VI_2 is attested or calculated for any of these monarchs during years 12–15 of their respective reigns; an intercalary month XII_2 is attested or calculated for year 13 of the reigns of each (Parker and Dubberstein 1956, 30–35).

the price equivalents here in Text 1 would not be out of place during the reigns of any of these Achaemenid monarchs, except Artaxerxes III.[43]

Although rather fragmentary, the price equivalents by and large fluctuate in resonance with the respective harvest seasons for each commodity, with the exception of mustard (see Summary: Text 1, below). Throughout year 12 and the first half of year 13, mustard price equivalents remained relatively constant and quite high, even months after the peak of the harvest in month VI (Slotsky 1997, 33). However, in year 14, perhaps as a result of a poor harvest, price equivalents peak at only half the earlier values and fall precipitously to one-tenth the harvest value towards the end of that year.

SUMMARY

(barley, dates, mustard, cress, and sesame qa per 1 shekel silver; wool mina per 1 shekel silver)

Year	*Month*	*Barley*	*Dates*	*Mustard*	*Cress*	*Sesame*	*Wool*
[...]							
[11	$m_{1'}$		]	270	[		]
[12	$m_{1''}$		]⸢(+)15⸣	270	[		]
	[$m_{2''}$		]	270	[		]
	[$m_{3''}$		]	270	9	[	]
	V	30	[ ]	270	9	9(+)	[ ]
	VI	33	45	270	7	[	]
	VII	22½	42	⸢210(+)⸣	9	[	]
	VIII	22	36	270	[		]
	IX	22	30	270	7½	6	2½
	X	19.9(+)	30	240	8	9	3
	XI	21	30	210	7	[	]
	XII	18	24	240	7	9	3
13	I	[ ]+1½	25½	240	7½	9.8(+)	3
	II	⸢15(+)⸣	25½	240	7?/7½?	[ ]	3
	III	33	24	180	[ ]	6	[ ]
	IV	[ ]	18	180	15	12(+)	[ ]
	V	[ ]	18	240	15	[	]
	VI	[	]	270	15	[	]

43 The extant price equivalents for IX–XII/12 Artaxerxes III (AD I -346) are in all cases substantially and significantly higher than the corresponding equivalents for months IX–XII, year 12 in Text 1 (see conveniently, Slotsky 1997, 134).

Year	*Month*	*Barley*	*Dates*	*Mustard*	*Cress*	*Sesame*	*Wool*
	[VII						]
	[...]						
[14	VI]	63	36	150	24	6	2½
	[VII]	60	36 @e 60	120	24	9	2
	[VIII	]	60	180	21	[ ]	1½
	[IX]	⸢(+)15⸣	60	30	[ ]	4	2½
	X	⸢(+)6⸣	60	18	21	7	[ ]
	XI	⸢(+)6⸣	⸢42(+)⸣	< >	30	7	[ ]
	XII	⸢120⸣	60	24	30	[	]
[15]	I	⸢(+)18⸣	60(+)	21(+)	[		]
	[II]	120	90	[ ]	36	[	]
	[III]	120	[	]⸢(+)3⸣	48	[	]
	[IV		]	120	48	[	]
	[V		]	120	48	[	]
	[VI		]	180	48	[	]
	[VII		]	225	[		]
	[...]						

	Barley	Dates	Mustard	Cress	Sesame	Wool
High:	120	90	270	48	12(+)	3
Low:	18	18	18	7	4	1½

TEXT 2

BM 36847 (80–6–17,587) (+) BM 37353 (80–6–17,1110)
Date: 23 – 26$^{?}$ S.E. (289/8 – 286$^{?}$/5$^{?}$ BCE)
Dimensions: 4.6 x 5.9 x 3.4; 4.0 x 3.1 x 2.2
Commodities: barley, dates, mustard [...]
Equivalence: 1 mina silver
Publication: Wiseman, *Sachs Mem. Vol.*, 368 [BM 37353]; 369 [BM 36847]
Unpublished Sachs transliteration (BM 36847 + BM 37353)
Photo: Plate III

obv.

o.1 EN.NUN *šá* KI.LAM [ ]
o.2 BAR ŠE.BAR 37 G[UR]
o.3 GU$_4$ ŠE.BAR 44 GUR [ ]
o.4 SIG ŠE.BAR AŠ SAG ITU ⸢20(+)(g)⸣ [ ]
o.5 ŠU ŠE.BAR 38 G[UR]
o.6 NE ŠE.BAR AŠ S[AG ITU]
o.7 ⸢KIN ŠE⸣.[BAR]
o.8 [DU$_6$ ŠE.BAR]
o.9 [APIN ŠE.BAR] ⸢ZÚ⸣ 30(+)(g) [ ]
o.10 [GAN ŠE.BAR TI]L ITU 38(g) [ ]
o.11 [AB ŠE.BAR 3]8(g) AŠ TIL ITU 40(g) ZÚ$^{!}$ 3⸢4(+)(g) [ ]
o.12 [ZÍZ ŠE.BAR nn](+)10(g) ZÚ 38(g) AŠ TIL ITU 40(g) *k*[*às*]
o.13 ŠE Š[E.BA]R 40(g) ZÚ 40(g) AŠ TIL ITU 30(+)x(g) [ ]
o.14 DIRI.ŠE ŠE.BAR 40(g) ZÚ 43(g) *kàs* 13(+)(g) [ ]

---

o.15 MU.24.KÁM ^{m}*se* BAR ŠE.BAR 40(g) ZÚ 44(g) *kà*[*s*]
o.16 GU$_4$ ŠE.BAR 40(g) ⸢ZÚ⸣.LUM 45(g) *kàs* [ ]
o.17 [SIG] ⸢ŠE.BAR 20(+)(g)⸣ ZÚ 45(g) *kà*[*s*]
o.18 [ŠU ŠE.BAR] ⸢ZÚ 34(+)(g)⸣ [ ]

(*remainder lost*)

rev.

r.1' ⸢KIN⸣ [ ]
r.2' DU$_6$ ŠE.⸢BAR⸣ [ ]
r.3' APIN ŠE.BAR 3⸢6(g) ZÚ⸣ [ ]
r.4' GAN ŠE.BAR 31(g) ZÚ 38(g) *k*[*às*]
r.5' AB ŠE.BAR 24(g) ZÚ 34(g) *kà*[*s*]
r.6' ZÍZ ŠE.BAR 30(g) ZÚ 30(g) *k*[*às*]

r.7' ⸢ŠE ŠE⸣.BAR 28(g) ZÚ 30(g) [ ]

---

r.8' [MU.26(?).KÁM] ⸢m⸣*se* BAR ŠE.BAR 28(g) ZÚ 30(g) [ ]

r.9' [GU$_4$ ŠE].BAR 26(g) ZÚ 30(+)(g) [ ]

r.10' [SIG ŠE.BAR] ⸢20(g)⸣ ZÚ ⸢10(+)(g)⸣ [ ]

r.11' [ŠU ŠE.BAR](+)1(g) ZÚ [ ]

r.12' ⸢NE⸣ [ŠE.BAR]

r.13' KIN Š[E.BAR]

r.14' DU$_6$ ŠE.BAR ⸢12(+)(g)⸣ [ ]

r.15' APIN ŠE.BAR 12(g) AŠ TIL I[TU]

r.16' GAN ŠE.BAR 10(g) [ ]

r.17' AB ŠE.BAR 11(g) [ ]

r.18' ZÍZ ŠE.BAR ⸢7(+)(g)⸣ [ ]

r.19' Š[E]

r.20' [DIRI.ŠE(?)]

TRANSLATION

o.1 Watch of the (market) equivalent [… (year 23 S.E.) …].

o.2 Month I: barley 37 k[ur …].

o.3 Month II: barley 44 kur […].

o.4 Month III: barley at the beginning of the month 20(+) kur […].

o.5 Month IV: barley 38 k[ur …].

o.6 Month V: barley at the beg[inning of the month …].

o.7 Month VI: bar[ley …].

o.8 [Month VII: barley …].

o.9 [Month VIII: barley …]; dates 30(+) kur […].

o.10 [Month IX: barley … en]d of the month 38 kur […].

o.11 [Month X: barley 3]8 kur, at the end of the month 40 kur; dates 34(+) kur […].

o.12 [Month XI: barley nn](+)10 kur; dates 38 kur, at the end of the month 40 kur; mus[tard…].

o.13 Month XII: b[arle]y 40 kur; dates 40 kur, at the end of the month 30(+nn) kur […].

o.14 Month XII$_2$: barley 40 kur; dates 43 kur; mustard 13(+) kur […].

---

o.15 Year 24, Se(leucus I). Month I: barley 40 kur; dates 44 kur; must[ard …].

o.16 Month II: barley 40 kur; dates 45 kur; mustard […].

o.17 [Month III]: barley 20(+) kur; dates 45 kur; must[ard …].

o.18 [Month IV: barley …]; dates 34(+) kur […]

(*remainder lost*)

r.1' (year $25^?$ S.E.) Month VI: [barley …].

o. 5'

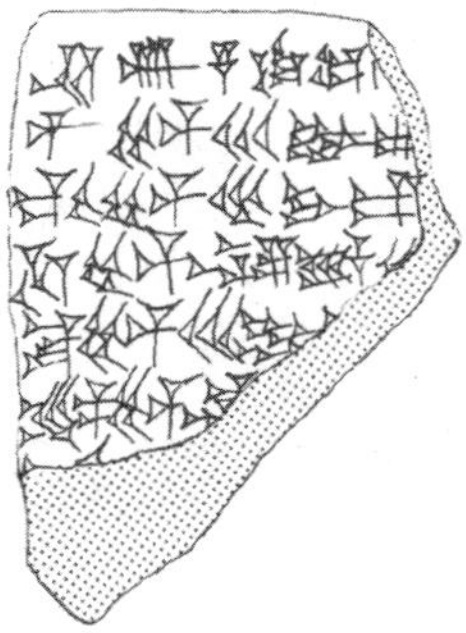

o. 10'

o. 15'

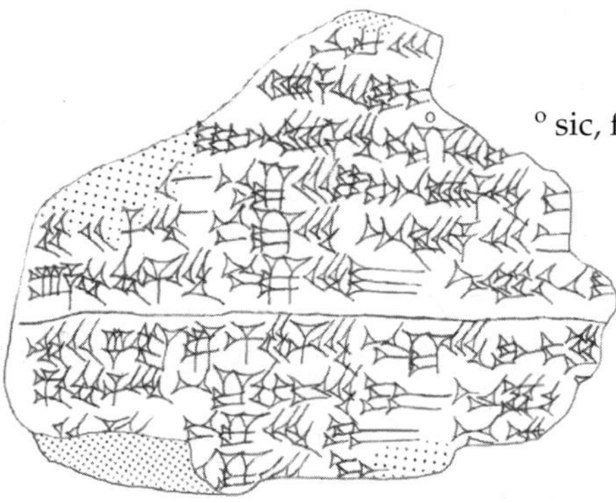

° sic, for ZÚ

BM 36847 (+) BM 37353 obverse

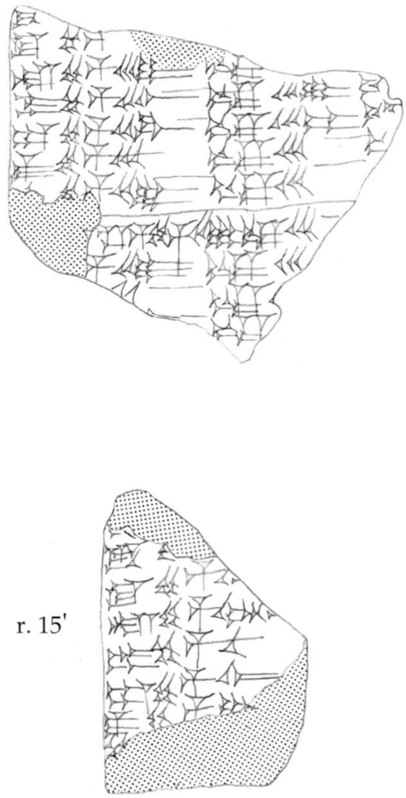

r. 5'

r. 10'

r. 15'

BM 36847 (+) BM 37353 reverse

r.2' Month VII: barley [...].
r.3' Month VIII: barley 36 kur; dates [...].
r.4' Month IX: barley 31 kur; dates 38 kur; mus[tard ...].
r.5' Month X: barley 24 kur; dates 34 kur; must[ard ...].
r.6' Month XI: barley 30 kur; dates 30 kur; mus[tard ...].
r.7' Month XII: barley 28 kur; dates 30 kur [...].

---

r.8' [Year 26$^{?}$], Se(leucus I). Month I: barley 28 kur; dates 30 kur [...].
r.9' [Month II: bar]ley 26 kur; dates 30(+) kur [...].
r.10' [Month III: barley] 20 kur; dates 10(+) kur [...].
r.11' [Month IV: barley ...](+)1 kur; dates [...].
r.12' Month V: [barley ...].
r.13' Month VI: ba[rley ...].
r.14' Month VII: barley 12(+) kur [...].
r.15' Month VIII: barley 12 kur, at the end of the m[onth ...].
r.16' Month IX: barley 10 kur [...].
r.17' Month X: barley 11 kur [...].
r.18' Month XI: barley 7(+) kur [...].
r.19' Month X[II: barley ...].
r.20' [Month XII$_2$(?): barley ...].

NOTES

o.1 The line begins with what may have been the title of these commodity price lists, *maṣṣartu ša maḫīri* "market watch," comparable to the title of the Astronomical Diaries, *maṣṣartu ša ginê* "regular watch."

COMPARANDA

(barley, dates, and mustard qa per 1 shekel silver)

XII$_2$/23 S.E.	*Barley*	*Dates*	*Mustard*
Text 2: o.14	120	129	39(+)
-288: r.10'[a]	120	126	48

a. AD I -288: r.10' ... ŠE].IM 3(p) 2(b) ZÚ.LUM 3(p) 3(b) *kàs* 1(p) 2(b) ...

The 40 kur/mina (i.e., 120 qa/shekel) for barley given in Text 2 is exactly sixty times the equivalence given in AD I -288 (120 qa/shekel); the equated figures for dates, however, are only similar, not identical: 43 kur/mina in Text 2 (i.e., 129 qa/shekel) versus 126 qa/shekel in -288 (i.e., 42 kur/mina). The value for mustard in -288, 48 qa/shekel, suggests the plausible restoration of Text 2: o.14 ⸢13(+)⸣(g) to 1⸢6⸣(g).

COMMENTS

Text 2 is found on two clay tablet fragments that do not physically join to each other. The smaller piece, BM 37353, preserves the beginnings of the first seven lines of the obverse (o.1–o.7) and eight lines at or near the bottom of the reverse (r.12'–r.19'). The larger piece, BM 36847, preserves portions of ten lines on the obverse (o.9–o.18) and eleven lines on the reverse (r.1'–r.11'). Taken together, the obverse of Text 2 shows portions of monthly price equivalents per mina[44] of silver for barley, dates, and mustard during the thirteen months of year 23 S.E. (date restored) and, separated by a ruled line, the first four months of 24 S.E. (date preserved). It seems likely, given the pattern of the commodities cited within the corpus at large, that the complete tablet would have contained data for all of the remaining standard commodities (cress, sesame, and wool); thus fully half of the tablet's width is likely missing. The reverse contains similar data for the last seven months of an unknown year and, separated by a ruled line, twelve months of the following year. If the tablet was as wide as just suggested then it was probably long enough to have contained at least two full years' worth of data on each side, arrayed one month per line. Note that there is sufficient space at the bottom of the reverse for data for an intercalary month XII_2, in which case the data on the reverse are likely to have been for either years 25 and 26 or 27 and 28 S.E., respectively. Unfortunately, with the exception of the data for XII_2/23 S.E. noted in the Comparanda above, none of the remaining data preserved in the fragmentary Astronomical Diaries for 23–28 S.E. can be correlated with the remaining data in Text 2 (see Table 7: Astronomical Diary Commodity Price Equivalents for 23 – 28 S.E.).

TABLE 7
ASTRONOMICAL DIARY COMMODITY PRICE EQUIVALENTS FOR 23 – 28 S.E.

AD I		*Barley*	*Dates*	*Mustard*	*Cress*	*Sesame*	*Wool*
-288: o.8–o.9	VII/23	[			](+)36	12	3
-288: r.10'	XII_2/23	120	126	48	66	18	[ ]
-287: o.10'	I/24	[		](+)42	36	20	[ ]
-286A: r.9'	VI/25	120	81	360	21	27	[ ]
-286A: r.18'	VII/25	120(+)	[				]
-284: o.15'	VII/27	[	]	180(+)	36	@b 24 @e [ ]	[ ]
-284: r.17'	X/27	[ ]	72(+)	[			]

44 See the note to line o.14 under Comparanda, above; see similarly Text 1.

AD I		*Barley*	*Dates*	*Mustard*	*Cress*	*Sesame*	*Wool*
-284: r.31'	XI/27	180	@b 72(+) [ ]	[			]
-283A: o.6–7	VII/28	[ ]	108	180	(+)36	24	4

(barley, dates, mustard, cress, and sesame qa per 1 shekel silver; wool mina per 1 shekel silver)

The data for barley only are sufficiently complete for the period covered (see Summary: Text 2) for any significant observations. Note that throughout years 23 and 24 the price equivalents for barley hold relatively steady at moderate levels whereas during years $y_{1'}$ (25 S.E.?) and $y_{2'}$ (26 S.E.?) they decline steadily and sharply despite the presumed harvest in months I and II of year $y_{2'}$. Plutarch (*Life of Demetrius* 46:4–47:5) reports that in 286 BCE (25/26 S.E.), in response to a letter from Demetrius Poliorcetes in which he sought to alleviate the suffering of his troops from the famine and pestilence they were enduring following their invasion of Asia the previous year, Seleucus I ordered his lieutenants in the region to supply Demetrius with sufficient provisions as befit a king and his army. However, Seleucus' adviser Patrocles soon convinced him of the danger Demetrius presented to his own realm and so Seleucus marched that year into Cilicia with a great army, capturing Demetrius the next year in 285 BCE. Such an undertaking may well have required Seleucus to draw down heavily on the supplies of barley available, especially from Babylon, thus causing the dramatic drop in the price equivalent of barley noted above (assuming, of course, that the conditions producing the famine in western Anatolia were not also mirrored in Babylonia).

SUMMARY

(Barley, dates, mustard, cress, and sesame qa per 1 shekel silver; wool mina per 1 shekel silver)

Year	*Month*	*Barley*	*Dates*	*Mustard*	*Cress*	*Sesame*	*Wool*
[23]	I	111	[				]
	II	132	[				]
	III	@b ⌜60(+)⌝	[				]
	IV	114	[				]
	V	@b [					]
	VI	[					]
	[VII						]
	[VIII		]⌜90(+)⌝[				]

Year	*Month*	*Barley*	*Dates*	*Mustard*	*Cress*	*Sesame*	*Wool*
	[IX	@e 114					]
	[X	]114 @e 120	[				]
	[XI	]⸢(+)30⸣	114 @e 120	[			]
	XII	120	120 @e ⸢90(+)⸣	[			]
	XII$_2$	120	129	⸢39(+)⸣[			]
24	I	120	132	[			]
	II	120	135	[			]
	[III]	⸢60(+)⸣	135	[			]
	[IV		]⸢102(+)⸣[				]
	[…]						
[y$_{1'}$]	VII	[					]
	VIII	108	[				]
	IX	93	114	[			]
	X	72	102	[			]
	XI	90	90	[			]
	XII	84	90	[			]
[y$_{2'}$]	I	84	90(+)[				]
	[II]	78	90(+)[				]
	[III]	60	⸢30(+)⸣[				]
	[IV	](+)3	[				]
	V	[					]
	VI	[					]
	VII	⸢36(+)⸣[					]
	VIII	48	[				]
		@e [ ]					
	IX	30	[				]
	X	33	[				]
	XI	⸢21(+)⸣[					]
	XII	[					]
[…?]							

	Barley	Dates
High:	132	135
Low:	30	90

TEXT 3

BM 32937b (78-5-31,26b)
Date: 46 – 48 S.E. (266/5 – 264/3 BCE)
Dimensions: 5.1 x 4.6 x 1.6
Commodity: barley
Equivalence: 1 shekel silver
Photo: Plate IV

obv.
o.1' [2(p)] ⸢1(b)⸣ AŠ!/EN!(ta) MURUB$_4$ ITU ⸢2 PI⸣
o.2' [ ] x lum? 2(p) 1(b) 2 *qa*
o.3' [ ] 2 PI AŠ TIL ITU 2 PI 1½ *qa*
o.4' [ ] 2(p) ⸢nn(b)⸣ 1 *qa* AŠ MURUB$_4$ <ITU> 2 PI AŠ TIL ITU 1(p) 5(b) 1 *qa*
o.5' MU.47 BAR ŠE 1(p) 3(b) AŠ MURUB$_4$ <ITU> 1(p) 4(b) [ ]
o.6' AŠ TIL ITU 1(p) 4(b)
o.7' GU$_4$ 1(p) 4(b) TA 20⸢(+) EN⸣ TIL [I]TU 1(p) ⸢nn(b)⸣ [ ]
o.8' SIG 2(p) 3(b)
(remainder lost)

rev.
r.1' [*(traces)*]
r.2' ⸢DU$_6$⸣ [ ] x x [*(traces)*]
r.3' EN 20 x x [TA] 21 EN [ ]
r.4' 1(p) 5(b) AŠ TIL [IT]U 1(p) 4(b)
r.5' APIN 1(p) 4(b) TA 7 EN 16 1(p) 2(b) [ ]
r.6' EN TIL ITU 1(p) 3(b)
r.7' GAN AŠ SAG ITU 1(p) 3(b) AŠ MURUB$_4$ <ITU> 1(p) 2(b) 1 *qa*
r.8' AŠ TIL ITU 1(p) 2(b) (bl) <MU.>48 ŠE.IM
r.9' [BA]R 1 (p) 1(b) 3 *qa* AŠ MURUB$_4$ <ITU> 1(p) 2(b) AŠ TIL ITU 1(p) x [ ]
r.10' [GU$_4$] x 3 *qa* AŠ TIL ITU x [ ]
r.11' [ ] x šu? k[a?]
(remainder lost)

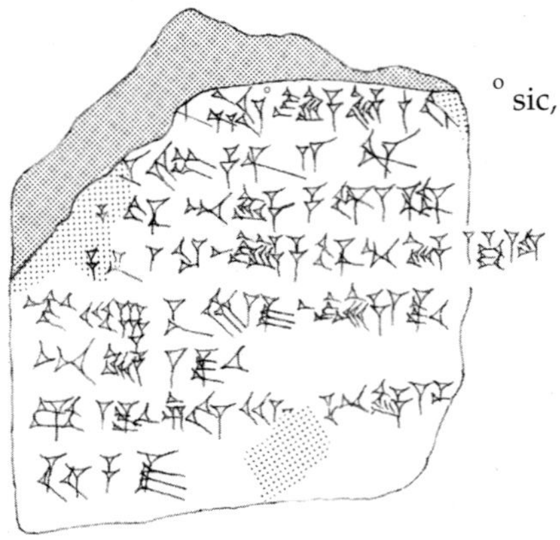

° sic, for EN or AŠ

o. 5'

BM 32937b obverse

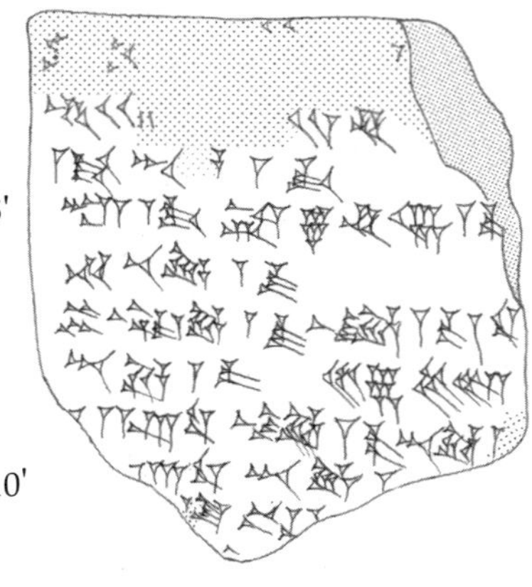

r. 5'

r. 10'

BM 32937b reverse

TRANSLATION

o.1' [(year 46 S.E.) (month $m_{1'}$) . . .] nn sūt, in!/to! the middle of the month 2 pān

o.2' [(month $m_{2'}$) . . .] . . . 2 pān 1sūt 2 qa

o.3' [(month $m_{3'}$) . . .] 2 pān, at the end of the month 2 pān 1½ qa.

o.4' [(month $m_{4'}$) . . .] 2 pān nn sūt 1 qa, in the middle <of the month> 2 pān, at the end of the month 1 pān 5 sūt 1 qa.

o.5' Year 47. Month I: barley 1 pān 3 sūt, in the middle <of the month> 1 pān 4 sūt [. . .],

o.6' at the end of the month 1 pān 4 sūt.

o.7' Month II: 1 pān 4 sūt, from the 20(+)th to the end of the month 1 pān nn sūt [. . .].

o.8' Month III: 2 pān 3 sūt.

(remainder lost)

r.1' [. . .]

r.2' Month VII: [. . .] . . . [. . . , from the . . .]

r.3' to the 20th . . . [. . . , from] the 21st to the [. . .]

r.4' 1 pān 5 sūt, at the end of the month 1 pān 4 sūt.

r.5' Month VIII: 1 pān 4 sūt, from the 7th to the 16th 1 pān 2 sūt [. . . , from the . . .]

r.6' to the end of the month 1 pān 3 sūt.

r.7' Month IX: at the beginning of the month 1 pān 3 sūt, in the middle <of the month> 1 pān 2 sūt 1 qa,

r.8' at the end of the month 1 pān 2 sūt. <Year> 48. Barley.

r.9' Month I: 1 pān 1 sūt 3 qa, in the middle <of the month> 1 pān 2 sūt, at the end of the month 1 pān . . . [. . .].

r.10' [Month II: . . .] . . . 3 qa, at the end of the month nn [. . .]

r.11' [. . .] . . . [. . .]

(remainder lost)

NOTES

o.1' The scribe wrote TA for the expected AŠ or EN.

o.2' Is] x lum to be restored Z]Ú.LUM . . . ?

r.11' Is šu to be read ŠU (i.e., month IV)? Is k[a? to be restored Z[Ú.LUM . . . ?

COMMENTS

Text 3 is found on a single tablet fragment preserved in part to its full width; perhaps a half dozen or more lines are lost from the top and one or two lines are lost from the bottom. The text, written in a vulgar diagonal tablet cursive, lists the monthly price equivalent, typically at the beginning, middle, and end of the month, but in several cases for shorter periods, per one shekel of silver for just a single commodity, barley.[45] On the obverse, there is fragmentary data for some four months in 46 S.E.[46] (date restored) and the first three months of 47 S.E. (date preserved). On the reverse, price equivalents for months VII through IX are abruptly followed by month I/48 S.E. (date preserved), i.e., months X – XII^2/ 47 S.E. are omitted. Inserting an abbreviated introductory formula without the expected preceding MU-sign for year 48 (compare o.5') in the space remaining at the end of line r.8' rather than beginning the new year on a fresh line as is typical suggests that the omission of the last four months of 47 S.E. may not have been intentional.[47] As a consequence of what appear to be numerous additional scribal lapses—note that in four of five occurrences of quotes involving the middle of the month, the scribe abbreviated the writing to simply AŠ MURUB$_4$ (ll. o.4', o.5', r.7', r.9'), perhaps a form of haplography given the similarity of the MURUB$_4$ and ITU signs in the Late Babylonian ductus; also note TA[*sic*] MURUB$_4$ ITU (o.1') instead of the expected AŠ or EN MURUB$_4$ ITU—it seems prudent not to attempt to identify the months ($m_{1'} – m_{4'}$) at the end of what is presumed to be 46 S.E. Unfortunately, the extent Astronomical Diaries for the period in question (AD I -264, -263) do not preserve any relevant price equivalents for purposes of comparison.

The first year monitored in Text 3, 46 S.E., some five years after the end of the First Syrian War, saw a curious transition of power occur. Following the death of Seleucus I in 31 S.E., Antiochus I, his son and coregent since 18 S.E., immediately appointed his own son Seleucus as co-regent. Between sometime in 45 S.E. and 5/ V/46 S.E. Antiochus had created a short-lived triumvirate by naming yet another son, Antiochus, as co-regent (Stolper Records of Deposit 46ff. 15:4'-5'). However, for reasons unknown, within two months Seleucus had been executed by his father (Trogus, *Prologues* 26) and the kingship was now in the hands of Antiochus I and the future Antiochus II (see conveniently Boiy 2004, 144–45).

---

45 Only barley, ŠE(.IM) is specified in the tablet (o.5', r.8'), in each case immediately following the identification of a new year. Although the lum-sign in o.2' and k[a]-sign (=ZÚ) in r.11' would ordinarily in this corpus readily lend themselves to being restored to read ZÚ(.LUM) "dates," in the areas of the tablet where continuous readings are possible, e.g., o.5'–o.8', r.5'–r.9', there is sufficient data for only a single commodity, presumably barley.

46 Although no royal name is associated with the year numerals, the Seleucid Era is assured as no Neo-Babylonian, Achaemenid, or Macedonian king enjoyed a reign of 48 years—Antiochus I reigned 31–51 S.E.

47 Compare Text 1:o.3'–o.5', which appears to be missing one of the first four months of year 12. Also note the omission of months I–VI/189 S.E. in Text 8, and I–VI/194$^?$ and I–VI/195$^?$ S.E. in Text 10.

Summary

(barley qa per 1 shekel silver)

Year	*Month*	*Barley*
[. . .]		
[46	$m_{1'}$	] 78
		→/@m! 72
	[$m_{2'}$	] 80
	[$m_{3'}$	] 72
		@e 73'
	[$m_{4'}$	] ⸢79(+)⸣
		@m 72
		@e 67
47	I	54
		@m 60(+)
		@e 60
	II	60
		20(+)→e ⸢36(+)⸣
	III	90
	[. . .]	
	VII	[ ]
		[ ]→20 [ ]
		21→[ ] 66
		@e 60
	VIII	60
		7→16 48(+)
		→e 54
	IX	@b 54
		@m 49
		@e 48
48	I	45
		@m 48
		@e 36(+)
	[II	]⸢(+)3⸣
		@e [ ]
	[. . .]	

High: 90
Low: 45

TEXT 3A

BM 95313 (1901–10–12,966)
Dimensions: 3.4 x 3.9 x 2.1
Date: 58 – [...] S.E.
Commodities: Barley, dates, mustard, cress [...]
Equivalence: 1(?) shekel silver
Photo: Plate V

obv.

o.1 ⸢MU.58.KÁM ^{m}*an-ti-*ʾ⸣ x [ ]
o.2 (bl) ⸢*kas*$_x$⸣ 1 GUR 2(p) 4(b) ⸢*saḫ*⸣[ ]
o.3 ITU.GU$_4$ ŠE.BAR ⸢2⸣ PI! ZÚ x [ ]
o.4 ITU.SIG ŠE.BAR 2 PI ZÚ 1(p) x [ ]
o.5 ITU.ŠU ŠE.BAR 2 PI ZÚ 1(p) x [ ]
o.6 ITU.NE ŠE.BAR ⸢2 PI⸣ ZÚ x [ ]
o.7 ITU.KIN$_x$ ŠE.BAR [ ]
(*remainder lost*)

rev.

r.1' [ ]
r.2' (bl) [ ] x
r.3' ⸢ITU⸣.ZÍZ? ŠE.BAR ⸢1⸣ GUR 1(p) x [ ]
r.4' (bl) *saḫ* x x [ ]
r.5' [ ]

TRANSLATION

o.1 Year 58 Antio[chus (II) ...];
o.2 (month I) mustard 1 kur 2 pān 4 sūt; cress [...].
o.3 Month II: barley 2 pān; dates ... [...].
o.4 Month III: barley 2 pān; dates 1 pān [...].
o.5 Month IV: barley 2 pān; dates 1 pān ... [...].
o.6 Month V: barley 2 pān; dates ... [...].
o.7 Month VI: barley [...].
(*remainder lost*)
r.1' [...]
r.2' [...] ....
r.3' (year $y_{1'}$) Month XI?: barley 1 kur 1pān ... [...];
r.4' cress ... [...]
r.5' [...].

NOTES

The edition presented here was prepared entirely from photographs generously supplied by Paola Corò and Christopher Walker, thus no handcopy is offered. Collations were most kindly provided at our request by Christopher Walker and Irving Finkel, however we remain entirely responsible for their interpretation.

r.3' For ⌜ITU⌝.ZÍZ$^{?}$ the alternate reading ⌜ITU⌝.ŠU$^{!}$ (Month IV) is not excluded.

COMMENTS

Text 3A is found on a small fragment of the upper left corner of a tablet with portions of the uninscribed upper and left edges preserved. The text is written in well-spaced lines in a clear script with diagonal tendencies, especially evident on the reverse; damage to both the obverse and reverse surfaces makes many of the signs difficult to read with certainty. On the obverse price equivalents for barley, dates, mustard, and cress are variously preserved for what appears to be month I through month VI of year 58 S.E., during the reign of Antiochus II; on the less-well preserved reverse, in what appear to have been the last few lines of the tablet, are a partial value for barley and indications of a now-lost value for cress, both for month XI$^{?}$ of an unspecified year $y_{1'}$, perhaps the following year, 59 S.E. Elsewhere in this corpus (Texts 1, 5, 6, 12) barley, dates, mustard, and cress only occur together in lists of price equivalents containing all six standard commodities and so it may be assumed that this tablet also originally treated the remaining two commodities, sesame and wool, in the now lost portions of the tablet. In this light it may be estimated that at least half of both the width and length of the tablet are now lost, and that the original tablet may have held data for at least two (full?) years. The price equivalent is not preserved, but comparisons with the contemporary Astronomical Diaries suggest that it is per one shekel of silver.

The year 58 S.E., together with the year(s) immediately following may have been of particular interest to the ancient scribe of Text 3A because during month VII (whose data might have been expected on the now-lost line o.8) of that year the sale of dates was suspended at the market in Babylon—this is the second of just two certain occurrences of the suspension of the sale of dates as evidenced by the Astronomical Diaries[48] (Slotsky 1997, 30–31). For the possible assignment of Text 14 to the very years 58 S.E. and following, the broader historical context surrounding the suspension of the sale of dates in V/58 S.E. towards the end of the Second Syrian War (260 – 253$^{?}$ BCE), and the evidence for the possible regulation of the market in its immediate aftermath, see Text 14, Comments, below.

---

48 AD II -253B_1: o.4' (VII/58 S.E.); earlier (325 BCE), the sale of all commodities was cut off until the 5th day of month II, year 12 Alexander III (AD I -324B: o.12' … K]I.LAM ŠE-*e u* KI.LAM *mim-ma gab-bi* (o.13') EN U_4.5 AŠ SILA.ME E^{ki} TAR-*is*); also note AD III –82A: r.17' […] ⌜x⌝ *a tú* KUD-*a*, "[…] … were cut off."

In addition to providing fragmentary data for the commodity dates during 58 S.E., Text 3A also provides barley price equivalents for months II to V—the period at and immediately following the barley harvest—which remain fixed for four consecutive months at 72 qa per shekel of silver. When seen in the light of the Astronomical Diary data for this, the period of the Second Syrian War (see Table 7A), the relatively low and stable price equivalents during the war followed by higher and more volatile price equivalents in the years after the war, suggest considerable economic hardship for the local population as the war progressed (see further, Text 14, Comments).

TABLE 7A

ASTRONOMICAL DIARY PRICE EQUIVALENTS FOR BARLEY, DATES, AND MUSTARD DURING 260 – 247 BCE/52 – 64 S.E.

		barley	*dates*	*mustard*
260 BCE -259	X/52 S.E.	90	114	222(+)
258 BCE -257A	I/54	[ ]	82½ @e 84	[ ]
	II/54	[ ]	124	198(+)
257 BCE -256	III/55	36	51	108
256 BCE	XI/55	24	51 @e 45	[ ]
-255A	I/56	24	45	225
	II/56	@e 42	45	225
	VI/56	42	60	180
	VI_2/56	42	72	180
255 BCE -254	IX/57	[ ]	(+)60	270
	X/57	[	]	270
254 BCE -253	VII/58	120	cut off	180
	IX/58	108	[	]
253 BCE	XII_2/58	[	]	108
252 BCE -251	VII/60	240 @e 237	new: 108	270
251 BCE	XII/60	[	]	300
250 BCE -249A	IV/62	[	]	60 [*sic*]
249 BCE -249B	X/62	[	]	360
	XI/62	[ ]	@e 120	396(+)
	XII/62	[ ]	(+)33	450
248 BCE -247B	VII/64	45	120	450
247 BCE -247C	X/64	150	135	540

		barley	*dates*	*mustard*
	XI/64	132	[	]
-247B	XII_2/64	198 @m 216	114 @m [ ]	[ ]

(Barley, dates, and mustard qa per 1 shekel silver)

SUMMARY

(barley, dates. and mustard qa per 1(?) shekel silver)

Year	*Month*	*Barley*	*Dates*	*Mustard*	*Cress*	[ ]
58	I	[ ]	60	276	[ ]	[ ]
	II	72	[			]
	III	72	36(+)[			]
	IV	72	36(+)[			]
	V	72	[			]
	VI	[				]
	[...]					
[$y_{1'}$]	XI	216(+)[		]	[ ]	[ ]
	[...]					

	Barley	Dates	Mustard	Cress	
High:	216(+)	60	(276)	[	]
Low:	72	36(+)	(276)	[	]

TEXT 4

BM 36730 (80–6–17,463)
Date: 69$^?$(71$^!$) – 71[*sic*] S.E. (243/2$^?$(241/0$^!$) – 241/0$^?$ BCE)
Dimensions: 10.3 x 8.0 x 3.0
Commodities: barley, dates
Equivalence: 1 shekel silver
Publication: Wiseman, *Sachs Mem. Vol.*, 367–68, 373.
Photo: Plate VI

obv.

1' [*(traces)*]
2' ⸢NE⸣ [KI.MIN 1(p)] ⸢4(b)⸣ ZÚ 2(p) 3(b) [ ]
3' KIN KI.MIN 1(p) 3(b) AŠ MURUB$_4$ ITU 1(p) 4(b) ZÚ [ ]
4' DU$_6$ KI.MIN 1(p) 1(b) 3 *qa* ZÚ 2(p) 2(b)
5' APIN KI.MIN 1(p) 1(b) 3 *qa* AŠ MURUB$_4$ ITU x x [A]Š TIL ITU 1(p) x
6' [G]AN KI.MIN 1(p) 1(b) 3 *qa* ZÚ 1(p) 5(b) [nn *q*]*a*
7' [A]B KI.MIN 1(p) 2(b) AŠ MURUB$_4$ ITU 1(p) 1(b) 3 *q*[*a* Z]Ú 2 PI
8' ZÍZ KI.MIN AŠ SAG ITU 1(p) 1(b) 3 *qa* AŠ MU[RUB$_4$ I]TU 1 PI
9' ŠE KI.MIN 1(p) 1(b) 3 *qa* AŠ MURUB$_4$ ITU [ ] 3 *qa* AŠ TIL IT[U]
10' ZÚ 2 PI AŠ MURUB$_4$ ITU 1(p) ⸢4(+)(b)⸣

11' MU.1,10.KÁM ^{m}*se-lu-ku* LU[GAL]
12' BAR KI$^!$.LAM ŠE.IM
13' GU$_4$ *(erasure)*
14' SIG *(erasure)*

rev.

15' ŠU *(erasure)*
16' NE *(erasure)*
17' KIN *(erasure)*
18' DU$_6$ *(erasure)*
19' API[N] *(erasure)* i- MU.38.KÁM [ ]
20' GAN *(erasure)* ii- SIG UD.1.KÁM KI.[LAM$^?$]
21' AB *(erasure)* iii- *šá* EBUR x x [ ]
22' ZÍZ *(erasure)*
23' ŠE *(erasure)*

24' MU.1,11.KÁM ^{m}*se-lu-*[*ku* LUGAL]
25' BAR KI.LAM ŠE.IM 3(p) [ ]
26' GU$_4$ ⸢KI.MIN⸣ x x x [ ]
(*remainder lost*)

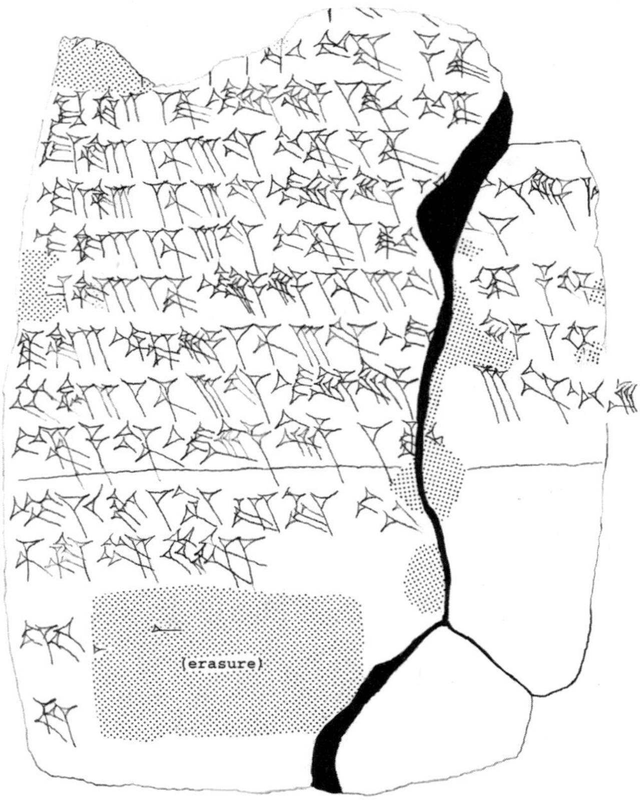

BM 36730 obverse

r. 5'

r. 10'

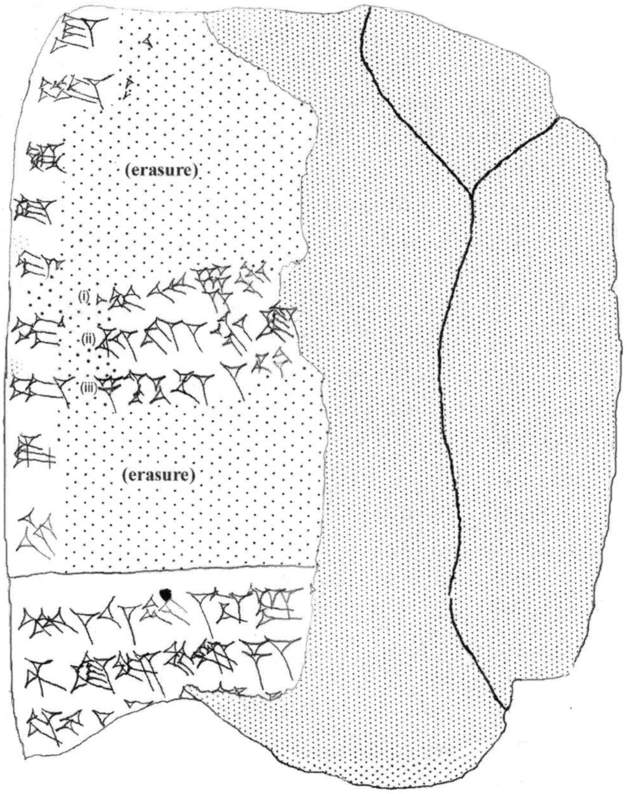

BM 36730 reverse

TRANSLATION

o.1' […]
o.2' (year 69 S.E.) Month V: [ditto (barley) 1 pān] 4 sūt; dates 2 pān 3 sūt [. . .].
o.3' Month VI: ditto 1 pān 3 sūt, in the middle of the month 1 pān 4 sūt; dates [. . .].
o.4' Month VII: ditto 1 pān 1 sūt 3 qa; dates 2 pān 2 sūt.
o.5' Month VIII: ditto 1 pān 1 sūt 3 qa, in the middle of the month . . . [a]t the end of the month 1 pān . . . .
o.6' [Mo]nth IX: ditto 1 pān 1 sūt 3 qa; dates 1 pān 5 sūt [nn q]a.
o.7' [Mon]th X: ditto 1 pān 2 sūt, in the middle of the month 1 pān 1 sūt 3 q[a; da]tes 2 pān [. . .].
o.8' Month XI: ditto at the beginning of the month 1 pān 1 sūt 3 qa, in the mid[dle of the mo]nth 1 pān [. . .].
o.9' Month XII: ditto 1 pān 1 sūt 3 qa, in the middle of the month [nn] 3 qa, at the end of the mon[th . . .];
o.10' dates 2 pān, in the middle of the month 1 pān 4(+) sūt.

---

o.11' Year 70, Seleucus (II), king.
o.12' Month I: the equivalent of barley
o.13' Month II: (erasure)
o.14' Month III: (erasure)
r.15' Month IV: (erasure)
r.16' Month V: (erasure)
r.17' Month VI: (erasure)
r.18' Month VII: (erasure)
r.19' Month [VIII]: (erasure)
r.20' Month IX: (erasure)
r.21' Month X: (erasure)
r.22' Month XI: (erasure)
r.23' Month XII: (erasure)

i- Year 38 […]
ii- Month III, day 1, equi[valent[?]…]
iii- of the crop … […]

---

r.24' Year 71, Seleu[cus (II), king]
r.25' Month I: the equivalent of barley 3 pān […]
r.26' Month II: ditto … […]
(*remainder lost*)

COMMENTS

Text 4 is written in a clear but vulgar diagonal tablet cursive on a moderately well preserved tablet missing perhaps just four lines from the top edge; the right half of the surface of the reverse is also lost. The text appears originally to have listed monthly price equivalents for barley and dates per 1 shekel of silver for three consecutive years; the second and third years are labeled 70 and 71 S.E., thus the first year is presumably to be restored [69] S.E. Each line of the tablet begins a new month (except for l. 10'), with each year separated from the next by a horizontal ruling. Exceptionally in this corpus, the sign for month I (BAR, ll. 12', 25') is followed by the formula KI.LAM ŠE.IM ("the equivalent of barley"), reminiscent of the formula that typically introduces the commodity price equivalent portion of the Astronomical Diaries, ITU BI KI.LAM ŠE.IM ("that month the equivalent of barley"); for the succeeding months in Text 4 (ll. 3'–9'), the formula is replaced, uniquely here, by the month name followed by KI.MIN ("ditto," i.e., the equivalent of barley).[49]

Most remarkable about this tablet is the fact that all of the price equivalence data for what is labeled 70 S.E. (lines 12'–23') has been erased, leaving only the signs for the month names at the beginning of each line. In this erased area, near lines 19'–21' in the middle of the reverse, three lines of a cuneiform graffito were written over the erasure in a similar but smaller script: only the first few signs of each of these line are preserved but they quite clearly refer to the price equivalent(s) for day 1, month III, year 38, and to the summer crop or harvest.

TABLE 8
ASTRONOMICAL DIARY COMMODITY PRICE EQUIVALENTS
FOR 69 – 71 S.E.

AD II	*Date (S.E.)*	*Barley*	*Dates*
-242: o.12'	XI/69	204	[ ]
-241: o.7'	II/70	225	[ ]
-240: o.19'	IX/71	[	](+)33
-240: r.9	X/71	[@b] 48 @m 45	72

(Barley, dates qa per 1 shekel silver)

Comparisons with the corresponding data in the Astronomical Diaries for 69 through 71 S.E. (see Table 8: Astronomical Diary Commodity Price Equivalents for 69 to 71 S.E.) suggest that the scribe committed a series of lapses of the stylus while copying data from his original source(s) for what he had intended to be 69 to 71 S.E. Self evidently, before the tablet had fully dried the presumably

49 Compare Text 9, which gives ITU MN KI.LAM ŠE.IM throughout.

erroneous data entered for 70 S.E. were recognized and all but the month name headings were deleted. However, there was apparently another serious lapse that was not observed, or if it was, no attempt was made to correct it. Note that the corresponding data points for the presumed year 69 S.E. in Text 4 (see Summary: Text 4, below) are completely incongruent with those in the Diary for 69 S.E.,[50] but are identical to those in the Diary for 71 S.E.[51] In this light, the remaining preserved values for months V to XII (ll. 2'–10') are better taken to be those for 71 S.E., as per AD II -240, rather than 69 S.E. Strengthening this likelihood is the fact that there are no data offered in Text 4 for the intercalary month XII_2 of the presumed 69 S.E. whereas 71 S.E. was in fact a regular 12 lunar-month year.[52] What the scribe of Text 4 might have originally written for the year labeled 71 S.E. cannot be divined as that part of the tablet is now lost.

The additional reference in the graffito to year 38 is without parallel within the corpus. Although it is by no means certain that year 38 of the Seleucid Era was intended here, it might be conjectured that the scribe may have been noting equivalents from that year that were broadly similar to some of the data he had recorded for 71 S.E., which he mislabeled 69, although they are certainly no match.[53] On the other hand, the graffito may be nothing more than a doodle of no significance to the tablet at hand whatsoever.

The intended span of years, 69 to 71 S.E., that held interest for the ancient scribe of Text 4 were the last three years of the Third Syrian (Laodikean) War.[54] At the conclusion of the Second Syrian War, circa 253 BCE, Antiochus II put aside his wife Laodike with whom he had had five children and married Berenike, the daughter of his former enemy Ptolemy II. Laodike, seeking to ensure that her son Seleucus would inherit the throne, conspired to have Antiochus as well as Berenike and her son by Antiochus murdered—each variously met their fate in 246 BCE whereupon Seleucus (II) was recognized as king in Babylonia. Berenike's brother, Ptolemy III, who that same year inherited his father's throne in Egypt, now launched an invasion of the Seleucid kingdom that apparently

---

50 AD II -242: o.12' offers for XI/69 S.E. for barley the equivalent of 204 qa/shekel—1(g) 4(b)—in contrast to the value in Text 4:8 of just 45 qa/shekel—1(p) 1(b) 3 *qa*—at the beginning of the month.

51 AD II -240: r.9 for X/71 S.E. gives equivalents for barley of 48 and 45 qa/shekel at the beginning and middle of the month, respectively, and the equivalent for dates of 72 qa/shekel—1(p) 2(b) AŠ $MURUB_4$ ITU 1(p) 1(b) 3 *qa* ZÚ 2 PI—which are identical to those in Text 4:7' for month X of the year preceding the one labeled 70 S.E.

52 AD II -240 is quite securely dated by several planetary observations and the mention of a solar eclipse at the end of month VIII (Sachs and Hunger 1989, 79–83).

53 Note the equivalents for barley and dates for VII/38 S.E. are 36 and 72 qa/shekel respectively—AD I -273B: o.9 … ITU BI KI.LAM Š[E.I]M 1 PI ZÚ.LUM 2 PI …; and for XII/38 S.E., 36 and 90 qa/shekel, respectively—AD I -273B: r.26' … ITU BI KI.LAM ŠE.IM 1 PI [Z]Ú.LUM 2(p) 3(b).

54 For a general overview and statement on the difficulties in reconstructing the events of this war, see Heinen 1984, 420–21; see also Boiy 2004, 149–53.

carried him to Babylon and the eastern capital at Seleucia on the Tigris (Appian, 65).[55] Taking advantage of the upheaval, the Parthians in neighboring Iran seized the opportunity to throw off the Seleucid yoke. The next year, 245 BCE, saw an uprising in Egypt forcing Ptolemy to abandon his campaign and return to Egypt; Seleucus then unsuccessfully pursued the war in Syria until its conclusion in 241 BCE.

SUMMARY

(barley and dates qa per 1 shekel silver)

Year	*Month*	*Barley*	*Dates*
[. . .]			
[69$^?$/71$^!$]	V	⸢60⸣	90
	VI	54 @m 60	[ ]
	VII	45	84
	VIII	45 @m [ ] @e 36(+)	[ ]
	IX	45	⸢96–101⸣
	X	48 @m 45	72
	XI	@b 45 @m 36(+)	[ ]
	XII	45 @m ⸢(+)3⸣ @e [ ]	72 @m 60(+)
	<XII$_2^?$		>
70[*sic*]	I	<	>
	II	<	>
	III	<	>
	IV	<	>
	V	<	>
	VI	<	>
	VII	<	>

55 Finkel and Van der Spek BCHP 11 have recently suggested that an undated chronicle in the British Museum (BM 34428) contains a reference to Ptolemy's unsuccessful siege of Babylon (http://www.livius.org/cg-cm/chronicles/bchp-ptolemy_iii/bchp_ ptolemy _iii_01.html).

Year	*Month*	*Barley*	*Dates*
	VIII	<	>
	IX	<	>
	X	<	>
	XI	<	>
	XII	<	>
71[*sic*]	I	108(+)[	]
	II	[	]
	[...]		

High:		108(+)	96(+)
Low:		45	72

TEXT 5

BM 35089 (Sp II 627) + BM 45724 (81–7–6,131)
Date: … 142 – 143 S.E. (… 170/69 – 169/8 BCE)
Dimensions: 14.7 x 7.3 x 3.7
Commodities: barley, dates, mustard, cress, sesame, wool
Equivalence: 2 shekels silver
Unpublished Pinches hand copy (Sp II 627; BM 45724)
Photo: Plates VII–VIII

obv.
col. i'

1' [(*traces*)]
2' [(*traces*)]
3' [(*traces*)]
4' [(*traces*)]
5' [ ] x x [(*traces*)] x ⸢SÍG.ḪÁ 4(+) MA.NA⸣ AŠ TIL ⸢ITU⸣ [ ]
6' [(*traces*)] x ⸢*kàs* 8⸣ GUR ⸢*saḫ*⸣ [ ]
7' [ŠE.GIŠ] AŠ SA[G ITU] x x [1(p)] ⸢4(b)⸣ AŠ TIL ITU 1(p) 3(b) SÍG.[ḪÁ]
8' [AŠ SAG] ITU ⸢1 GUR⸣ x x [ ] x x EN TIL ITU 1 GU[R] x [nn GU]R 2 PI
9' [*k*]*às* 8 GUR ⸢*saḫ*⸣ x [ ] nn GUR x x x [ŠE.G]IŠ 1(p) ⸢3(+)(b)⸣ SÍG.ḪÁ ⸢8⸣ [MA.N]A
10' ⸢NE ŠE.BAR 1 GUR ZÚ 2 GUR x x *kàs*⸣ [ ] ⸢ITU⸣ 5 GUR *saḫ* 4(p) [ ]
11' [Š]E.GIŠ [(*traces*) SÍG.Ḫ]Á 8 MA.NA KIN ŠE.BAR 1 GUR x [ ] ⸢2(+)(p) 2(b)⸣
12' [(*traces*)] AŠ TIL ITU nn GUR 1 PI ZÚ AŠ SAG ITU 2 G[UR] ⸢3(b)⸣
13' [(*traces*) IT]U 2 GUR 4 PI *kàs* 7(g) [ ]
14' [(*traces*) IT]U 4 PI ŠE.GIŠ 1(p) 3(b) SÍG.Ḫ[Á nn MA.N]A
15' [DU$_6$ ŠE.BAR E]N TIL ITU 1 GUR 1 *qa* ZÚ AŠ SA[G ITU]
16' [*kà*]*s* 5 GUR *saḫ-l*[e_{10} Š]E.GIŠ.⸢Ì⸣ 1(p) 2(b) [ ]
17' [(*traces*)]
(*remainder lost*)

col. ii'

1' [ ] x [ ]
2' [IT]U 1 GUR 4(p) 2(b) ⸢ZÚ GIBIL⸣.MEŠ 5 GUR [ ]
3' [*sa*]*ḫ* 4(p) 4(b) ŠE.GIŠ x [SÍ]G.ḪÁ 11 MA.NA GA[N ŠE.BAR]
4' EN TIL ⸢ITU⸣ 1 GUR 4(p) x [ ] ⸢5(+)⸣ GUR ⸢2(+)⸣ PI ⸢*kàs*⸣ ⸢3(+)(g)⸣ [ ]

5' ⸢ŠE.GIŠ⸣ 2(p) 5(b) SÍG.ḪÁ 11 MA.NA AB ŠE.BAR EN MURUB$_4$ ITU x [ ]

6' EN TIL ITU 2 GUR ZÚ 5 GUR 1(p) 4(b) *kàs* 6 GU[R]

7' ŠE.GIŠ 2(p) 5(b) SÍG 10 MA.NA ZÍZ ŠE.BAR 2 GUR ZÚ 5 G[UR]

8' AŠ TIL ITU 4 GUR 2 PI ⸢*kàs*⸣ 6 GUR *saḫ* ⸢1 GUR⸣ ŠE.GIŠ 2(p) 5(b) ⸢3⸣ [*qa*]

9' SÍG.ḪÁ 10 MA.NA ŠE ŠE.BAR AŠ SAG ITU 2$^?$ GUR AŠ MURUB$_4$ ITU 3 GUR

10' AŠ TIL [IT]U [ZÚ AŠ SAG ITU] 5 GUR 1 PI AŠ MURUB$_4$ ITU 5 GUR [ ]

11' AŠ TIL ITU 4 GUR 4 PI *kàs* 4 GUR *saḫ* ⸢1 GUR⸣ ŠE.GIŠ 3 P[I]

12' ⸢DIRI⸣.ŠE ŠE.BAR EN MURUB$_4$ ITU nn GUR EN TIL ITU 2 GUR 5(b) ZÚ

13' 4 GUR 4 PI AŠ [MURUB$_4$ ITU] ⸢4⸣ GUR 2 PI AŠ TIL ITU 4 [GU]R 1 P[I]

14' [*k*]*às* 6 GUR *saḫ* 1 GUR 4(b) ⸢ŠE.GIŠ⸣ [ ] 4(b) SÍG 10 MA.NA

15' MU.1 ME 43.KÁM BAR ⸢ŠE⸣.BAR EN MURUB$_4$ ITU 2 G[UR] ⸢4(b)⸣ AŠ TIL ITU 2 GU[R]

16' ZÚ AŠ SAG ITU 3 G[UR] x x AŠ TIL ITU 4 GUR 1 PI *kà*[*s*]

17' ⸢1⸣ GUR 1 [PI] ⸢ŠE⸣.GIŠ 2(p) 4(b) SÍG.⸢ḪÁ⸣ [ ] 12 MA.NA GU$_4$ ŠE.BAR AŠ SAG I[TU]

18' [TI]L ITU 2 GUR 3(p) 2(b) ZÚ 4 GU[R *k*]*às* 8 GUR *saḫ* x [ ]

19' [ ] ⸢(+)2(p)⸣ 2(b) 3 *qa* SÍG.ḪÁ 12 MA.NA SIG ⸢ŠE⸣.BAR 2 GUR 3(p) [ ]

20' [ ] 4(g) [ ] x [ ] 2(p) 2(b) [ ]

(*remainder lost*)

rev.

col. i'

1' [IT]U 6 G[UR]

2' [ ](+)3 GUR x x [ ]

3' [ ] ITU x [ ]

4' [ ] x [ ]

(*remainder lost*)

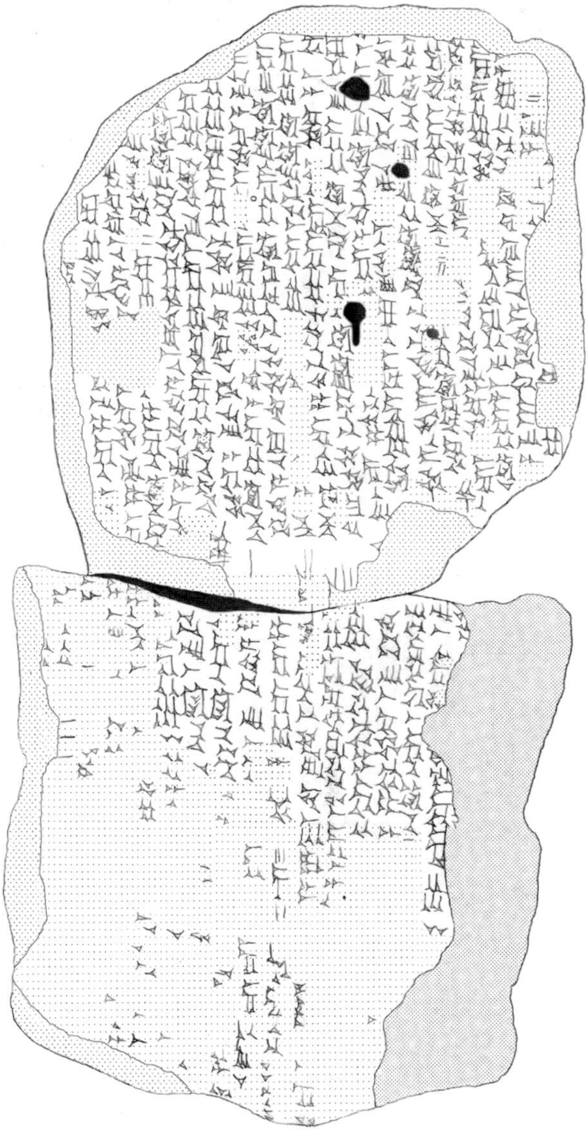

BM 35089 + BM 45724 obverse

BM 35089 + BM 45724 reverse

TRANSLATION

obv. i'

1'–4' […]

5' [… (year $y_{1'}$) (month II) …] … ; wool 4(+) mina, at the end of the month […]

6' [(month III) …] … ; mustard 8 kur; cress […];

7' [sesame] at the begin[ning of the month] … [… 1 pān] 4 sūt, at the end of the month 1pān 3 sūt; wo[ol …]

8' [(month IV) … (barley) at the beginning of] the month 1 kur … […] … to the end of the month 1kur$^{!}$ … [… (dates) nn ku]r 2 pān;

9' [mus]tard 8 kur; cress … […] nn kur … ; [sesa]me 1 pān 3(+) sūt; wool 8 [min]a.

10' Month V: barley 1 kur; dates 2 kur … ; mustard [… of] the month 5 kur; cress 4 pān;

11' [se]same [… ; woo]l 8 mina. Month VI: barley 1 kur … […] 2(+) pān 2 sūt,

12' […] at the end of the month nn kur 1 pān; dates at the beginning of the month 2 k[ur …] 3 sūt,

13' [… of the mon]th 2 kur 4 pān; mustard 7 kur […]

14' [… (cress) … of the mon]th 4 pān; sesame 1 pān 3 sūt; woo[l nn min]a.

15' [Month VII: barley … t]o the end of the month 1 kur 1 qa; dates at the begin[ning of the month …]

16' [… ; mustar]d 5 kur; cres[s … ; s]esame 1 pān 2 sūt […]

17' […]

(*remainder lost*)

obv. ii'

1' […] … […]

2' [(year 142 S.E.) (month VIII) (barley) … of the mont]h 1 kur 4 pān 2 sūt; dates, new 5 kur […];

3' [cre]ss 4 pān 4 sūt; sesame … [w]ool 11 mina. Mon[th IX: barley …]

4' to the end of the month 1 kur 4 pān … [… (dates) …](+)5 kur 2(+) pān; mustard 3(+) kur […];

5' sesame 2 pān 5 sūt; wool 11 mina. Month X: barley to the middle of the month … […],

6' to the end of the month 2 kur; dates 5 kur 1 pān 4 sūt; mustard 6 ku[r …];

7' sesame 2 pān 5 sūt; wool 10 mina. Month XI: barley 2 kur; dates 5 k[ur …],

8' at the end of the month 4 kur 2 pān; mustard 6 kur; cress 1 kur; sesame 2 pān 5 sūt 3 qa];

9' wool 10 mina. Month XII: barley at the beginning of the month 2$^{?}$ kur, in the middle of the month 3 kur,

10' at the end of the [mon]th [… ; dates at the beginning of the month] 5 kur 1 pān, in the middle of the month 5 kur […],

11' at the end of the month 4 kur 4 pān; mustard 4 kur; cress 1 kur; sesame 3 pā[n …].

12' Month XII$_2$: barley to the middle of the month nn kur, to the end of the month 2 kur 5 sūt; dates

13' 4 kur 4 pān in [the middle of the month] 4 kur 2 pān, at the end of the month 4 kur 1 p[ān ...];

14' [mus]tard 6 kur; cress 1 kur 4 sūt; sesame [...] 4 sūt; wool 10 mina.

15' Year 143. Month I: barley to the middle of the month 2 k[ur] 4 sūt, at the end of the month 2 ku[r ...];

16' dates at the beginning of the month 3 k[ur ...] ... at the end of the month 4 kur 1 pān; must[ard ...]

17' (cress) 1 kur 1 [pān]; sesame 2 pān 4 sūt; woo[l] 12 mina. Month II: barley at the beginning of the mo[nth ...]

18' [... en]d of the month 2 kur 3 pān 2 sūt; dates 4 ku[r ... ; mus]tard 8 kur$^{!}$; cress ... [...]

19' [...(sesame)... nn](+)2 pān 2 sūt 3 qa; wool 12 mina. Month III: barley 2 kur 3 pān [...]

20' [...] 4 kur [...] ... [...] 2 pān 2 sūt [...]

(*remainder lost*)

rev. i'

1' [... of the mon]th 6 k[ur ...]

2' [...](+)3 kur ... [...]

3' [... of the] month ... [...]

4' [...] ... [...]

(*remainder lost*)

NOTES

o.i':5' Conjectured reading as suggested by traces in Pinches' copy.

COMMENTS

Text 5 is found on two fragments of a larger tablet that originally had at least two columns of text on its obverse. The two fragments remain at present unglued but fit together quite well, with the "firing holes" that run horizontally between the adjacent side edges of the tablet fragments aligning perfectly along their interface. No original tablet edges are preserved and there is considerable surface erosion, especially to the left half of obverse column i' (35089)—as a result, the readings of these lines are quite provisional. On the reverse (45724), just four fragmentary lines are preserved. The text gives month by month price equivalences for all six commodities for one or more years before 142 (date restored) and after 143 S.E. (date preserved). Price fluctuations within the month, especially for the beginning, middle, and end of the month, are commonly recorded for barley and dates, and occasionally for sesame and wool. The equivalence rate may be assumed to be per two shekels of silver when the values for months I to III/143 S.E. in Text 5 (see Summary: Text 5, below) are compared to price equivalences per one shekel of silver for the succeeding months V, VI, and VIII/143 S.E. in the Astronomical Diaries (see Table 9: Astronomical Diary Commodity Price Equivalents for 143 S.E. [AD II -168A, D]).

TABLE 9
ASTRONOMICAL DIARY COMMODITY PRICE EQUIVALENTS
FOR 143 S.E. (AD II -168A, D)

Year	*Month*	*Barley*	*Dates*	*Mustard*	*Cress*	*Sesame*	*Wool*
143	V	246	230 @e 360	540	96	45	[ ]
	VI	252	378	720 (var. 540$^{?}$)	96$^{?}$ (var. 84)	48 (var. 42)	6
	VIII	@b 210 @m 180(+) @e 204	@b 432 →e 420	606	84	@b 40½ @e 39	5

(barley, dates, mustard, cress, and sesame qa per 1 shekel silver; wool mina per 1 shekel silver)

If the original tablet was in fact just two columns wide and began at or no more than a line or two above o.i': 1', and the present fragments represent the upper third or so of the original tablet, then col. i' probably contained data for months I to XII/141 S.E. and months I to VI(?) of 142 S.E., and col. ii' covered months VII(?) to XII_2/142 S.E. and I to XII/143 S.E. The reverse may have similarly treated the next three years. Unfortunately, the data preserved for months III to VII/$y_{1'}$ (see Summary: Text 5, below) are suggestive of but cannot be correlated precisely with the data in the diary for 141 S.E. (see Table 10: Astronomical Diary Commodity Price Equivalents for 141 S.E. [AD II -170A,H]).

TABLE 10
ASTRONOMICAL DIARY COMMODITY PRICE EQUIVALENTS
FOR 141 S.E. (AD II -170A,H)

Year	*Month*	*Barley*	*Dates*	*Mustard*	*Cress*	*Sesame*	*Wool*
141	II	[			]	24	4½
	III	[		]	48	21	[ ]
	IV	[			]	30	4
	VII	@b 156 @e [ ]	[		]	36	4½

(barley, dates, mustard, cress, and sesame qa per 1 shekel silver; wool mina per 1 shekel silver)

Several significant historical events are to be noted for the years 142 and 143 S.E. In V/142 S.E. Antiochus IV, for reasons unknown, ordered the killing of his son[56] and co-ruler, Antiochus.[57] An Astronomical Diary for the following year (V/143 S.E.), reports that "Antiochus (IV) marched victoriously through the cities of Meluḫḫa (Egypt)."[58] This, the so-called Sixth Syrian War (170 – 168 BCE),[59] was brought to a sudden end as a result of the well-reported confrontation between Antiochus and the Roman ambassador C. Popilius Laenas.[60]

SUMMARY

(barley, dates, mustard, cress, and sesame qa per 1 shekel silver; wool mina per 1 shekel silver)

Year	*Month*	*Barley*	*Dates*	*Mustard*	*Cress*	*Sesame*	*Wool*
	[…]						
$y_{1'}$	II	[					] 2(+) @e [ ]
	III	[@e [ ]	]	720	[ ]	@b [ ] [ ] 30 @e 27	[ ]
	IV	[@b] 90(+) @e 126(+)	[ ]+36	720	[ ]	27(+)	4
	V	90	180(+)	450	72(+)	[ ]	4
	VI	90(+) [@e 108(+)	@b 192(+)] 252	540(+) [ ]	72	27	[ ]
	VII	[ ] →e 90½	@b [ ] [ ]	450	[ ]	24(+)[	]
	[…]						

56 Following the assassination of Seleucus IV, his chancellor Heliodorus proclaimed the king's son Antiochus, age 4–5, as king and the dowager queen Laodike regent. Seleucus' brother Antiochus, supported by Eumenes II of Pergamum, proclaimed himself king, marrying his brother's widow, adopting her son, and tolerating him as co-ruler (Habicht 1989, 340–41, and n. 57).

57 Sachs and Weisman, *Iraq* 16, 202ff.: r.12 [MU.1 ME] 42 KÁM NE AŠ *a-mat* ᵐ*an* LUGAL ᵐ*an* LUGAL A-*šú di-ik-ku* (r.13) [MU.1 ME.4]3 KÁM ᵐ*an* LUGAL; for a bibliography of this tablet (BM 35603 = Sp. II 113) see Del Monte 1997, 208 [Lista Reale n.6], to which add Glassner 2004, 134–37 [4].

58 AD II -168A:15; see further Geller 1991.

59 See conveniently, Habicht 1989, 343–46.

60 Polybius, *Histories* 29, 27; Livius, *History* VI, 45.12; Justin 34, 3; Appian, *Syrian Wars*, 66, 164.

Year	*Month*	*Barley*	*Dates*	*Mustard*	*Cress*	*Sesame*	*Wool*
[142]	VIII	[[ ] 168	new: 450(+)	]	84	[ ]	5½
	IX	[ ] →e 112(+)	486(+)	270(+)[	]	51	5½
	X	→m [ ] →e 180	480	540	[ ]	51	5
	XI	180	450(+) @e 396	540	90	52½	5
	XII	@b 180 @m 270 @e [ ]	[ ] 468 @m 450(+) @e 432	360	90	54	[ ]
	XII$_2$	→m 180 →e 195	[ ] 432 [ ] 396 @e 378(+)	540	102	[ ]	5
143	I	→m 252 @e 180(+)	@b 270(+) [ ] @e 378	[ ]	108	48	6
	II	@b [ ] [ ]e 240	360	720	[ ]	43½	6
	III	234(+)[					]
	[…]						
$y_{1'}$	$m_{1'}$	[	]	540	[		]
	[…]						
High:		270	486(+)	720	108	54	6
Low:		90	252	450	72	27	4

TEXT 6

BM 34073 (Sp 169 + Sp II 653) + BM 35123 (Sp II 666)
Date: 173 – 175 S.E. (139/8 – 137/6 BCE)
Dimensions: 16.9 x 7.6 x 3.8
Commodities: Barley, dates, mustard, cress, sesame, wool
Equivalence: 2 shekels silver
Unpublished Pinches hand copy (BM 35123)[61]
Unpublished Sachs transliteration (BM 34073 + 35123)
Photo: Plates IX–X

obv.

o.1'	[MUR]UB$_4$ ITU 4(p) x [ ]
o.2'	[*saḫ-l*]*e*$_x$ 2 PI ŠE.GIŠ.Ì [ ]
o.3'	[MURU]B$_4$ ITU 4(p) 2(b) AŠ TIL ITU 4(p) [ ]
o.4'	[ ] TIL ITU 8 GUR 2(p) x [ ]
o.5'	[TIL] ITU 1(p) 2(b) 3 *qa* ŠE.GIŠ.[Ì]
o.6'	[ ] TIL ITU 3(p) 5(b) ZÚ AŠ SA[G ITU]
o.7'	[*kà*]*s* AŠ ⸢SAG⸣ ITU 8 GUR x [ ]
o.8'	[ŠE.GIŠ].⸢Ì⸣ AŠ SAG ITU 5(b) AŠ MURUB$_4$ [IT]U [ ]
o.9'	[nn M]A.NA DU$_6$ ŠE.BAR AŠ SAG ITU [ ]
o.10'	[ ] ZÚ 3 GUR 1 PI AŠ M[URUB$_4$ ITU]
o.11'	[ ] *saḫ-le*$_x$ ⸢AŠ SAG⸣ ITU 1(p) 2(b) ⸢3 *qa*⸣ [ ]
o.12'	[IT]U 5(b) 3 *qa* EN TIL ITU 5(b) SÍG.[ḪÁ]
o.13'	[IT]U 3(p) 2(b) {AŠ} 11 3(p) 1(b) 12 3 P[I]
o.14'	[1]⸢8⸣ 19 3 PI TA 20 EN ṬIL [ITU]
o.15'	[ ] x x x ⸢EN⸣ MURUB$_4$ ITU 2 GUR 3(p) x [ ]
o.16'	[ ] x [1]⸢8⸣ 19 2 GUR 4 PI TA 20 E[N]
o.17'	[*saḫ-l*]*e*$_x$ 1 PI 4 *qa* ŠE.GIŠ.Ì 5(b) SÍG.ḪÁ [ ]
o.18'	[ ] 3(p) 1(b) EN TIL ITU 3 PI NU.DÙ.MEŠ [ ]
o.19'	[ ] x ⸢*kàs*⸣ 8 GUR ⸢*saḫ*⸣-[*le*$_x$]
o.20'	[ŠE.GIŠ.Ì] ⸢5(b) 3⸣ *qa* SÍG.[ḪÁ]
o.21'	[3 G]UR 1 PI AŠ MURUB$_4$ ITU ⸢3(g)⸣ [ ]
o.22'	[ ] x 30 3 GUR 1 PI *k*[*às*]
o.23'	[ŠE].GIŠ.Ì 5(b) NU.DÙ.MEŠ [ ]
o.24'	[ ] ⸢3⸣ PI AŠ MURUB$_4$ ITU 2(p) 5(b) x [ ]
o.25'	[3(g)] 1 PI AŠ MURUB$_4$ ITU 3 GUR 1(p) ⸢3(+)(b)⸣ [ ]

61 Wiseman 1988, 365, n. 16.

o.26' [*saḫ*]-*le*$_x$ 1 PI ŠE.GIŠ.Ì AŠ SA[G ITU]

o.27' [SÍ]G.ḪÁ 5 MA.NA ŠE ŠE.BAR A[Š]

o.28' [ZÚ AŠ S]AG ITU 3 GUR 1 PI AŠ MURUB$_4$ IT[U]

o.29' [*saḫ*-*le*$_x$] 1 PI 4 *qa* ŠE.GIŠ.Ì EN MU[RUB$_4$ ITU]

---

o.30' [MU.1 ME 1,14.KÁM BAR ŠE.B]AR AŠ SAG ITU 3 PI AŠ MURUB$_4$ ITU ⸢3(p)⸣ [ ]

o.31' [ ] AŠ TIL ITU 3(p) 5(b) ZÚ EN MURUB$_4$ ⸢ITU⸣ 3 GU[R]

o.32' [1] PI ŠE.GIŠ.Ì AŠ SAG ITU 5(b) 2 *qa* AŠ M[URUB$_4$ ITU]

o.33' [SÍG.Ḫ]Á 5 MA.NA GU$_4$ ŠE.BAR AŠ ⸢SAG⸣ ITU 4 PI AŠ ⸢MURUB$_4$ ITU nn⸣

o.34' [ZÚ AŠ] SAG ITU 3 GUR 1(p) 2(b) EN TIL ⸢ITU⸣ 3 GUR 1(p) 4(b) *kàs* 6 GUR

o.35' [ŠE.GI]Š.Ì 4(b) 4 *qa* SÍG.ḪÁ 5 MA.NA AŠ TIL ITU 6 MA.NA

o.36' [SIG ŠE.BAR 4(p)] ⸢4(b)⸣ TA 11 EN 14 4(p) 5(b) 15 4(p) 4(b) 16 17 4(p) 3(b)

o.37' [TA 19 E]N TIL ITU 4 PI ZÚ AŠ SAG ITU 3 GUR 1(p) 4(b) AŠ MURUB$_4$ ITU 3 G[UR]

o.38' [*k*]*às* 6 GUR *saḫ*-*le*$_x$ 5(b) ŠE.GIŠ.Ì 4(b) 1 *qa* SÍG.ḪÁ 5 [MA.NA]

o.39' [ŠU] ŠE.BAR EN MURUB$_4$ ⸢ITU⸣ 4 PI EN TIL ITU 4(p) 1(b) NU.DÙ.MEŠ 4(p) 2(b) [ ]

o.40' [3] GUR 3(p) 4(b) EN TIL ITU 3 GUR 2(p) 3(b) *kàs* 5 GUR *saḫ*-*l*[*e*$_x$]

o.41' [AŠ] MURUB$_4$ ITU 3(b) 2 *qa* AŠ TIL ITU 3(b) 1 *qa* SÍG.ḪÁ 6 MA.[NA]

o.42' [E]N MURUB$_4$ ITU 3 GUR 2(p) 3(b) EN TIL ITU 3 GUR 2(p) ⸢4(b)⸣ [ ]

o.43' [ ] ⸢5⸣ GUR *saḫ*-*le*$_x$ 1 PI ŠE.GIŠ.Ì AŠ SAG ITU ⸢3(b)⸣ [ ]

o.44' [ ] ⸢6 MA⸣.NA KIN ŠE.BAR ⸢EN⸣ MURUB$_4$ ITU 4(p) x [ ]

o.45' [ ] ⸢2⸣6 3(p) 4(b) EN TIL ITU 3(p) 2(b) [ ]

o.46' [nn P]I *kàs* AŠ SAG ITU 6 GU[R]

o.47' [ ] ⸢x x *qa*⸣ SÍG.Ḫ[Á]

(*remainder lost*)

rev.

r.1' [nn MA.N]A ŠE ŠE.[BAR]

r.2' [ ] x EN 5 2 G[UR]

r.3' [ ] x 13 2 GUR ⸢1(+)(p)⸣ [ ]

r.4' [*kàs*] ⸢8 GUR⸣ [*sa*]*ḫ*-*le*$_x$ 4(b) 2 *qa* [ ]

r.5' [ ] 3(b) AŠ TIL I[TU nn] *qa* SÍG.ḪÁ 4 M[A.NA]

---

r.6' [MU.1 ME] ⸢1⸣,15.KÁM ⸢BAR⸣ [ŠE.BAR AŠ] SAG ITU [nn] ⸢PI⸣ [ ] MU[RUB$_4$ ITU]

r.7' [ ] x x 4(b) *kàs* 8 GUR *saḫ-*⸢*le*$_x$⸣ 2(b) 2 *qa* [ ]

r.8' [nn M]A.NA GU$_4$ ŠE.BAR AŠ SAG ITU ⸢(+)2(p)⸣ 2(b) TA 7 E[N]

r.9' [TA] 15 EN 20 2(p) 2(b) TA ⸢21⸣ EN TIL ITU ⸢2(+)(p)⸣ [ ]

r.10' [ ] x ⸢AŠ MURUB$_4$ ITU 2 GUR AŠ TIL ITU⸣ 2 GUR 4(b) ⸢*kàs*⸣ [ ]

r.11' [IT]U 3(b) ⸢EN⸣ TIL ITU 4(b) ⸢ŠE⸣.GIŠ.Ì AŠ SAG ITU [ ]

r.12' [ ] x [SÍG].ḪÁ 4 MA.NA SIG ŠE.BAR AŠ KÙ.BABBAR *bab-b*[*a-né-é-tú*]

r.13' [*i*]*s-ta-ter-ra-an-na* ⸢*šá*⸣ $^{[m]}$⸢*de*⸣*-meṭ-ri-*[*su*]

r.14' [ ] ITU 2(p) 2(b) ⸢*ù*⸣ AŠ *is-ta-ter-ra-an-na*

r.15' [^{m}*ar-šá-ka*]*-a* LUGAL 2 PI ZÚ AŠ SAG ITU 2 GUR ⸢2(+)(p)⸣ AŠ ⸢MURUB$_4$⸣ I[TU]

r.16' [SUMU]N.MEŠ 2 GUR 1(p) 4(b) ⸢*kàs*⸣ 6 GUR *s*[*aḫ-le*$_x$]

r.17' [ ] x 4(b) 4 *qa* ŠE.GIŠ.Ì AŠ SAG ITU 2(b) 4 *q*[*a*]

r.18' [M]A.NA ŠU ŠE.BAR AŠ SAG ITU 2(p) 2(b) EN TIL I[TU]

r.19' [ ] x ZÚ 1 GUR 4 PI SUMUN.MEŠ 2 GUR [ ]

r.20' [ ] ⸢*kàs*⸣ 6 GUR *saḫ-le*$_x$ 4(b) 4 *qa* Š[E.GIŠ.Ì]

r.21' [SÍG.Ḫ]Á 4 MA.NA NE ŠE.BAR ⸢3(+)(p)⸣ [ ]

r.22' [*kà*]*s* 7 GUR *saḫ-le*$_x$ 1 P[I]

r.23' [KIN ŠE.BAR] AŠ SAG ITU 2(p) 2(b) 3 *q*[*a*]

r.24' [ ] ⸢1⸣ PI 4 *qa* ŠE.GIŠ.[Ì]

r.25' [ ] ⸢DU$_6$⸣ ŠE.BAR 2(p) ⸢nn(b)⸣ [ ]

r.26' [M]URUB$_4$ ITU ⸢2⸣ G[UR]

r.27' [ ] x x [ ]

r.28' [ ]

r.29' [ ] x 2(p) ⸢5(b)⸣ [ ]

r.30' [ŠE.GIŠ].Ì AŠ SAG ITU 5(b) E[N]

r.31' [ ] ZÚ 3 GUR 1 PI *kà*[*s*]

r.32' [nn MA].NA AB ŠE.BAR 2(p) 5(b) AŠ T[IL ITU]

r.33' [ZÚ AŠ SAG IT]U 3 GUR 1 PI EN TIL IT[U]

r.34' [ ] x ŠE.GIŠ.Ì 5(b) 4 *qa* [ ]

r.35' [ ] x ITU 3 GUR 1 PI E[N]

r.36' [ ] ⸢ITU 2 GUR 4 PI⸣ *k*[*às*]

r.37' [ŠE.GIŠ.Ì AŠ SA]G ITU 5(b) 4 *qa* AŠ ⸢MURUB$_4$⸣ [ITU]

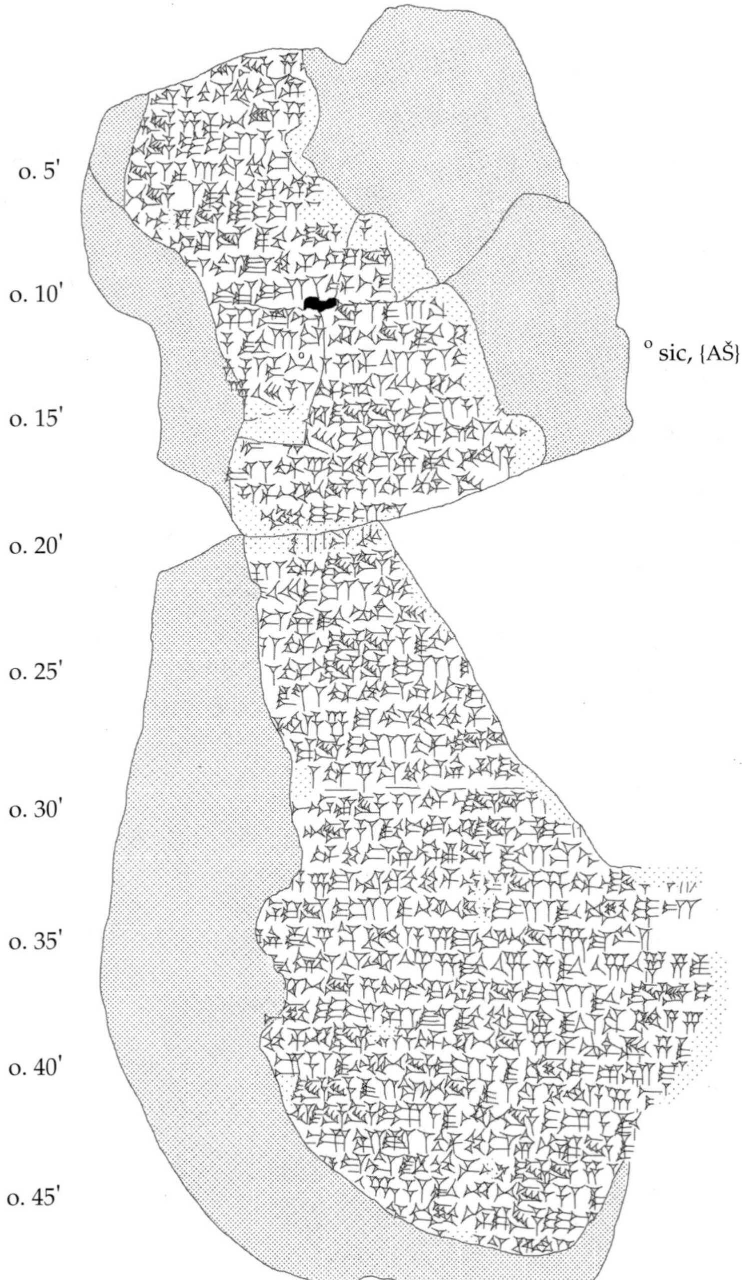

BM 34073 + BM 35123 obverse

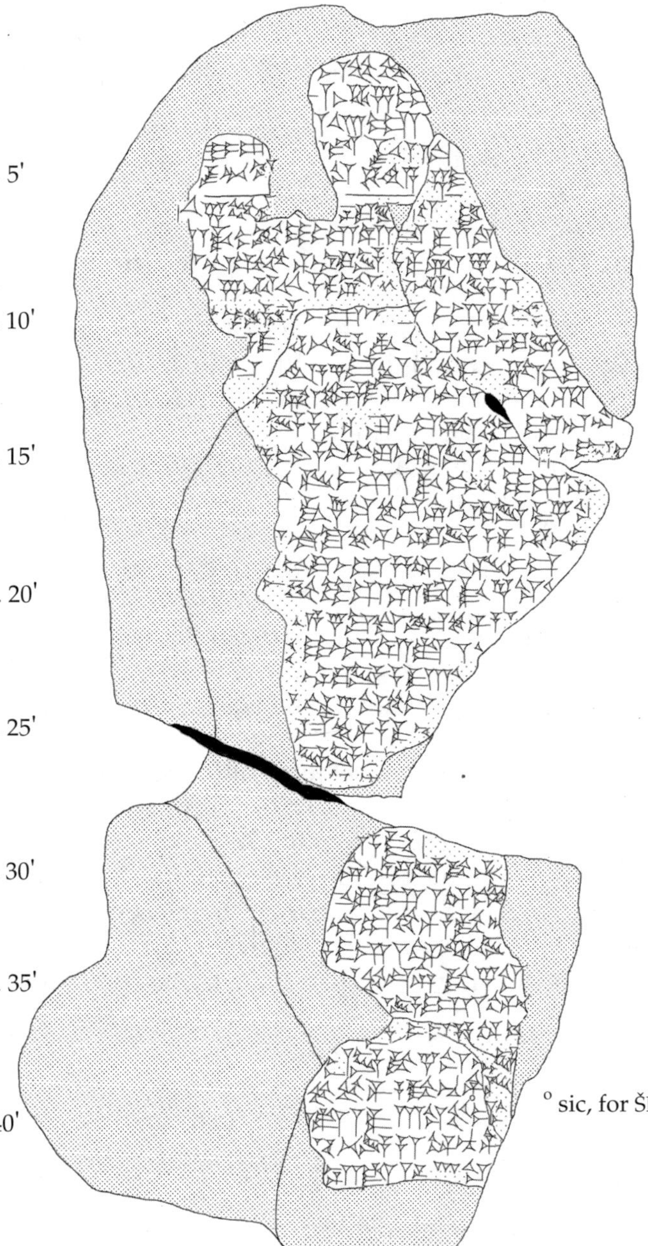

° sic, for ŠE

BM 34073 + BM 35123 reverse

r.38' [ ] ŠE ŠE.BAR 2(p) 5(b) NU.DÙ.MEŠ [ ]
r.39' [*sa]ḫ-le*$_x$ 1(p) 2(b) 3 *qa* ŠE!.GIŠ.⸢Ì⸣ [ ]
r.40' [E]N TIL ITU 3 PI NU.DÙ.[MEŠ]
r.41' [ ] ⸢*saḫ*⸣-*le*$_x$ ⸢1(p) 2(b) 3⸣ *qa* [ ]
(*remainder lost*)

TRANSLATION

o.1' [(year 173 S.E.) (month IV) (barley) … the mid]dle of the month 4 pān … […]
o.2' [… ; cres]s 2 pān; sesame […]
o.3' [(month V) (barley) … the midd]le of the month 4 pān 2 sūt, at the end of the month 4 pān […]
o.4' [… (mustard) …] the end of the month 8 kur 2 pān … […]
o.5' [… (cress) … the end of] the month 1 pān 2 sūt 3 qa; sesam[e …]
o.6' [… (month VI) (barley) …] the end of the month 3 pān 5 sūt; dates at the begin[ning of the month …]
o.7' [… ; must]ard at the beginning of the month 8 kur … […]
o.8' [… ; sesam]e at the beginning of the month 5 sūt, in the middle of the [mon]th […]
o.9' [… (wool) … nn m]ina. Month VII: barley at the beginning of the month […]
o.10' […]; dates 3 kur 1 pān, in the mi[ddle of the month …]
o.11' […]; cress, at the beginning of the month 1pān 2 sūt 3 qa […]
o.12' [… (sesame) … of the mon]th 5 sūt 3 qa, to the end of the month 5 sūt; wool […]
o.13' [… (month VIII) (barley) … of the mon]th 3 pān 2 sūt, {on} the 11th 3 pān 1 sūt, the 12th 3 p[ān …]
o.14' [… 1]8th (and) 19th 3 pān, from the 20th to the end of the [month …]
o.15' [… (dates) …] … to the middle of the month 2 kur 3 pān … […]
o.16' […] … 18th (and) 19th 2 kur 4 pān, from the 20th t[o …]
o.17' [… ; cres]s 1 pān 4 qa; sesame 5 sūt; wool […]
o.18' [… (month IX) (barley) …] 3 pān 1 sūt, to the end of the month 3 pān, poor quality […]
o.19' […] … ; mustard 8 kur; cre[ss …]
o.20' [… ; sesame] 5 sūt 3 qa; wo[ol …]
o.21' [… (month X) … (dates) … 3 k]ur 1 pān in the middle of the month 3[kur …]
o.22' […] … 30th 3 kur 1 pān; mu[stard …]
o.23' [… ; se]same 5 sūt, poor quality […]
o.24' [… (month XI) (barley) …] 3 pān, in the middle of the month 2 pān 5 sūt … […]
o.25' [… (dates) … 3 kur] 1 pān in the middle of the month 3 kur 1 pān 3(+) sūt […]
o.26' [… ; cre]ss 1 pān; sesame at the begin[ning of the month …]
o.27' [… ; w]ool 5 mina. Month XII: barley at [the …]

o.28' [... ; dates at the be]ginning of the month 3 kur 1 pān, in the middle of the mon[th ...]
o.29' [... ; cress] 1 pān 4 qa; sesame to the mid[dle of the month ...].

---

o.30' [Year 174. Month I: barl]ey at the beginning of the month 3 pān, in the middle of the month 3 pān [...]
o.31' [...] at the end of the month 3 pān 5 sūt; dates to the middle of the month 3 ku[r ...]
o.32' [... (cress) ... 1] pān; sesame at the beginning of the month 5 sūt 2 qa, in the m[iddle of the month ...]
o.33' [... ; woo]l 5 mina. Month II: barley at the beginning of the month 4 pān, in the middle of the month ...
o.34' [... ; dates at the] beginning of the month 3 kur 1 pān 2 sūt, to the end of the month 3 kur 1 pān 4 sūt; mustard 6 kur
o.35' [... ; sesa]me 4 sūt 4 qa; wool 5 mina, at the end of the month 6 mina.
o.36' [Month III: barley ... 4 pān] 4 sūt, from the 11th to the 14th 4 pān 5 sūt, the 15th 4 pān 4 sūt, the 16th (and) 17th 4 pān 3 sūt
o.37' [... from the 19th t]o the end of the month 4 pān; dates at the beginning of the month 3 kur 1 pān 4 sūt, in the middle of the month 3 k[ur ...]
o.38' [... ; mus]tard 6 kur; cress 5 sūt; sesame 4 sūt 1 qa; wool 5[mina]
o.39' [.... Month IV]: barley to the middle of the month 4 pān, to the end of the month 4 pān 1 sūt, poor quality 4 pān 2 sūt [...]
o.40' [... (dates) ... 3] kur 3 pān 4 sūt, to the end of the month 3 kur 2 pān 3 sūt; mustard 5 kur; cres[s ...]
o.41' [... (sesame) ... in] the middle of the month 3 sūt 2 qa, at the end of the month 3 sūt 1 qa; wool 6 mi[na]
o.42' [... (month V) ... (dates) ... t]o the middle of the month 3 kur 2 pān 3 sūt, to the end of the month 3 kur 2 pān 4 sūt [...]
o.43' [... (mustard) ...] 5 kur; cress 1 pān; sesame at the beginning of the month 3 sūt [...]
o.44' [... ; wool] 6 mina. Month VI: barley to the middle of the month 4 pān ... [...]
o.45' [...] the 26th 3 pān 4 sūt, to the end of the month 3 pān 2 sūt [...]
o.46' [... (dates) ... nn p]ān; mustard at the beginning of the month 6 ku[r ...]
o.47' [... (sesame) ...] nn qa; woo[l ...]
(*remainder lost*)
r.1' [... (month XI) ... (wool) ... nn min]a. Month XII: bar[ley...]
r.2' [... (dates) ...] ... to the 5th 2 k[ur ...]
r.3' [...] ... the 13th 2 kur 1(+) pān [...]
r.4' [... ; mustard] 8 kur [... cr]ess 4 sūt 2 qa [...]
r.5' [... (sesame) ...] 3 sūt, at the end of the m[onth ... nn] qa; wool 4 m[ina ...].

---

r.6' [Year 1]75. Month I: [barley at] the beginning of the month [nn] pān [...] the mi[ddle of the month ...]
r.7' [... (dates) ...] ... 4 sūt; mustard 8 kur; cress 2 sūt 2 qa [...]

r.8' [… (wool) … nn m]ina. Month II: barley at the beginning of the month 2(+) pān 2 sūt, from the 7th t[o the …]
r.9' [… from] the 15th to the 20th 2 pān 2 sūt, from the 21st to the end of the month 2(+) pān […]
r.10' [… (dates) …] … in the middle of the month 2 kur, at the end of the month 2 kur 4 sūt; mustard […]
r.11' [… (cress) … of the mon]th 3 sūt, to the end of the month 4 sūt; sesame at the beginning of the month […]
r.12' […] … ; [wo]ol 4 mina. Month III: barley in silver in go[od condition]
r.13' [… s]taters of Demetri[us …]
r.14' [… of] the month 2 pān 2 sūt, and in staters
r.15' [… Arsac]es, the king, 2 pān; dates at the beginning of the month 2 kur 2(+) pān, in the middle of the m[onth]
r.16' [… , ol]d 2 kur 1 pān 4 sūt; mustard 6 kur; c[ress]
r.17' […] … 4 sūt 4 qa; sesame at the beginning of the month 2 sūt 4 q[a …]
r.18' [… (wool) … nn m]ina. Month IV: barley at the beginning of the month 2 pān 2 sūt, to the end of the m[onth …]
r.19' […] … ; dates 1 kur 4 pān, old 2 kur […]
r.20' […]; mustard 6 kur; cress 4 sūt 4 qa; s[esame …]
r.21' [… ; woo]l 4 mina. Month V: barley 3(+) pān […]
r.22' [… ; musta]rd 7 kur; cress 1 p[ān …]
r.23' [… . Month VI: barley] at the beginning of the month 2 pān 2 sūt 3 q[a …]
r.24' [… (cress) …] 1 pān 4 qa; sesa[me …]
r.25' […]. Month VII: barley 2 pān nn sūt […]
r.26' [… (dates) … the m]iddle of the month 2 k[ur …]
r.27' […] … […]
r.28' […]
r.29' [… (Month VIII: barley) …] … 2 pān 5 sūt […]
r.30' [… ; sesa]me at the beginning of the month 5 sūt, t[o …]
r.31' [… (month IX) …]; dates 3 kur 1 pān; must[ard …]
r.32' [… (wool) … nn mi]na. Month X: barley 2 pān 5 sūt, at the e[nd of the month …]
r.33' [… ; dates at the beginning of the mon]th 3 kur 1 pān, to the end of the mon[th …]
r.34' […] … ; sesame 5 sūt 4 qa […]
r.35' [… (month XI) … (dates) …] … of the month 3 kur 1 pān f[rom …]
r.36' [… of] the month 2 kur 4 pān; mu[stard …]
r.37' [… ; sesame at the begin]ning of the month 5 sūt 4 qa, in the middle of [the month …]
r.38' […]. Month XII: barley 2 pān 5 sūt, poor quality […]
r.39' [… ; cr]ess 1 pān 2 sūt 3 qa; sesa[me …]
r.40' [… (month XII_2) (barley) … t]o the end of the month 3 pān, poor quali[ty …]
r.41' […]; cress 1 pān 2 sūt 3 qa […]

(remainder lost)

NOTES

o.5' Pinches' copy shows: ti]l
o.20' Pinches' copy shows:] 5(b)$^{?}$ 3 qa síg-ḫ[á
o.29' Pinches' copy shows: -l]e_x
o.32' Pinches copy shows:] 𒁹 PI
o.37' TA 19] restored as per AD III -137B: r.16'
o.41' Pinches' copy shows:] ina múrub itu ...
r.9' Pinches' copy shows: t]a
r.33' ZÚ AŠ SAG IT]U restored as per AD III -136C: o.14'

COMPARANDA

(Barley, dates, mustard, cress, and sesame qa per 1 shekel silver; wool mina per 1 shekel silver)

II/174 S.E.	*Barley*	*Dates*
Text 6: o.33'–o.34'	@b 72; @m [ ]	@b 294; →e 300
-137A: o.13'[a]	[…]; 20→25 84; 26–28 72(+); 29–30 [ ]	→m 336$^{?}$; →e 180(+)

a. AD III -137A: o.13' […] TA 20 EN 25 2(p) 2(b) 26 27 28 2(p) [x x] 29 30 [x x Z]Ú.LUM EN $MURUB_4$ ITU 1 GUR 4(p)$^{?}$ 2(b)$^{?}$ EN TIL ITU 1 GUR […]

For barley the data in Text 6 and the Astronomical Diary (-137A) do not overlap, but are reasonably close. For dates note that Text 6 gives two quotes, one at the beginning of the month and a second to the end of the month while the Diary quotes prices to the middle of the month and to the end of the month—the apparent discrepancies might be resolved by rereading the questionable quote to the middle of the month in the Diary as 1(g) 3(p)$^{!}$ 2(b)$^{!}$ (= 300 qa) or 1(g) 3(p)$^{!}$ 1(b)$^{!}$ (= 294 qa).

III/174 S.E.	*Barley*	*Dates*	*Sesame*	*Wool*
Text 6: o.36'–o.38'	[…] 84; 11→14 87; 15 84; 16–17 81; […]→e 72	@b 300; @m 270(+); [ ]	12½	2½
-137B: r.16'–r.17'[a]	[…]17 81; 18 78; 19→e 72	@b [ ]	12½	2; @e 2½

a. AD III -137B: r.16' [. . . 1]7 2(p) 1(b) 3 *qa* 18 2(p) 1(b) TA 19 EN TIL ITU 2(p) ZÚ.LUM AŠ SA[G ITU . . . (r.17') . . . ŠE.GIŠ.Ì 2(b) ½ *qa* SÍG.ḪÁ 2 MA.NA AŠ TIL ITU 2½ MA.NA

Text 6 and -137B provide congruent data for barley for the (16th and) 17th and (from the 19th) to the end of the month, and for sesame for the month; for wool the single monthly value in Text 6 corresponds to the Diary end of the month quotation.

IV/174 S.E.	*Barley*	*Sesame*
Text 6: o.40'–o.41'	→m 72; →e 75; pq 78(+)	[ ]; @m 10; @e 9½
-137A: r.2'[a]	[ ]	@b 12; @m 10; @e [ ]

a. AD III -137A: r.2' [...] x *saḫ-le*$_{10}$ 3(b) ŠE.GIŠ AŠ SAG ITU 2(b) AŠ MURUB$_4$ <ITU> 1(b) 4 *qa* AŠ TIL ⸢ITU⸣ [...]

Text 6 and -137A provide congruent data for sesame in the middle of the month. Also note that the quote for regular barley in Text 6 at the end of the month is congruent with the single value for the following month V in AD III -137C.[62]

XII/174 S.E.	*Dates*	*Mustard*
Text 6: r.2'–r.5'	[...]→5 180(+); [...]13 198(+)	720
-137E: r.4'[a]	210	720

a. AD III -137E: [...] (r.3') 1(p) 2(b) 3 *qa* AŠ TIL ITU [...] (r.4') 1 GUR 5(b) *kàs* 4$^?$ G[UR ...]

The single monthly value for dates in -137E is in reasonable agreement with the more finely detailed but fragmentary values in Text 6; Text 6 and -137E give congruent data for mustard.

VIII/175 S.E.	*Sesame*
Text 6: r.30'	@b 15; →[ ]
-136B: o.9'[a]	15

a. AD III -136B: o.9' [*k*]*às* 2 GUR 1(p) 3(b) *saḫ-le*$_{10}$ 3(b) 2 *qa* ŠE.GIŠ.Ì 2(b) 3 *qa* SÍG.[ḪÁ ...]

The single monthly value for sesame in -136B is in agreement with the single preserved value in Text 6 for the beginning of the month.

X/175 S.E.	*Barley*	*Dates*
Text 6: r.32'–r.33'	51; @e [ ]	@b 288; →e [ ]
-136C: o.14'[a]	[ ] 57	@b 288; @m 300

a. AD III -136C: o.14' [...] 1(p) 3(b) 3 *qa* ZÚ AŠ SAG ITU 1 GUR 3 PI AŠ MURUB$_4$ ITU 1 GUR 3(p) 2(b)

62 AD III -137C: o.17 [... ŠE].IM 2 PI 3 *qa* Z[Ú ...]

For barley -136C preserves only a single unspecified value, which differs by 1 sūt from the single preserved value in Text 6. For dates both texts give congruent values at the beginning of the month, however, the Diary follows with a value in the middle of the month whereas Text 6 follows with a value to the end of the month.

XI/175 S.E.	*Dates*
Text 6: r.35'–r.37'	[ ] 288; [ ] 252
-136C: r.10'[a]	[...]; 28–29 252

a. AD III -136C: r.9' ... ŠE.IM EN MURUB$_4$ ITU 1(p) 3(b) EN TIL ITU 1(p) 2(b) 4½ *qa* (r.10') [...] 28 29 1 GUR 2 PI *kàs* AŠ SAG ITU 3 GUR EN TIL ITU 4 GUR

The second of two equivalences for dates in Text 6 is congruent with the single preserved value in -136C for the last two days of the month.

XII$_2$/175 S.E.	*Cress*
Text 6: r.41'	25½
-136B: r.17'[a]	27

a. AD III -136B: r. 17' *kàs* 4 GUR *saḫ-le$_{10}$* 4(b) 3 *qa* ŠE.GIŠ.Ì 1(b) 4 *qa* SÍG.ḪÁ 2 MA.NA

The traces in Text 6 suggest the single monthly price equivalent for cress differs by 1½ qa/shekel from that of -136B.

COMMENTS

Text 6 is found on three joined fragments of a comparatively large tablet; a small portion of the right edge is preserved between lines o.33'–o.43'. The text, written in a small clear script, presents monthly price equivalences for all six standard commodities for the years 173 (restored), 174 (restored), and 175 S.E. (partially restored). The data in Text 6 are often broken down to monitor fluctuations at the beginning, middle, and end of the month, especially for barley and dates; for some months the quotes are on a virtually day-by-day basis. The price equivalent, in light of the comparable data from the Astronomical Diaries for 174 S.E. (-137) and 175 S.E. (-136), is given at the rate of two shekels of silver. Where the data in Text 6 can be compared directly with those in these Astronomical Diaries, congruencies as well as minor difference in both the recording periods and the price equivalents are to be noted throughout (see Comparanda).

In a curious departure from the form typical of this corpus where the silver equivalence is described simply as KÙ.BABBAR (see Texts 7, 9, 11, 15) without any further qualifications, Text 6: r.12'–r.15', although fragmentary, quite clearly quotes two distinct price equivalents for barley in III/175 S.E. (27 May – 25 June 137 BCE), which depend upon the species of payment: the first, 42 qa/shekel in "staters of Demetri[us] (II)"; and the second, 36 qa/shekel in "staters of [Arsac]es (i.e., Phraates II)." Describing the silver of payment as "staters of RN" (with or without additional qualifiers of purity and condition) is otherwise only found in the contemporary archival documents, whereas throughout the market quotations in the Astronomical Diaries dated through the reign of Seleucus I the silver equivalence is sporadically qualified as *qalû* and, thereafter, *epšu*,[63] the latter likely reflecting changes in royal coinage instituted early in the reign of Antiochus I (281 – 261 BCE) intended to unify the typology of royal issues and bring weight norms for precious metals under strict control.[64] This unique specification of specific types of coins in Text 6, especially of Seleucid coinage with a greater purchasing power,[65] less than five years after Babylon had first fallen into the hands of the Parthian king Mithradates I in 171 S.E. (141 BCE) (Habicht 1989, 371), it will be suggested, is to be connected to one of several reversals of fortune endured by the Parthians during the nearly two decades they required to fully subdue Babylonia.

Following the initial capture of Babylon by the Parthians, the Seleucid king Demetrius II responded by marching against the Parthians (140 BCE). But despite initial successes, he was defeated and captured, the date of which is generally taken to be 139 BCE (Habicht 1989 371, and n.178), although Eusebius gives the date as the third year of the 160th Olympiad, i.e., 138 BCE.[66] This latter date in fact is to be preferred in the light of a report of the king's capture in the Astronomical Diary for the summer of that year (IV/174 S.E. = 8 July – 5 Aug. 138 BCE) (Del Monte 1997, 111):

> (r.8') … That month, I heard as follows: … king Demetrius who before […] his troops from the cities of … […] (r.9') […] made […] of Babylonia, and this king Arsaces went from the cities of Media to Babylonia, and … […] (r.10') […]

---

63 First attested in AD -277 and occurring regularly thereafter.

64 Golenko 1995, 51–53.

65 The increased purchasing power (+6%) of the Demetrius staters is almost identical to the greater average weight of silver tetradrachms minted at Seleucia on the Tigris by Demetrius II (+6.7%) over those of Mithradates, as determined by a survey of nearly a score of coins published online by the American Numismatic Society (http://www.numismatics.org/search/) and Parthia.com (http://parthia.com/mithradates1.htm).

66 … Demetrius, the son of Demetrius … defeated Antiochus the son of Alexander, who was based in Syria and the city of Antioch, and started to reign in the first year of the 160th Olympiad (140 B.C.). In his second year, he collected an army and set off for Babylon and the eastern regions, to fight against Arsaces. In the next year, which was the third year of the 160th Olympiad (138 B.C.), he was captured by Arsaces, who sent him to be held prisoner in Parthia … (Eusebius *Chronicle* [http://www.attalus.org/translate /eusebius.html]).

> brought about [the defeat] of his troops, and seized him and his nobles, saying, "King Arsaces [...] good peace for you? from ... [...] (r.11') [...] in plenty, happiness and good peace in the cities of Media next to king Arsaces ... [...]."[67]

Justin adds the following details:

> [§38.9.2] ... Demetrius had attacked the Parthians and had emerged the victor in numerous engagements, but he was suddenly caught in an ambush and taken prisoner, with the loss of his army. [3] The Parthian king, Arsacides (Mithridates I), displayed a kingly magnanimity and sent him to Hyrcania, where he not only provided him with the mode of life of a king but also gave him the hand of his daughter[68] in marriage, promising to restore to him the throne of Syria, which Trypho had seized in his absence. [4] After Arsacides' death, Demetrius despaired of ever returning. He could not bear his captivity, he was weary of the life of a commoner, luxurious though it was, and he secretly planned an escape to his kingdom. [5] He was encouraged and accompanied by his friend Callimander, who, after Demetrius' capture, had hired guides and come from Syria to Babylon, through the Arabian deserts, dressed as a Parthian. [6] However, Arsacides' successor, Phrahates (II), took a shorter route along minor roads and, thanks to the speed of his horsemen, overtook the fugitive Demetrius and brought him back.[69]

The unique inclusion here in Text 6 of such a specific statement regarding payment in either Seleucid or Arsacid species suggests the imminently anticipated if not actual presence of Demetrius in Babylon in the late spring of 137 BCE. As a consequence, the dates of Mithridates' death and Phraates' succession to the throne must fall between the summer of 138 and the spring of 137 BCE.[70]

---

67 AD III -137A r.8' ... ITU BI *al-te-me um-ma* x x x [m]*de-meṭ-ri* LUGAL *šá* AŠ IGI-*ma* $ERIN_2$-*šú* TA URU.MEŠ [...] (r.9') [...] URI[ki] DÙ-*uš u* [m]*ar-šá-ka-a* LUGAL *an-na-a* TA URU.MEŠ *šá* KUR *ma-da-a-a* DIŠ KUR URI[ki] GIN-*ma* x [...] (r.10') [...M]EŠ $ERIN_2$-*ni-šú* GAR-*ma šá-a-šú u* [lú]GAL.MEŠ-*šú* AŠ ŠU[II] *iṣ-bat um-ma* [m]*ar-šá-ka-a* LUGAL *sa-lim* SIG_5-*ka* TA x [...] (r.11') [...] AŠ *nu-ḫu-uš* DÙG.GA ŠÀ-*bi u sa-lim* SIG_5 AŠ URU.MEŠ *šá* KUR *ma-da-a-a* AŠ *ta-ḫu* [m]*ar-šá-ka-a* LUGAL *šak*-[...].

68 Cf. App. *Syr*. 67 "... [Demetrius] was taken prisoner by [the Parthians] and lived in the palace of king Phraates, who gave him his sister, Rhodogyne, in marriage."

69 Justin, *Epitome of the Philippic History of Pompeius Trogus*. Translated by J.C. Yardley, with Introduction and Explanatory Notes by R. Devlin. Classical Resources Series 3 (Atlanta: Scholars Press, 1994), 244–45.

70 Cf. ca. 139/38 BCE, e.g., Schippmann 1987a, 527.

SUMMARY

(barley, dates, mustard, cress, and sesame qa per 1 shekel silver; wool mina per 1 shekel silver)

Year	*Month*	*Barley*	*Dates*	*Mustard*	*Cress*	*Sesame*	*Wool*
173	[…]						
	IV	[ ]m 72(+)	[	]	36	[	]
	V	[ ]m 78 @e 72(+)	[ ]	[ ]e 756	25½	[	]
	VI	[ ]e 79	@b [ ]	@b 720(+)	@b 15 @m [ ]	[	]
	VII	@b [	] 288 @m [ ]	[ ]	@b 25½	[ ] 16½ →e 15	[ ]
	VIII	[ ] 60 11 57 12 54(+) 18–19 54 20→e [ ]	→m 234(+) 18–19 252 20→[ ]	[ ]	20	15	[ ]
	IX	[ ] 57 →e 54 pq [ ]	[ ]	720	[ ]	16½	[ ]
	X	[	] 288 @m 288(+) [ ] 30 288	[	]	15 pq [ ]	[ ]
	XI	[ ] 54 @m 51(+)	[ ] 288 @m 297(+)	[ ]	18	@b [ ]	2½
	XII	@[ ]	@b 288 @m [ ]	[ ]	20	→m [	]
174	I	@b 54 @m 54(+) @e 69	→m 270(+)	[ ]	18	@b 16 @m [ ]	2½
	II	@b 72 @m [ ]	@b 294 →e 300	540	[ ]	14	2½ @e 3
	III	[ ] 84 11→14 87 15 14 16–17 81 [ ]→e 72	@b 300 @m 270(+)	540	15	12½	2½
	IV	→m 72 →e 75 pq 78(+)	[ ] 336 →e 315	450	[ ]	[ ] @m 10 @e 9½	3
	V	[ ]	→m 315 →e 318(+)	450	18	@b 9(+)	3
	VI	→m 72(+) [ ] 26 66 →e 60(+)	[ ]	@b 540	[		]

Year	*Month*	*Barley*	*Dates*	*Mustard*	*Cress*	*Sesame*	*Wool*
	[…]						
	XI	[					]
	XII	[ ]	[ ]→5 180(+) [ ] 13 198(+)	720	13	9 @e [ ]	2
175	I	@b [	]	720	7	[	]
	II	@b 42 7→[ ] 15→20 42 21→e 36(+)	@m 180 @e 192	[	] 9 →e 12	[ ]	2
	III	stD 42 stA 36	@b 218(+) @m [ ] old 210	540	14	@b 8 [ ]	[ ]
	IV	@b 42 →m [ ]	162 old 180(+)	540	14	[ ]	2
	V	54(+)	[ ]	630	18(+)	[	]
	VI	@b 43½	[	]	19	[	]
	VII	36(+)	[ ]m 180(+)	[			]
	VIII	[ ] 51(+)	[		]	@b 15? →[ ]	[ ]
	IX	[	] 288	[			]
	X	51 @e [ ]	@b 288 →e [ ]	[	]	17	[ ]
	XI	[	] 288 [ ] 252	[	]	@b 17 @m [ ]	[ ]
	XII	51 pq [ ]	[	]	25½	[	]
	XII_2	→e 54 pq [ ]	[	]	25½	[	]

	Barley	Dates	Mustard	Cress	Sesame	Wool
High:	87	336	756	36	17	3
Low:	36	162	450	7	8	2

TEXT 7

BM 34598 (Sp II 72)
Date: Month VIII, 178 – 185 S.E. (Oct./Nov. 134 – Nov. 127 BCE)
Dimensions: 6.6 x 5.8 x 2.1
Commodities: [dates]
Equivalence: 2 shekels silver
Unpublished Pinches hand copy (Sp II 72)
Photo: Plate XI

obv.

1 [ ] TA MU.1 ME 1,18.KÁM
2 [EN MU.1 ME 1],25.KÁM *šá* DIŠ 2 GÍN KÙ.BABBAR
3 [APIN AŠ SAG] ⸢ITU⸣ 4 GUR 1 PI
4 [MURUB$_4$ ITU] 4 GUR
5 [TIL ITU] 3 GUR 4 PI
6 [APIN AŠ SAG] ITU 3 GUR 4 PI
7 MURUB$_4$ ITU 3 GUR 3(p) 2(b)
8 TIL ITU 3 GUR *(erasure)*
9 APIN *(erasure)* 4 GUR
10 APIN AŠ SAG ITU 3 GUR 3 PI
11 MURUB$_4$ ITU 3 GUR 2(p) 3(b)
12 [T]IL ITU 3 GUR 2 PI
13 [AP]IN AŠ SAG ITU 3 GUR

lo.e.

14 [MURUB$_4$ IT]U 2 ⸢GUR⸣ 4(p) 3(b) *(erasure)*
15 [TIL IT]U 2 GUR 4(p) 4(b)
16 ⸢APIN⸣ [AŠ] ⸢SAG ITU⸣ [nn] ⸢GUR⸣

rev.

17 [MURUB$_4$ IT]U *(erasure)* 3(p) 2(b)
18 [TIL IT]U 2 GUR 2(p) 1(b)
19 [API]N AŠ SAG ITU 4(p) 3(b)
20 [MURUB$_4$ IT]U 4 PI
21 [TIL IT]U 3(p) 2(b)
22 [ ] APIN AŠ SAG ITU 1 GUR
23 [MURUB$_4$] ITU 4(p) 3(b)
24 [TIL I]TU 4 PI

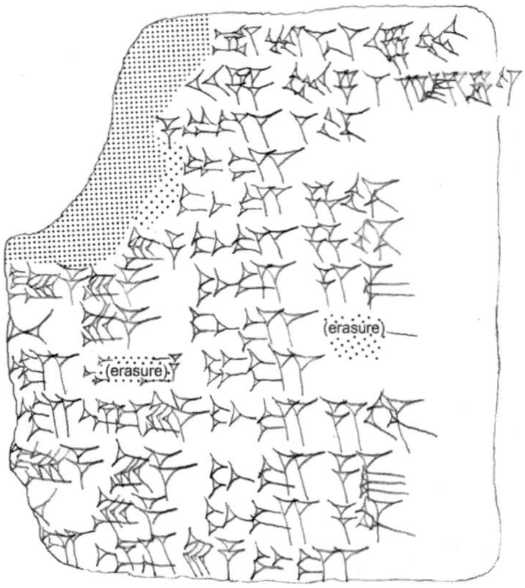

BM 34598 obverse

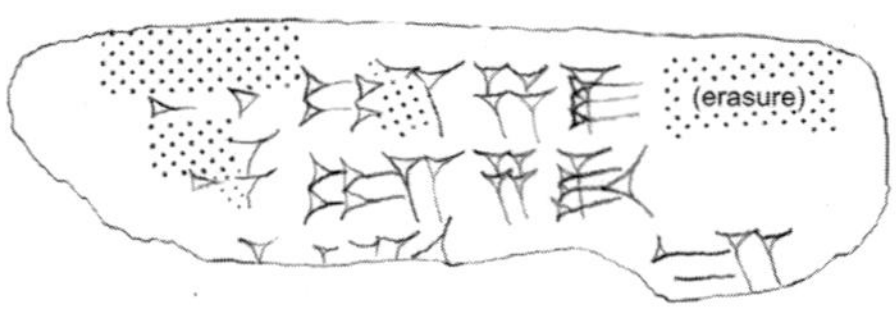

BM 34598 lower edge

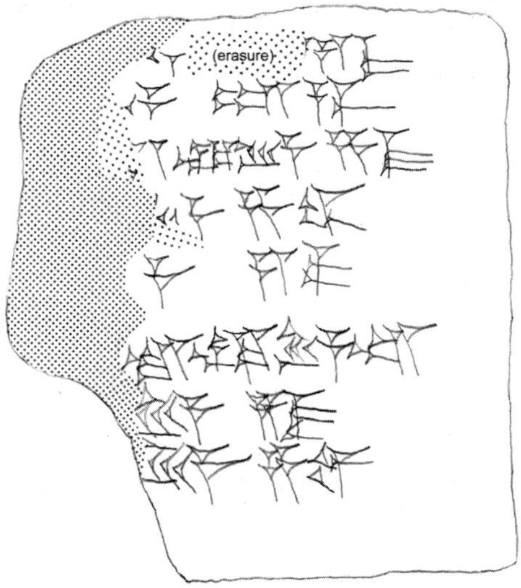

BM 34598 reverse

TRANSLATION

1 […] from year 178
2 [to year 1]85, which is for 2 shekels of silver.
3 [(Year 178) Month VIII: (dates) at the beginning of] the month 4 kur 1 pān,
4 [(in) the middle of the month] 4 kur,
5 [(at) the end of the month] 3 kur 4 pān.
6 [(Year 179) Month VIII: (dates) at the beginning of] the month 3 kur 4 pān,
7 (in) the middle of the month 3 kur 3 pān 2 sūt,
8 (at) the end of the month 3 kur.
9 (Year 180) Month VIII: (dates) 4 kur.
10 (Year 181) Month VIII: (dates) at the beginning of the month 3 kur 3 pān,
11 (in) the middle of the month 3 kur 2 pān 3 sūt,
12 [(at) the e]nd of the month 3 kur 2 pān.
13 [(Year 182) Mo]nth VIII: (dates) at the beginning of the month 3 kur,
14 [(in) the middle of the mon]th 2 kur 4 pān 3 sūt,
15 [(at) the end of the mon]th 2 kur 4 pān 4 sūt.
16 (Year 183) Month VIII: [(dates) at] the beginning of the month [nn] kur,
17 [(in) the middle of the mon]th 3 pān 2 sūt,
18 [(at) the end of the mon]th 2 kur 2 pān 1 sūt.
19 [(Year 184) Month VIII]: dates) at the beginning of the month 4 pān 3 sūt,
20 [(in) the middle of the mon]th 4 pān,
21 [(at) the end of the mon]th 3 pān 2 sūt.
22 […] (Year 185) Month VIII: (dates) at the beginning of the month 1 kur,
23 [(in) the middle of] the month 4 pān 3 sūt,
24 [(at) the end of the mo]nth 4 pān.

NOTES

1 A possible restoration for the beginning of the line is suggested by Text 2:1 EN.NUN *šá* KI.LAM … .

9 Pinches noted that he could see beneath the erasure traces of AŠ SAG ITU.

17 Traces of 2 GUR appear beneath the erasure.

COMPARANDA

(Dates qa per 1 shekel silver)

VIII/179 S.E.	*Dates*
Text 7: 6–8	@b 342; m 330; e 270
-132C: r.26'–28'[a]	→12 180(+)[…]; 21–23 306, 24[…] 270
-132D_2: o.5'[b]	→12 324; 13→18 330; 19[–20] 315; […]

a. AD III -132C: r.26' … ZÚ.LUM EN 12 1 GUR […] (r.27') TA 21 EN 23 1 GUR 3(p) 3(b) 24 […] (r.28') [1 G]UR 2(p) 3(b)

b. AD III -132D_2: o.5' … ZÚ.L[UM] EN 12 1 GUR 4 P[I] TA 13 EN 18 1 GUR 4(p) 1(b) 19 [(20)[?] 1 GUR] 3(p) 4(b) 3 *qa*

Text 7 shows a price equivalent at the beginning of VIII/179 S.E. of 342 qa/shekel whereas the Astronomical Diaries first quote a price through the 12th of 324 qa/shekel (-132D_2). The Diary price equivalents for the 13th to 18th (-132D_2) and for what is certainly the end of the month (-132C) are congruent with the values for the middle and end of the month in Text 7: 330 and 270 qa/shekel, respectively.

VIII/185 S.E.	*Dates*
Text 7: 22–24	@b 90; m 81; e 72
Text 8: o.5'	84
-126A: o.2'–o.3'[a]	[…]; 22→24 72; […]

a. AD III -126A: o. 2' [… T]A 22 EN 24 2 PI (o.3') ⸢TA⸣ […]

The Diary value for the 22nd through the 24th (72 qa/shekel) is in agreement with the end of the month value in Text 7. Contrast the single equivalence for dates during VIII/185 S.E. of 84 qa/shekel given in Text 8: o.5', with the values in Text 7 at the beginning and middle of the month of 90 and 81 qa/shekel, respectively[71]; the small difference may be due in part to what day was taken to be the "middle" of the month.

COMMENTS

Text 7 is written on a small well-preserved tablet of which only a portion of its upper left is missing. The text charts market quotations for an unnamed commodity at the beginning, middle, and end of month VIII for eight consecutive years from 178 through 185 S.E.; only for 180 S.E. is there given but a single value for the month.[72] The price equivalent is stated (l. o.2) to be per two shekels of silver. Comparison with the quantities given in the price equivalents in the Astronomical Diaries for these years readily permits the commodity tracked in Text 7 to be identified as dates. Dates were harvested in the fall, i.e., by or in month VIII—typically October or November in the Julian calendar. The text charts a five- to six-fold increase in the price (i.e., drop in quantity per unit price) of dates, with the most precipitous changes occurring between 182 and 184 S.E.—from an average of 323 qa/shekel for the years 178–182 S.E. to an average of just 76 qa/shekel for 184–185 S.E. Unfortunately the absence for 183

71 The single monthly price equivalences in Text 8 may represent the end of the month quotations, but more often than not appear to be randomly distributed throughout the more detailed monthly data in the Diaries and Text 9.

72 The traces of AŠ SAG ITU beneath the erasure in l. 9 suggest that the scribe had intended to provide more finely detailed price equivalents for 180 S.E. but could only locate a single monthly value in his sources.

S.E. of a value for the beginning of the month, the low value for the middle of the month (60 qa/shekel, but note the erasure of 2 GUR) resembling the values for the later years, and the high value at the end of the month (269 qa/shekel) resembling the data for the earlier years make interpretation of the situation in that critical year rather difficult. Nonetheless the data clearly show the drop in the price equivalent of dates in this period to be far more sudden than suggested by the data previously available in the Astronomical Diaries.[73] Monthly price equivalents for barley and dates for I–XII/185 S.E. are partially preserved in Text 8.

During the first five years (178 – 182 S.E.) the price equivalents for dates in month VIII were at relatively moderate and stable levels.[74] During 182 S.E. (130 BCE), after some eight years of relative political stability within Babylonia under Parthian rule, with the former Seleucid king Demetrius II held in captivity (see Text 6 Comments), the new Seleucid king, Demetrius' brother Antiochus VII, renewed hostilities.[75] In response to Antiochus' initial successes on the battle field and his occupation of Babylon itself in 183 S.E. (129 BCE),[76] the Parthian king Phraates II, in an effort to create a distraction, sent Demetrius back to Syria where he was able, briefly, to reoccupy the Seleucid throne and plot not the recovery of the eastern provinces but an attack on Egypt.[77] In the meantime, with Antiochus having been killed by Phraates, Babylonia was lost forever to the Seleucids and "Arsaces" was acknowledged once again as king in Babylon in VIII/183 S.E.[78]

During 184 S.E. (128 BCE)—the first year of the markedly more expensive dates in month VIII—Phraates was killed while campaigning against the Scythians while Babylon was in the hands of Phraates' appointee, the satrap Himerus, who was noted for his cruelty and his disdain for his subjects.[79] However, by 24/II/185 S.E. (30 May 127 BCE)[80]—the beginning of the second

---

73 Slotsky 1997, 59, concluded that beginning about 107 S.E. the quantities of dates in the price equivalents in the Astronomical Diaries began to rise rapidly, that is, prices for dates were falling; however, beginning about 193 S.E., and especially after 200 S.E., her analysis showed that price equivalents once again dropped off.

74 Note that less than three years earlier in month XII_2/175 S.E. "[…] there was … through devastation by Adad among the date-palms" (AD III -136B r. 11').

75 On the rise to power of Antiochus VII, see conveniently, Habicht 1989, 365–69.

76 Justin 38, 10:6. For texts with date formulas attesting to the dating of Antiochus' rule in Babylon (*terminus post quem*, 20 May 129 BCE; terminus ante quem, 5 November 129 BCE) see Boiy 2004, 172–73.

77 Justin 39, 1.

78 The report of a lunar eclipse for 13/VIII/183 S.E. identifies "Arsaces" as king (AD V 21).

79 Justin 42, 1:2–3; Posidonius (FGrHist 87 F13); Diodorus (34/35 21) cited by Boiy 2004, 174.

80 BOR 4 132:6.

year of the markedly more expensive dates in month VIII—Babylonia was briefly in the hands of Hyspaosines, the former Seleucid governor, then Parthian governor, and now king of Characene (Mesene), located to the south in the former Sealand at the head of the Persian Gulf.[81] But by month VIII itself, a historical anecdote in an Astronomical Diary for that month briefly reports the re-entry into Babylon of forces loyal to the Parthian king:

> (o.6') … That month, (on) the 4th, Timarchos (o.7'), who previously from beside Arsaces, the king, was appointed the guard commander and who in month IV (o.8') had escaped from Hyspaosines, came from beside Indupanē with Median troops (o.9') (and) they entered Babylon. That day, the administrator of E-sangil and the Babylonians provided him one bull and 3 (sheep) sacrifices (r.1) as an offering at the Gate of the Son of the Prince of E-sangil. (On) the 6th, they went to Borsippa. (On) the 8th, (r.2) they came out from Borsippa (and) went to the side of Indupanē on the outskirts of Seleucia on (r.3) the Tigris. (On) the 9th, the great dais that in month I had been put at … of the 'Pure Gate,' (r.4) its top was changed…. That month, (on) the 25th, the sacrifices, which had been interrupted in the Akītu Temple (r.5) … to Bēl, Bēltīya, and Ištar of Babylon (AD III -126A: o.6'–r.5).

SUMMARY

(dates qa per 1 shekel silver)

Year	*Month*	*Dates*
178	VIII	@b 378 m 360 e 342
179	VIII	@b 342 m 330 e 270
180	VIII	360
181	VIII	@b 324 m 315 e 306
182	VIII	@b 270 m 261 e 264
183	VIII	@b [ ] m 60 e 269

81 See conveniently Boiy 2004, 169–71, 175–76; for a recent monograph on the subject of this kingdom, see Schuol 2000.

Year	*Month*	*Dates*
184	VIII	@b 81 m 72 e 60
185	VIII	@b 90 m 81 e 72

High: 378
Low: 60

TEXT 8

BM 33479 (Rm IV 33) + BM 33639 (Rm IV 195)
Date: 184 – 190 S.E. (128/7 – 122/1 BCE)
Dimensions: 8.2 x 6.3 x 2.5
Commodities: barley, dates
Equivalence: 2 shekels silver
Unpublished Strassmaier hand copy 622a (Rm IV 195)
Unpublished Sachs transliteration (33479 + 33639)
Photo: Plate XI

obv.

o.1' x x [ ]

---

o.2' MU.1 ME 1,2⸢5⸣ [BAR ŠE(.IM)]
o.3' ZÚ 1 PI SIG 1(p) x [ ]
o.4' KIN 1(p) 2(b) ZÚ ⸢3(p)⸣ [ ]
o.5' ZÚ 4(p) 4(b) GAN 1(p) 5(b) Z[Ú]
o.6' ZÍZ 5(b) ⸢ZÚ⸣ 3 PI 2 *qa* Š[E]

---

o.7' MU.1 ME 1,2⸢6⸣ BAR ŠE 1(p) 2(b) ZÚ 2(+)(p) [ ]
o.8' ZÚ 3 PI SIG 2 PI ZÚ 4 PI [ ]
o.9' NE ⸢1(+)(p)⸣ 5(b) ZÚ 4 ⸢PI⸣ KIN 1(p) 5(b) Z[Ú]
o.10' APIN 1(p) 2(b) ⸢3 *qa* ZÚ⸣ [GA]N 1(p) 2(b) ZÚ [ ]
o.11' AB 1(p) 1(b) 3 *qa* Z[Ú] x [ ]
o.12' ŠE 1(p) 4(b) ZÚ 1 GUR 1(p) [ ]

---

o.13' MU.1 ME 1,2⸢7 BAR$^{!?}$⸣ ŠE.I[M]
o.14' SIG [2(p)] ⸢2(b)⸣ ZÚ 2 GUR [ ]
o.15' [ZÚ nn GU]R 3 P[I]

rev.

r.1 APIN 2(p) 1(b) ZÚ 1 GUR 3(b) [ ]
r.2 ZÍZ 5(b) ZÚ 4(p) 3(b) ŠE [ ]

---

r.3 MU.2[*sic*] ME 28 BAR ŠE 1(p) x [ ]
r.4 SIG 1(p) 1(b) ZÚ 2(p) 5(b) ⸢3⸣ [*qa*]
r.5 NE 1(p) 5(b) 3 ⸢*qa* ZÚ 2(p) 3(+)(b)⸣ [ ]
r.6 D[U$_6$] x x x [Z]Ú 1 GUR 3(b) API[N]
r.7 GAN 2(p) 1(b) ZÚ 1(g) 2(p) 4(b) AB 2(p) ⸢3(+)(b)⸣ [ ]

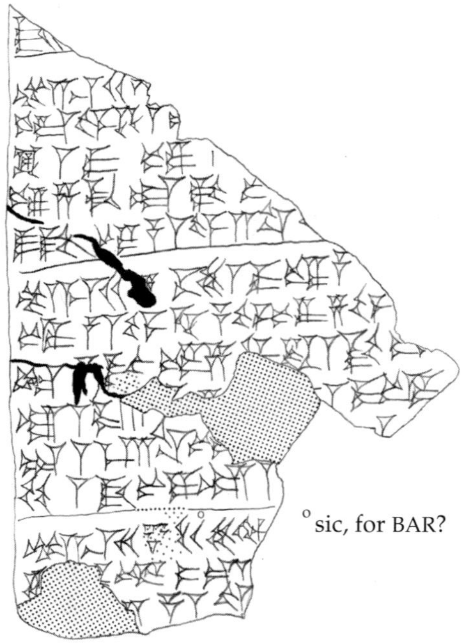

BM 33479 + BM 33639 obverse

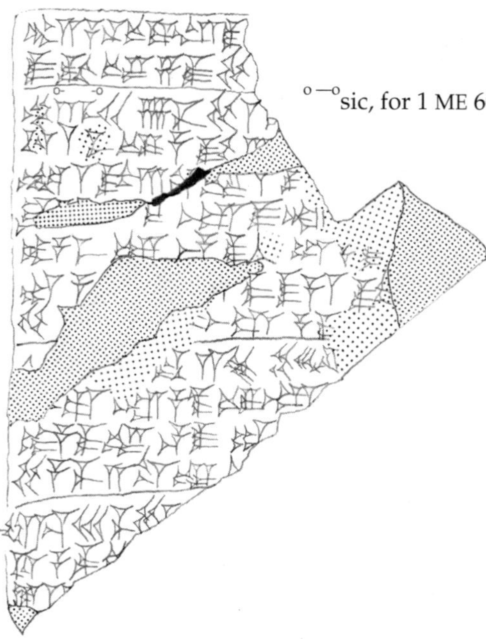

BM 33479 + BM 33639 reverse

r.8 AB 2(+)(p) [ ] x 2(b) ZÍZ 3(p) 5(b) [ ]
r.9 ŠE ⸢2(+)(p)⸣ [Z]Ú 1 GUR 2(p) 2(b) [ ]

---

r.10 M[U.1 ME 1,29] ⸢KIN⸣.2.KÁM ŠE.IM [ ]
r.11 ⸢1⸣ GUR APIN 2(p) 3(b) ZÚ 1 GUR [ ]
r.12 GAN 2(p) 2(b) ZÚ 1(g) 2(p) 3(b) AB [ ]
r.13 ŠE 2(p) 1(b) 2 *qa* ZÚ ⸢1(g)⸣ [ ]

---

r.14 MU.1 ME 1,30 BAR ŠE ⸢2(p)⸣ [ ]
r.15 SIG 2(p) 2(b) Z[Ú]
r.16 KIN 1(p) x [ ]
(remainder lost)

TRANSLATION

o.1' … […].

---

o.2' Year 185. [Month I: barley …];
o.3' (month II) dates 1 pān. Month III: (barley) 1 pān … […].
o.4' Month VI: (barley) 1 pān 2 sūt; dates 3 pān […];
o.5' (month VIII) dates 4 pān 4 sūt. Month IX: (barley) 1 pān 5 sūt; dat[es …].
o.6' Month XI: (barley) 5 sūt; dates 3 pān 2 qa. M[onth XII …].
o.7' Year 18[6]. Month I: barley 1 pān 2 sūt; dates 2(+) pān […];
o.8' (month II) dates 3 pān. Month III: (barley) 2 pān; dates 4 pān […].
o.9' Month V: (barley) 1(+) pān 5 sūt; dates 4 pān. Month VI: (barley) 1 pān 5 sūt; da[tes …].
o.10' Month VIII: (barley) 1 pān 2 sūt 3 qa; dates [.… Month I]X: (barley) 1 pān 2 sūt; dates […].
o.11' Month X: (barley) 1 pān 1 sūt 3 qa; da[tes …] … […].
o.12' Month XII: (barley) 1 pān 4 sūt; dates 1 kur 1 pān […].

---

o.13' Year 187. Month I[!]: barl[ey …].
o.14' Month III: [(barley) 2 pān] 2 sūt; dates 2 kur […]
o.15' [(month $m_{1'}$)… dates nn ku]r 3 pā[n …]
r.1 Month VIII: (barley) 2 pān 1 sūt; dates 1 kur 3 sūt […].
r.2 Month XI: (barley) 5 sūt; dates 4(p) 3(b). Month XII: [(barley)…].

---

r.3 Year 188[!]. Month I: barley 1 pān … […].
r.4 Month III: (barley) 1 pān 1 sūt; dates 2 pān 5 sūt 3 [qa …].
r.5 Month V: (barley) 1 pān 5 sūt 3 qa; dates 2 pān 3(+) sūt […].
r.6 Month VII: (barley) … [da]tes 1 kur 3 sūt. Month VIII […].
r.7 Month IX: (barley) 2 pān 1 sūt; dates 1 kur 2 pān 4 sūt. Month X: (barley) 2 pān 3(+) sūt […].

r.8 Month X: (barley) 2(+) pān […] … 2 sūt. Month XI: (barley) 3 pān 5 sūt […].

r.9 Month XII: (barley) 2(+) pān [… date]s 1 kur 2 pān 2 sūt […].

---

r.10 Ye[ar 189.] Month VI$_2$: barley […];

r.11 (month VII) (dates) 1 kur. Month VIII: (barley) 2 pān 3 sūt; dates 1 kur […].

r.12 Month IX: (barley) 2 pān 2 sūt; dates 1 kur 2 pān 3 sūt. Month X: [(barley)…].

r.13 Month XII: (barley) 2 pān 1 sūt 2 qa; dates 1 kur […].

---

r.14 Year 190. Month I: barley 2(+) pān […].

r.15 Month III: (barley) 2 pān 2 sūt; da[tes …].

r.16 Month VI: (barley) 1 pān … […]

(remainder lost)

NOTES

o.1' The traces might be read ZÍZ x or, and perhaps more likely, ⸢5(b)⸣, however all other preserved lines on the tablet begin with the year, month, or commodity, never the quantity of the commodity; note the first two signs of l. o.6' ZÍZ 5(b).

o.4' Reading ⸢3(p)⸣ as per traces in both Strassmaier's and Sachs' copies.

o.13' For BAR$^{!?}$ the traces on the tablet suggest the remains of [Š]E. Sachs transliterated the line as MU.1 ME 1,2⸢7⸣[.K]ÁM$^{?}$ ŠE.IM; however KÁM is nowhere else attested on this tablet following a year (cf. r.10 KIN.2.KÁM) and the patterns established elsewhere throughout the tablet would require the restoration of <BAR> immediately following the putative KÁM.

o.14' [2(p)] ⸢2(b)⸣ is reasonably restored in the light of comparable values in Text 9: r.1' and AD III -124A: o.32'.

r.3 The scribe inadvertently wrote 2 ME 28 (= 228) for the intended 1 ME 1,28 (= 188).

r.7–r.8 The data for month X (AB) at the end of line r.7 appear to be repeated at the beginning of line r.8.

r.9 Reading ⸢2(+)(p)⸣ as per traces in Sachs' copy.

COMPARANDA

(Barley and dates qa per 1 shekel silver)

VIII/185 S.E.	*Dates*
Text 8: o.5'	84
Text 7: 22–24	@b 90; m 81; e 72
-126A: o.1'[a]	[…]; 22→24 72; […]

a. AD III -126A: o.1' […] ⌜x 4(b) 3⌝ *q*[*a* …] (o.2') [… T]A 22 EN 24 2 PI (o.3') ⌜TA⌝[…]

Text 7 shows that the quantity of dates per shekel of silver declined throughout the month. The single equivalent for the month in Text 8 (84 qa/shekel) is slightly higher than the single preserved Astronomical Diary value for the 22nd to 24th (72 qa/shekel) and falls between the values at the beginning and middle of the month in Text 7. The small differences may be due in part to the specific day on which the value for Text 8 was recorded and what day was taken to be the "middle" of the month in Text 7.

I/186 S.E.	*Barley*	*Dates*
Text 8: o.7'	24	36(+)
Text 9: o.1–0.5	1 20; 2 21; 3-[…]7 30; 8→15 28; 16→20 30; 21[...2]4 22½; 25→e 18	@b 54(+); […]; 12→15 72; 16–17 81; 18–19 90; 20–2[2…] 90; →e 72
-125A: o.10–o.11[a]	1 20; 2 22½; 3–5 24; 6–7 30; 8→15 28; 16→20 30; 21–22 […]; 25→e 20	@b 96; […]→11 66; 12→15 72; 16–17 81; 18–19 90; 20–22 93; 23–24 90; →e 72

a. AD III -125A: o.10 … ŠE.IM 1 3(b) 2 *qa* 2 3(b) 4½ *qa* 3 4 5 4(b) 6 7 5(b) TA 8 EN 15 4(b) 4 *qa* TA 16 EN 20 5(b) 21 22 […] (o.11) [TA] 25 EN TIL ITU 3(b) 2 *qa* ZÚ AŠ SAG ITU 2(p) 4(b) [TA nn] ⌜EN⌝ 11 1(p) 5(b) TA 12 EN 15 2 PI 16 17 2(p) 1(b) 3 *qa* 18 19 2(p) 3(b) 20 21 22 2(p) 3(b) 3 *qa* 23 24 2(p) 4(b) 3 *qa* EN TIL ITU 2 PI

The single monthly value for barley in Text 8 (24 qa/shekel) is congruent with the Astronomical Diary's value for the 3rd to 5th. The single price equivalents, one each for barley and dates, in Text 8 completely ignore the rapidly fluctuating quantities for both commodities as seen in Text 9 and the Diary, which, with but two exceptions in the barley data (on the 2nd and the from the 25th to the end of the month) parallel each other perfectly.

II/186 S.E.	*Dates*
Text 8: o.8'	54
Text 9: o.8–o.9	→9 72; 10→[…] 69; 25–26 72; @e 81

The single monthly quantity of dates in Text 8 (54 qa/shekel) is substantially lower than any of the preserved values in Text 9. It is not impossible that this value originally corresponded to one or more of the missing values in the middle of the month in Text 9. Nonetheless note that emending Text 8 to read 4[!] PI would yield an appropriate price equivalent of 72 qa/shekel.

III/186 S.E.	*Barley*	*Dates*
Text 8: o.8'	36	72
Text 9: o.10–o.12	[...]; 3–5 39; 6–8 36; 9 39; 10→13 36; [...] 30; 23→e 33	@b 72; [... 17] 72; 18→[...]

The single monthly price equivalent for barley in Text 8 (36 qa/shekel) corresponds to the values for the 6th to 8th and 10th to 13th in Text 9, while the single monthly equivalent for dates in Text 8 (72 qa/shekel) corresponds to the value for the period ending on the 17th in Text 9.

V/186 S.E.	*Barley*	*Dates*
Text 8: o.9'	33	72
Text 9: o.15	[...] 30; 12→20 33; →e 36(+)	[...]
-125A: r.3'[a]	[...]	[@b] 60; @m 72; →e 81[?]

a. AD III -125A: r.3' [... ZÚ AŠ SAG I]TU 1(p) 4(b) AŠ MURUB$_4$ ITU 2 PI EN TIL ITU 2(p) 1(b) 3[?] *qa*

The single monthly price equivalent for barley in Text 8 (33 qa/shekel) corresponds to the value for the 12th to 20th in Text 9. The single monthly quantity of dates in Text 8 (72 qa/shekel) corresponds to the mid-month value in the Astronomical Diary.

VI/186 S.E.	*Barley*
Text 8: o.9'	33
Text 9: o.17–o.18	[...] 31½; @m 30; 18→2[0[?]]; [...]→e 28
-125A: r.18'[a]	[...] 30; 26→e 28

a. AD III -125A: r.18' [... IT]U 5(b) TA 26 EN TIL ITU 4(b) 4 *q*[*a*]

The single monthly value (33 qa/shekel) in Text 8 is slightly greater than any of the preserved data in Text 9 and the Astronomical Diary, both of which show an overall decrease in the price equivalent of barley throughout the course of the month; the value in Text 8 may have agreed with now lost data at or near the beginning of the month in Text 9 and the Diary. The first preserved value in the Diary (30 qa/shekel) is congruent with the value at the middle of the month in Text 9; the quantities to the end of the month in the Diary and Text 9 are also congruent (28 qa/shekel).

IX/186 S.E.	*Barley*
Text 8: o.10'	24
Text 9: o.24	[...]; 25→e 24

The single monthly equivalent for barley in Text 8 (24 qa/shekel) corresponds to the value for the 25th through the end of the month, the only preserved value, in Text 9.

X/186 S.E.	*Barley*
Text 8: o.11'	22½
Text 9: o.26	[...]; 5→15 22½; 16→2[0? ...]

The single monthly equivalent for barley in Text 8 (22½ qa/shekel) corresponds to the value for the 5th to 15th, the only preserved value, in Text 9.

XII/186 S.E.	*Barley*
Text 8: o.12'	30
Text 9: o.30–o.31	1–2 24; 3→[...]; pq 36; 23 30; 24–26 18(+); [...]
-124B: r.8'–r.9'[a]	@b 24(+); [@m] 28; @e 30

a. AD III -124B: r.8' ... ŠE.IM AŠ SAG ITU 4(b) [...] (r.9') [... MURUB$_4$ IT]U 4(b) 4 *qa* AŠ TIL ITU 5(b) Z[Ú ...]

The price equivalent for barley (30 qa/shekel) in Text 8 is equal to the end of the month quote in the Astronomical Diary and the quote for the 23rd of the month in Text 9.

III/187 S.E.	*Barley*	*Dates*
Text 8: o.14'	⌜42⌝	180(+)
Text 9: r.1'	[...] 51; 13 48; 14→[...]	[...]
-124A: o.32'[a]	[...]; 58; [...] 42?; @m 45; →e 42	@b 180(+)

a. AD III -124A: o.32' [...] ITU 1(p) 3(b) 4 *qa* [... I]TU 1(p) 1(b)? AŠ MURUB$_4$ ITU 1(p) 1(b) 3 *qa* EN TIL ITU 1(p) 1(b) ZÚ.LUM AŠ SAG ITU 1 GUR [...]

The single price equivalent for barley in Text 8 is restored on the basis of the equivalents in Text 9 and -124A where the values are quite similar but not identical. The quantities of dates in the single monthly price equivalent in Text 8 and the equivalent at the beginning of the month in the Astronomical Diary appear to be similar but in each case the text is broken immediately following the initial part of the quantity.

VIII/187 S.E.	*Barley*	*Dates*
Text 9: r.14'–r.15'	→18 18(+); [...]	1–2 90; 3–4 102; 5→[...]; [...] 16 120; 17→25 108(+); [...]
Text 8: r.1	39	96(+)

There is no significant overlap in the data.

XI/187 S.E.	*Barley*	*Dates*
Text 8: r.2	15	81
Text 9: r.23'–r.25'	15½	[...]10 90; 11 96; 12 81; 13→22 84; 23 78; 24 72; [...](+)9½; →e 66

The single monthly value for barley in Text 8 (15 qa/shekel) is close to the single preserved value for barley in Text 9 (15½ qa/shekel). The single monthly equivalent for dates in Text 8 (81 qa/shekel) is congruent with the value for the 12th of the month in Text 9.

III/188 S.E.	*Barley*	*Dates*
Text 8: r.4	21	52½
-123A: o.16'[a]	[...] 30; →e 27½; 27–29 [...]	52(+)

a. AD III -123A: o.16' [...] ⸢ITU⸣ 5(b) EN TIL ITU 4(b) 3½ *qa* 27 28 2[9 ...] ZÚ.LUM 1(p) 2(b) 4 [(nn?) *qa*]

The single value for barley in Text 8 (21 qa/shekel) is lower than either of the preserved equivalents in the Astronomical Diary (30 and 27½ qa/shekel). The single price equivalent for dates in Text 8 (52½ qa/shekel) is close to the value partially preserved in the Diary and suggests a plausible restoration there of 52[½] qa/shekel.

V/188 S.E.	*Barley*
Text 8: r.5	34½
-123A: r.20[a]	1→5 31½; 6→[...]
-123C: 10'[b]	[...] ⸢34½⸣; →m 32½; 21(+)→[...]

a. AD III -123A: r.20 ŠE.IM TA 1 EN 5 5(b) 1½ *qa* TA 6 E[N ...]

b. AD III -123C: 10' [... 5(b)] 4½ *qa* EN MURUB$_4$ ITU 5(b) 2½ *qa* TA 21(+)[x ...]

The single price equivalent for barley in Text 8 (34½ qa/shekel) corresponds to the first quote preserved in -123C at some undetermined point after the beginning (as per -123A) but prior to the middle of the month (as per -123C).

XII/189 S.E.	*Barley*	*Dates*
Text 8: r.13	40	90(+)
-122E: r.11'[a]	[...](+)3	1→20 108(+); [...]

a. AD III -122E: r.11' [...] 3 *qa* ZÚ.LUM TA 1 EN 20 3 P[I ...]

The data preserved in Text 8 and in the Diary are too fragmentary for meaningful comparison.

COMMENTS

Text 8 is found on two joined fragments forming the lower left segment of a larger tablet with portions of the left and lower edges preserved. Perhaps no more than four signs are missing from the end of the longest preserved line (o.9'), and a half dozen or so lines are lost from the top. The text appears to have originally given a single monthly price equivalent each for barley and dates for each full year from [184] S.E. through 190 S.E., except for 189 S.E., which gives monthly price equivalents for just the latter half of the year, i.e., intercalary month VI$_2$ through month XII.[82] The price equivalence rate per 2 shekels of silver is readily determined by comparisons with the comparable overlapping data in Texts 7 and 9[83] and the relevant Astronomical Diaries.[84] Comparisons with the data in these same texts also demonstrate that the single monthly price equivalents for barley and dates in Text 8 are not uniformly given for any one specific time of the month, rather they appear to be randomly distributed throughout the more detailed monthly data in these texts (see the Comparanda, above).

Several scribal lapses and other idiosyncrasies are notable in this text. In line r.3 the scribe wrote 2 ME 28 (228) for the intended year 1 ME 1,28 (188). The price equivalent for barley in month X/188 S.E. is repeated both at the end of r.7 and

82 Perhaps the tablet summarizing the data for the first half of the year was unavailable to the scribe. Compare Text 10, which only gives data for the latter halves of the years 194?–195? S.E. Also note Text 3, which omits data for months X – XII$_2$/47 S.E.

83 Price equivalents for dates during VIII/185 S.E. are also found in Text 7, and for barley, dates, and sesame during I/186 – XII/187 S.E. in Text 9.

84 Both Texts 7 and 9 specifically state that the equivalence rate is per 2 shekels of silver (7:2; 9: r31', U.E.) while the relevant Diaries (-125A; -124A, B; -123A, C, E) regularly quote quantities per 1 shekel of silver (e.g.,–125A: o.12).

the beginning of r.8. The scribe appears to have regularly alternated his writing for barley: ŠE in 186, 188, and 190 S.E., and ŠE.IM in 187 and 189 S.E.; in 187 he seems to have become confused and wrote something presently unintelligible for the expected month name BAR. Irrespective of the specific writing, the signs for "barley" were written only once per year at month I and were not written again thereafter for that year; ZÚ is repeated each month preceding the monthly quantity of dates.

The period covered by Text 8 is one of continued political instability in Babylonia, marked by generally quite low price equivalents for both barley and dates. In fact the scribe of the Astronomical Diary for I/186 S.E. notes after having given the standard market quotations: "That month ... garlic, leek and all ... crops were expensive."[85] Text 8 is presumed to have begun with 184 S.E. (128 BCE), when the Parthian king Phraates II was killed fighting the Scythians and Babylon was governed by his satrap Himerus, noted for his cruelty and his disdain for his subjects.[86] The first legible price equivalent for dates in month II of 185 S.E., during Hyspaosines' brief occupation of Babylon,[87] is the lowest price equivalent for dates (18 qa/shekel) in the extant record since the days of Alexander IV nearly two centuries earlier (17 qa/shekel).[88] The date price equivalents rise modestly through the year peaking at just 84 qa/shekel in month VIII, coincidentally the time of the date harvest and the re-entry into Babylon of troops loyal to the Parthian crown,[89] occupied now by Artabanus I who, during his brief reign (ca. 128/27 – ca. 124/3 BCE), would be preoccupied with the continued presence of Hyspaosines in southern Babylonia[90] and Scythian nomads in the east against whom he would fall.

Although the data here in Text 8 are not complete nor particularly detailed, a curious pattern nonetheless emerges from the price equivalents for dates for the period from 184 S.E. (128/7 BCE) through 188 S.E.(124/3 BCE): they rise steadily from a low of 60 qa/shekel in XI/185 S.E. to a peak of 180(+) qa/shekel in III/187 S.E. and then descend steadily to a new low of 45(+) qa/shekel in V/188 S.E. Text 9, which contains barley and date (and sesame) price equivalents for I/186 through XII/187 S.E. on a virtually day-by-day basis, confirms, despite short term monthly fluctuations, the larger scale phenomenon observed here. The Astronomical Diaries for this same overall period repeatedly refer to

85 AD III -125A: o.12; for a summary of the market quotations for this period, see conveniently Slotsky 1997, 143–44.

86 Justin 42, 1:2–3; Posidonius (FGrHist 87 F13); Diodorus (34/35 21), cited by Boiy 2004, 174.

87 See conveniently Boiy 2004, 169–71.

88 AD I -308: r.15' ... ZÚ.LUM AŠ SAG ITU 2(b) 5 *qa* .... .

89 AD III -126A: o.6'–r.5.

90 For a summary of this king's reign and sources, see conveniently Schippmann 1987b, 647.

plundering by Arabs,[91] who severely restricted travel to Borsippa and beyond and generally created panic; in IV/187 S.E., they reportedly "broke a hole into the wall of Babylon" (-124A: r.5'). By IV/188 S.E., following the death of Hyspaosines the previous month,[92] and amid reports of what must have been a plague of locusts,[93] there may well have been full-scale urban rioting:

> (r.6) ... The 28th, the chief of the guard and many city[?] people [...] from Borsippa to Babylon [...] (r.7) [...] fell upon them [...] they [...], they plundered them, and they killed this chief of the guard in Babylon. Panic [...] (AD III -123A)

Throughout the remainder of 188 S.E. (124/3 BCE) barley and date price equivalents begin to rise until the point where the scribe failed to record the data for the first six months of 189 S.E. (123 BCE). Nonetheless, the Astronomical Diary for I/189 S.E. reports that "that year *samānu*-disease[94] seized the barley during the harvest" (AD III -122A: o.8').

The data for the remainder of 189 (123/2 BCE) and 190 S.E. (122/1 BCE) are poorly preserved but the price equivalents for barley and dates show no significant changes from the previous five years. But now a new king, Mithradates II (124/3 to 88/7 BCE), is on the Parthian throne who during his long reign would raise Parthia to the level of a major international power.[95]

SUMMARY

(barley and dates qa per 1 shekel silver)

Year	*Month*	*Barley*	*Dates*
[...]			
185	[I		]
	II	[ ]	18
	III	18(+)	[ ]
	[IV		]
	[V		]
	VI	24	54(+)
	[VII		]
	[VIII	]	84

91 I/186 S.E. (AD III -125A: o.21); VI/186 S.E. (-125A: r.20'); I/187 S.E. (-124A: o.8'–o.9'); IV/187 (-124A: r.5'–r.7'); IX/124 S.E. (-124B: o.21'); II/188 S.E. (-123A: o.5', cf. -123C:12').

92 AD III -123A: o.18'–o.20'.

93 AD III -123A: o.28'; r.3.

94 Perhaps an ergot-like disease (CAD S, 112, s.v.).

95 See conveniently Boiy 2004, 180–84.

Year	*Month*	*Barley*	*Dates*
	IX	33	[ ]
	[X		]
	XI	15	60
	[XII		]
18[6]	I	24	36(+)
	II	[ ]	54
	III	36	72
	[IV		]
	V	33	72
	VI	33	[ ]
	[VII		]
	VIII	25½	[ ]
	IX	24	[ ]
	X	22½	[ ]
	[XI		]
	XII	30	108(+)
	[XII_2		]
18[7]	[I		]
	[II		]
	III	⸢42⸣	180(+)
	$m_{1'}$	[ ]	144(+)
	[...]		
	VIII	39	96(+)
	[IX		]
	[X		]
	XI	15	81
	[XII		]
188!	I	18(+)	[ ]
	[II		]
	III	21	52½
	[IV		]
	V	34½	45(+)
	[VI		]
	VII	[ ]	99
	[VIII		]

Year	*Month*	*Barley*	*Dates*
	IX	39	138
	X	45(+)	[ ](+)12
	XI	69	[ ]
	XII	36(+)	133½
[189]	VI_2	[	]
	[VII	]	90
	VIII	45	90(+)
	IX	42	135
	[X		]
	[XI		]
	XII	40	90(+)
190	I	36(+)	[ ]
	[II		]
	III	42	[ ]
	[IV		]
	[V		]
	VI	18(+)	[ ]
	[...]		

High:	15	180(+)
Low:	69	18

TEXT 9

BM 34686 (Sp II 173 + Sp II 956) + BM 35604 (Sp III 114)
Date: 186 – 187 S.E. (126/5 – 125/4 BCE)
Dimensions: 12.5 x 8.7 x 2.9
Commodities: barley, dates, sesame
Equivalence: 2 shekels silver
Unpublished Pinches hand copy (BM 34686)[96]
Unpublished Sachs transliteration (BM 34686 + 35604)
Photo: Plates XII–XIII

obv.

o.1 [MU.1 ME 1,26.KÁ]M ITU.BAR ⸢KI.LAM⸣ ŠE.IM 1 1 PI 4 *qa* 2 1(p) 1(b) ⸢3⸣ [4 5]

o.2 [6] 7 1(p) 4(b) TA 8 EN 15 1(p) 3(b) 2 *qa* TA 16 EN 20 1(p) 4(b) 21 [22]

o.3 [2]4 1(p) 1(b) 3 *qa* TA 25 EN TIL ITU 1 PI ZÚ.LUM AŠ SAG ITU 3(p) x

o.4 [ ] TA 12 EN 15 4 PI 16 17 4(p) 3(b) 18 19 1 GUR 20 21 ⸢2⸣[2]

o.5 [23 24 1 GU]R 3(b) ⸢EN⸣ TIL ITU 4 PI ŠE.GIŠ.Ì 1(p) 3(b) ITU.GU$_4$ KI.LAM ŠE.IM 1 1 P[I]

o.6 [1 P]I 4 *qa* TA 8 EN 10 1 PI TA 11 EN TIL ITU [1(p) 1(b) G]IBIL.MEŠ

o.7 [nn(p) 4(b)] 15 2 PI 16 17 2(p) 3(b) 18 2 PI TA 19 ⸢EN⸣ 22 1(p) 5(b)

o.8 [TA] 26 EN TIL ITU 2(p) 1(b) 2 *qa* ZÚ.LUM EN 9 4 PI TA 10

o.9 [24] ⸢3⸣ (p) 5(b) 25 26 4 PI AŠ TIL ITU 4(p) 3(b) ŠE.GIŠ 1(p) 1(b) ½ *qa*

o.10 [ITU.SIG KI.LAM ŠE.IM 1 2] 3 4 5 2(p) 1(b) 6 ⸢7⸣ 8 2 PI 9 2(p) 1(b) TA 10 EN 13 2 PI

o.11 [1(p)] ⸢4(b)⸣ TA 23 EN TIL ITU 1(p) 5(b) ZÚ.LUM AŠ SA[G IT]U ⸢4 PI⸣

o.12 [17] ⸢4⸣ PI TA 1⸢8⸣ [EN TIL ITU] ⸢ŠE⸣.[GIŠ]

o.13 [ ]

o.14 [1(p)] 5(b) Z[Ú].LUM 3(p) 4(b) AŠ TIL ITU 4 PI [ ]

o.15 [1(p)] ⸢4(b)⸣ TA ⸢12⸣ EN 20 1(p) 5(b) EN TIL ITU 2 P[I]

o.16 [ŠE].GIŠ AŠ SAG ⸢ITU⸣ 1(b) AŠ MURUB$_4$ ⸢ITU 1(b)⸣ 4 *qa* EN TIL IT[U]

o.17 [1 (p)] ⸢4(b)⸣ 3 *qa* AŠ MU[RUB$_4$ IT]U 1(p) 4(b) TA 18 EN 20(+) [ ]

o.18 [ ] TIL ITU 1(p) 3(b) ⸢2 *qa*⸣ ZÚ.LUM 4 PI ŠE.GIŠ 1(b) 1(+) [*qa*]

---

96 Reported by Wiseman 1988, 365, n. 16, but not presently available.

o.19 [ ] TA 5 EN 10 1(p) 1(b) 3 *qa* TA 11 EN 22(+) [ ]
o.20 [AŠ SAG] ITU 4 PI AŠ MURUB$_4$ ITU ⸢GIBIL⸣.MEŠ 1 ⸢GUR 1 PI⸣ [ ]
o.21 [ ] 11 1(b) 1 *qa* TA 12 EN TIL ITU 1(b) ITU.API[N KI.LAM ŠE.IM]
o.22 [AŠ SA]G ITU 1 GUR 1 PI EN MURUB$_4$ ITU 1 GUR 2(b) AŠ MURUB$_4$ [ITU]
o.23 [ ] x EN TIL ITU 4(p) 2(b) ŠE.GIŠ 1(b) 1 *qa* ITU.GAN [KI.LAM ŠE.IM]
o.24 [nn] *qa* TA 25 EN TIL ITU 1(p) 2(b) ZÚ.LUM AŠ SA[G ITU]
o.25 [EN] 22 1 GUR 4(b) TA 23 EN TIL ITU 1 GUR [ ]
o.26 [TA] 5 EN 15 1(p) 1(b) 3 *qa* TA 16 EN 20(+) [ ]
o.27 [AŠ S]AG ITU 1 GUR 2(b) TA 7 EN 12 1 GUR TA [13]
o.28 ⸢TA⸣ 26 EN TIL ITU 1 GUR 1(p) 5(b) ŠE.GIŠ 1(b) 1½ [*qa*]
o.29 AŠ MURUB$_4$ ITU 1 GUR 2(p) 4(b) AŠ TIL ITU 1 GUR 2 PI ŠE.GI[Š]
o.30 ITU.ŠE KI.⸢LAM ŠE⸣.IM 1 2 1(p) 2(b) TA 3 E[N]
o.31 ⸢NU⸣.DÙ.MEŠ 2 PI 23 1(p) 4(b) ⸢24 25⸣ 26 1(p) [ ]
o.32 [ ] x EN 10 1 GUR 1(p) 4(b) ⸢11 12 13⸣ 1 GUR 2(p) ⸢2(b)⸣ [ ]
o.33 [ ] x x x x [ ]

(*remainder lost*)

rev.

r.1' [2(p)] ⸢5(b) 13 2(p) 4(b) TA 14 EN⸣ [ ]
r.2' [*q*]*a* A[Š TIL ITU] 1(b) 2 *qa* ITU.ŠU KI.LAM ŠE.IM EN x [ ]
r.3' ⸢TA⸣ 12 EN 15 2(p) 1(b) 2 *qa* TA 16 EN TIL ITU 2 PI 4 *qa* Z[Ú.LUM]
r.4' EN 22 1 GUR 3(p) 4(b) AŠ TIL ITU 1 GUR 4 PI ŠE.GIŠ AŠ SAG ITU 1(b) 2(+) [*qa*]
r.5' ITU.NE KI.LAM ŠE.IM AŠ SAG ITU $2^{!?}$ PI 4 *qa* TA 14 EN 2⸢4⸣ [ ]
r.6' 27 28 1(p) 5(b) 29 30 1(p) 4(b) ZÚ.LUM AŠ SAG ITU 1 GUR 3(p) 2(b) T[A]
r.7' 28 29 30 1 GUR 2(p) 3(b) ŠE.GIŠ AŠ SAG ITU 2(b) AŠ MURUB$_4$ ITU 1(b) 4 *qa* AŠ TIL ITU [ITU.KIN KI.LAM ŠE.IM]
r.8' [AŠ S]AG ITU 1(p) 3(b) 5 *qa* EN MURUB$_4$ ITU 1(p) 2(b) EN TIL ITU 1(p) 2(b) 4 *qa* ZÚ.LUM x [ ]
r.9' [10] 11 12 1 GUR TA 13 EN 23 1 GUR 1 PI TA 24 EN TIL ITU 1 GUR [ ]
r.10' [TA 2]0 EN 23 3(b) TA 24 EN 27 3(b) 2 *qa* 28 29 3(b) ITU.DU$_6$ K[I.LAM ŠE.IM]
r.11' [1(p)] ⸢3(b)⸣ 3 *qa* TA 12 EN 19 1(p) 2(b) TA 20 EN 25 1(p) 1(b) 3 *q*[*a*]
r.12' [ ] ⸢ITU⸣ [ ] (+)1 *qa* TA 12 EN 20 1 GUR 1(p) 2(b) GIBIL.MEŠ AŠ SAG ITU x [ ]

r.13' [T]A 23 EN 26 1 GUR 2(p) 2(b) EN TIL ITU 1 GUR 1(p) ⸢2(b)⸣ [ ]

r.14' [I]TU 2(b) 2 *qa* ITU.APIN KI.LAM ŠE.IM EN 18 1(p) [ ]

r.15' [ ] *qa* ZÚ.LUM 1 2 1 GUR 3 4 1 GUR 4(b) TA 5 E[N]

r.16' [1]6 1 GUR 1(p) 4(b) TA {EN} 17 EN 25 1 GUR 1 (p) [ ]

r.17' [ ] x x ⸢ITU.GAN KI.LAM⸣ ŠE.IM AŠ SAG ITU 1 PI [ ]

r.18' [AŠ] ⸢MURUB$_4$ ITU⸣ 1 GUR 1PI T[A 16 EN]

r.19' [ŠE].GIŠ(.Ì) AŠ SAG IT]U 3(b) 1 *qa* EN T[IL IT]U ⸢3(b) 2 *qa*⸣ I[TU.AB KI.LAM ŠE.IM]

r.20' [nn] ⸢*qa* 6⸣ 7 1 PI 4 *qa* TA 8 EN 1⸢8⸣ [ ]

r.21' [EN] TIL ITU 5(b) 2 *qa* ZÚ.LUM 1 2 1 GUR 1(p) ⸢3(+)(b)⸣ [ ] ⸢5 6⸣ [7]

r.22' [ ] ⸢3(b)⸣ TA 11 EN 17 1 GUR 2(b) 18 19 20 4(p) 4(b) [1 G]UR AŠ TIL ITU 1 G[UR]

r.23' [IT]U 3(b) 1 *qa* TA 16 EN 25 2(b) 4½ *qa* [EN TIL IT]U ⸢2(b)⸣ 4 *qa* ITU.ZÍZ KI.LAM ŠE.IM 5(b) 1 *qa*

r.24' [ ] 10 1 GUR 11 1 GUR 2(b) 12 4(p) 3(b) TA 13 EN ⸢2⸣2 4(p) 4(b) 23 4(p) 2(b) 24 4 PI

r.25' [ ] 3(b) 1 *qa* EN TIL ITU 3(p) 4(b) ŠE.GIŠ 1 2 2(b) 4½ *qa* TA 3 EN 15 2(b) ⸢3 *qa*⸣ TA 16

r.26' [EN] ⸢2(b)⸣ 2 *qa* EN TIL ITU 2(b) 1½ *qa* ITU.⸢ŠE KI.LAM ŠE.IM⸣ EN 10 5(b) 11 12 13 5(b) 2 *qa*

r.27' [14 15 1]6 5(b) 4 *qa* 17 ⸢18 1 PI⸣ 19 1(p) 1(b) 20 1(p) 2(b) TA 21 EN 25 1(p) 2(b) 4 *qa* TA!(en) ⸢26⸣ x

r.28' [AŠ SA]G ITU 3(p) ⸢4(b) 6⸣ 7 8 9 3(p) 2(b) 10 11 12 3(p) 2(b) 4 *qa* 13 14 15 3 (p) [ ]

r.29' [TI]L ⸢ITU⸣ 4(p) 1 (b) ŠE.GIŠ 1 2 3 2(b) 1 *qa* TA 4 EN 15 2(b) ⸢½ *qa*⸣ TA 16 E[N]

r.30' [ ] ⸢2(b)⸣ 3 *qa* 28 29 2(b) 4 *qa*

---

r.31' [*n*]*a-dan šá a-na* 2 GÍN KÙ.BABBAR AŠ KUR SU[M]

u.e.

[MU.1].ME 1,26.KÁM *u* MU.1 ME 1,27.KÁM *šá*!(diš) ⸢*a-na* 2 GÍN⸣ [KÙ.BABBAR]

le.e.

[ZÚ.LU]M *u* ŠE.GIŠ.Ì *šá* MU.1 ME 1,26.[KÁM]

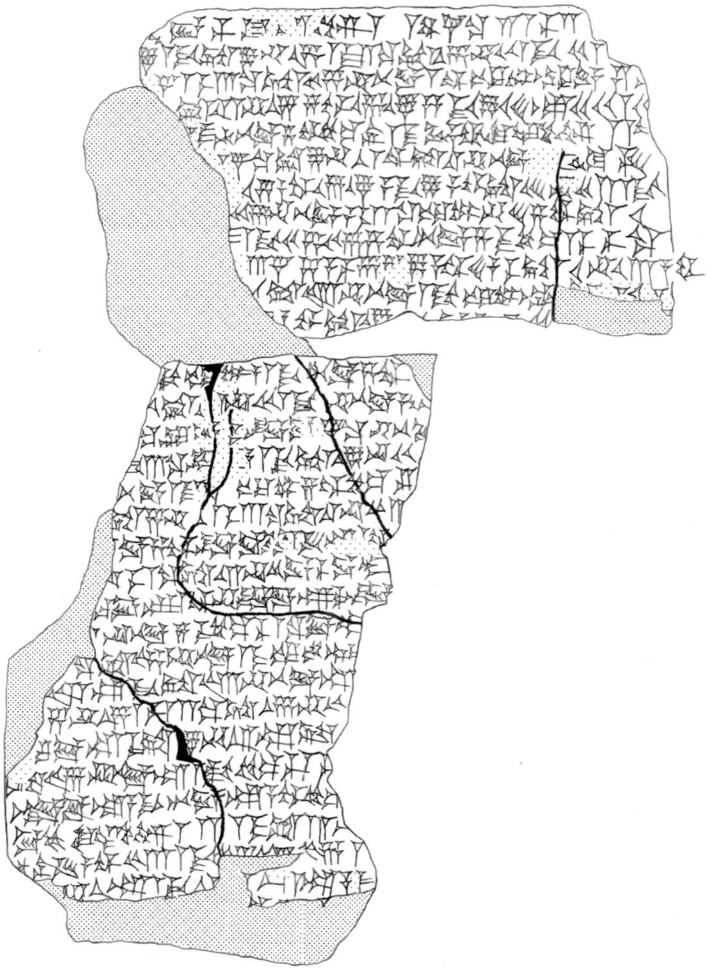

BM 34686 + BM 35604 obverse

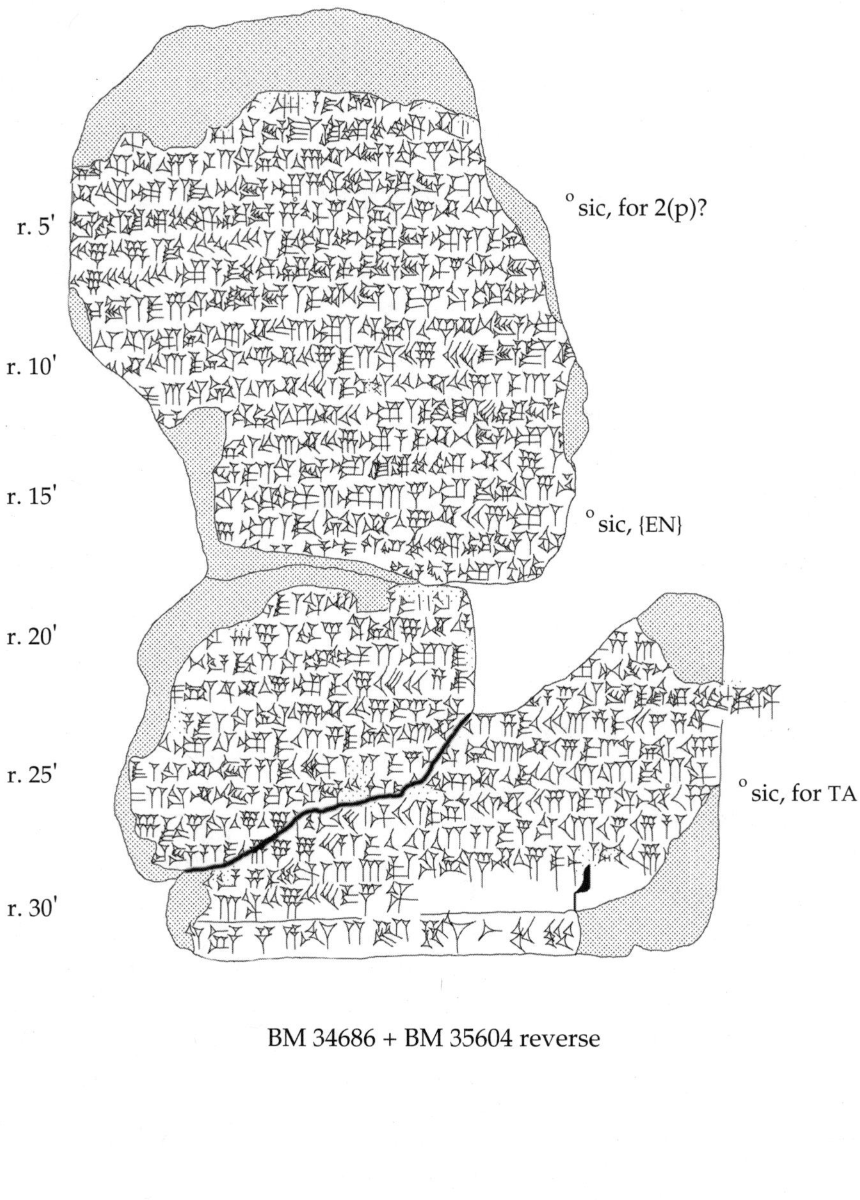

BM 34686 + BM 35604 reverse

BM 34686 + BM 35604 left edge

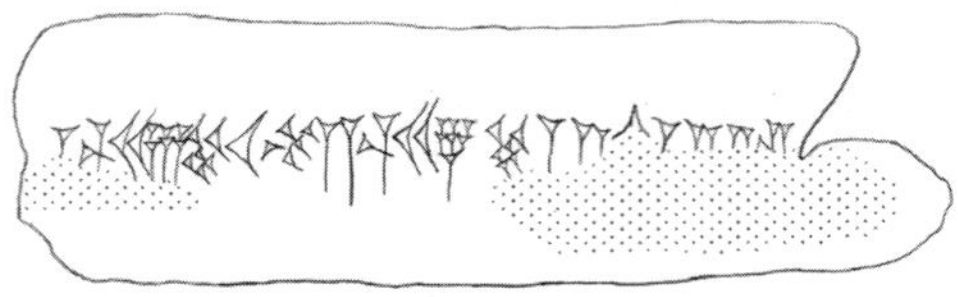

BM 34686 + BM 35604 upper edge

TRANSLATION

o.1 [Year 186]. Month I market rate: barley (on) the 1st 1 pān 4 qa, the 2nd 1 pān 1 sūt, the 3rd, [4th (and) 5th …]

o.2 [… the 6th (and)] 7th 1 pān 4 sūt, from the 8th to the 15th 1 pān 3 sūt 2 qa, from the 16th to the 20th 1 pān 4 sūt, the 21st [(and) 22nd …]

o.3 [… the 2]4th 1 pān 1 sūt 3 qa, from the 25th to the end of the month 1 pān; dates at the beginning of the month 3 pān …

o.4 […], from the 12th to the 15th 4 pān, the 16th (and) 17th 4 pān 3 sūt, the 18th, (and) 19th 1 kur, the 20th, 21st (and) 2[2nd]

o.5 [… the 23rd (and) 24th 1 ku]r 3 sūt, to the end of the month 4 pān; sesame 1 pān 3 sūt. Month II market rate: barley (on) the 1st 1 pā[n …]

o.6 [… 1 pā]n 4 qa, from the 8th to the 10th 1 pān, from the 11th to the end of the month [1 pān 1 sūt, n]ew

o.7 [… nn pān 4 sūt], the 15th 2 pān, the 16th (and) 17th 2 pān 3 sūt, the 18th 2 pān, from the 19th to the 22nd 1 pān 5 sūt

o.8 [… from] the 26th to the end of the month 2 pān 1 sūt 2 qa; dates to the 9th 4 pān, from the 10th

o.9 [… 24th] 3 pān 5 sūt, the 25th (and) 26th 4 pān, at the end of the month 4 pān 3 sūt; sesame 1 pān 1 sūt ½ qa.

o.10 [Month III market rate: barley (on) the 1st (and) 2nd …], the 3rd, 4th (and) 5th 2 pān 1sūt, the 6th, 7th (and) 8th 2 pān, the 9th 2 pān 1 sūt, from the 10th to the 13th 2 pān o.11 [… 1 pān] 4 sūt, from the 23rd to the end of the month 1 pān 5 sūt; dates at the beginn[ing of the mon]th 4 pān

o.12 [… 17th] 4 pān, from the 18th [to the end of the month …]; se[same …]

o.13 […]

o.14 [… (month IV) (barley) 1pān] 5 sūt; d[a]tes 3 pān 4 sūt, at the end of the month 4 pān […]

o.15 [… (month V) (barley) 1 pān] 4 sūt, from the 12th to the 20th 1 pān 5 sūt, to the end of the month 2 pā[n …]

o.16 [… ; ses]ame at the beginning of the month 1 sūt, in the middle of the month 1 sūt 4 qa, to the end of the mon[th …]

o.17 [… (month VI) (barley) 1 pān] 4 sūt 3 qa, in the mid[dle of the mon]th 1 pān 4 sūt, from the 18th to the 20(+) […]

o.18 […] end of the month 1 pān 3 sūt 2 qa; dates 4 pān; sesame 1 sūt 1(+) [qa …]

o.19 [… (month VII) (barley)] from the 5th to the 10th 1 pān 1 sūt 3 qa, from the 11th to the 22(+) […]

o.20 [… (dates) at the beginning of] the month 4 pān, in the middle of the month, new 1 kur 1 pān […]

o.21 [… (sesame)] the 11th 1 sūt 1 qa, from the 12th to the end of the month 1 sūt. Month VIII [market rate: barley …]

o.22 [… at the beginn]ing of the month 1 kur 1 pān, to the middle of the month 1 kur 2 sūt, in the middle of the [month …]

o.23 […(month IX) (dates)] … to the end of the month 4 pān 2 sūt; sesame 1 sūt 1 qa. Month IX [market rate: barley …]

o.24 [… nn] qa, from the 25th to the end of the month 1 pān 2 sūt; dates at the begin[ning of the month …]

o.25 [… to the] 22nd 1 kur 4 sūt, from the 23rd to the end of the month 1 kur […]

o.26 [(month X) (barley) from the] 5th to the 15th 1 pān 1 sūt 3 qa, from the 16th to the 20(+) […]

o.27 [(dates) at the beg]inning of the month 1 kur 2 sūt, from the 7th to the 12th 1 kur, from [the 13th to the …],

o.28 from the 26th to the end of the month 1 kur 1 pān 5 sūt; sesame 1 sūt 1½ [qa …],

o.29 (month XI) (dates) in the middle of the month 1 kur 2 pān 4 sūt, at the end of the month 1 kur 2 pān; sesa[me …].

o.30 Month XII market rate: barley (on) the 1st (and) 2nd 1 pān 2 sūt, from the 3rd t[o …],

o.31 poor quality 2 pān, the 23rd 1 pān 4 sūt, the 24th, 25th (and) 26th 1 pān […]

o.32 […] … (dates) to the 10th 1 kur 1 pān 4 sūt, the 11th, 12th (and) 13th 1 kur 2 pān 2 sūt […]

o.33 […] x x x x […]

(*remainder lost*)

r.1' [… (year 187) (month III) (barley) 2 pān] 5 sūt, the 13th 2 pān 4 sūt, from the 14th to the […]

r.2' [… (sesame) nn q]a, a[t the end of the month] 1 sūt 2 qa. Month IV market rate: barley from … […],
r.3' from the 12th to the 15th 2 pān 1 sūt 2 qa, from the 16th to the end of the month 2 pān 4 qa; d[ates …],
r.4' to the 22nd 1 kur 3 pān 4 sūt, at the end of the month 1 kur 4 pān; sesame at the beginning of the month 1 sūt 2(+) [qa …].
r.5' Month V market rate: barley at the beginning of the month 2[!] pān 4 qa, from the 14th to the 24th […]
r.6' the 27th (and) 28th 1 pān 5 sūt, the 29th (and) 30th 1 pān 4 sūt; dates at the beginning of the month 1 kur 3 pān 2 sūt, fr[om …]
r.7' the 28th, 29th (and) 30th 1 kur 2 pān 3 sūt; sesame at the beginning of the month 2 sūt, in the middle of the month 1 sūt 4 qa, at the end of the month [… . Month VI market rate: barley]
r.8' [at the be]ginning of the month 1 pān 3 sūt 5 qa, to the middle of the month 1 pān 2 sūt, to the end of the month 1 pān 2 sūt 4 qa; dates … […]
r.9' [the 10th,] 11th (and) 12th 1 kur, from the 13th to the 23rd 1 kur 1 pān, from the 24th to the end of the month 1 kur […]
r.10' [(sesame) from the 2]0th to the 23rd 3 sūt, from the 24th to the 27th 3 sūt 2 qa, the 28th (and) 29th 3 sūt. Month VII ma[rket rate: barley …]
r.11' [… 1 pān] ⌜3 sūt⌝ 3 qa, from the 12th to the 19th 1 pān 2 sūt, from the 20th to the 25th 1 pān 1 sūt 3 q[a …]
r.12' [… (dates) of the] month […] (+)1 qa, from the 12th to the 20th 1 kur 1 pān 2 sūt—new at the beginning of the month … […]
r.13' [… fr]om the 23rd to the 26th 1 kur 2 pān 2 sūt, to the end of the month 1 kur 1 pān 2 sūt […]
r.14' [… (sesame) of the mo]nth 2 sūt 2 qa. Month VIII market rate: barley to the 18th 1 pān […]
r.15' [… nn] qa; dates (on) the 1st (and) 2nd 1 kur, the 3rd (and) 4th 1 kur 4 sūt, from the 5th t[o …]
r.16' [… 1]6th 1 kur 1 pān 4 sūt, from {to} the 17th to the 25th 1 kur 1 pān […]
r.17' […] … . Month IX market rate: barley at the beginning of the month 1 pān […]
r.18' […(dates) in] the middle of the month 1 kur 1 pān, fr[om the 16th to the …]
r.19' [… ; sesame at the beginning of the mon]th 3 sūt 1 qa, to the e[nd of the mon]th 3 sūt 2 qa. Mo[nth X market rate: barley …]
r.20' [… nn] qa, the 6th (and) 7th 1 pān 4 qa, from the 8th to the 18th […]
r.21' [… to] the end of the month 5 sūt 2 qa; dates (on) the 1st (and) 2nd 1 kur 1 pān 3(+) sūt […] the 5th, 6th [(and) 7th …]
r.22' […] 3 sūt, from the 11th to the 17th 1 kur 2 sūt, the 18th, 19th (and) 20th 4 pān 4 sūt [… 1 k]ur, at the end of the month 1 k[ur …]
r.23' [… (sesame) of the mon]th 3 sūt 1 qa, from the 16th to the 25th 2 sūt 4½ qa, [to the end of the mon]th 2 sūt 4 qa. Month XI market rate: barley 5 sūt 1 qa,
r.24' [… (dates)] the 10th 1 kur, the 11th 1 kur 2 sūt, the 12th 4 pān 3 sūt, from the 13th to the 22nd 4 pān 4 sūt, the 23rd 4 pān 2 sūt, the 24th 4 pān

r.25' […] 3 sūt 1 qa, to the end of the month 3 pān 4 sūt; sesame (on) the 1st (and) 2nd 2 sūt 4½ qa, from the 3rd to the 15th 2 sūt 3 qa, from the 16th

r.26' [to the …] 2 sūt 2 qa, to the end of the month 2 sūt 1½ qa. Month XII market rate: barley to the 10th 5 sūt, the 11th, 12th (and) 13th 5 sūt 2 qa,

r.27' [the 14th, 15th (and) 1]6th 5 sūt 4 qa, the 17th (and) 18th 1 pān, the 19th 1 pān 1 sūt, the 20th 1 pān 2 sūt, from the 21st to the 25th 1 pān 2 sūt 4 qa, from$^{!}$ the 26th […]

r.28' [… (dates) at the beginn]ing of the month 3 pān 4 sūt, the 6th, 7th, 8th (and) 9th 3 pān 2 sūt, the 10th, 11th (and) 12th 3 pān 2 sūt 4 qa, the 13th, 14th (and) 15th 3 pān […]

r.29' [… the en]d of the month 4 pān 1 sūt; sesame (on) the 1st, 2nd (and) 3rd 2 sūt 1 qa, from the 4th to the 15th 2 sūt ½ qa, from the 16th t[o …]

r.30' […] 2 sūt 3 qa, the 28th (and) 29th 2 sūt 4 qa.

---

r.31' […] …which was giv[en] in the land for 2 shekels of silver […]

u.e. [… year 1]86 and year 187 for 2 shekels of [silver …]

le.e. [… dat]es and sesame for year 186 […]

NOTES

o.1–o.2 Restorations from context, reinforced by AD III -125A: o.10.

o.5 [23 24 1 GU]R restored from context, reinforced by AD III -125A: o.11'.

o.6 The restoration [1(p) 1(b)] is suggested by Sachs' copy.

o.7 [nn(p) 4(b)] restored as per Sachs' copy.

o.11 ⸢4(b)⸣ … SA[G IT]U ⸢4 PI⸣ restored as per traces in Sachs' copy.

o.12 All restorations as per traces in Sachs' copy.

o.14 [1(p)] restored as per traces in Sachs' copy.

o.15 [1(p)] ⸢4(b)⸣ restored from context and as per traces in Sachs' copy.

o.25 [EN] restored as per traces in Sachs' copy.

o.27 [13] restored as per Sachs' copy and reinforced by context

r.1' [2(p)] ⸢5(b)⸣ restored from context and traces in Sachs' copy.

r.2' Restoration at beginning of line suggested by Sachs.

r.5' $2^{!?}$ PI: the text clearly shows 4(p), i.e., 72 qa/shekel, a seemingly anomalous spike when seen in context.

r.9' [10] restored as per Sachs' copy.

r.18' Restorations as suggested by AD III -124B: o.17'.

r.19' Beginning of line restored as suggested by AD III -124B: o.17'; end of line restored as per traces in Sachs' copy.

r.21' [EN] … [7 restored as per Sachs' copy and reinforced by AD III -124B: r.9'.

U.E. For *šá*$^{!}$(diš) Sachs offered "looks like 𒁹 but may be *šá*"; cf. Slotsky 1997, 12.

COMPARANDA

(Barley, dates, and sesame qa per 1 shekel silver)

I/186 S.E.	*Barley*	*Dates*
Text 9: o.1–o.5	1 20; 2 21; 3-[…]7 30; 8→15 28; 16→20 30; 21[…2]4 22½; 25→e 18	@b 54(+); […]; 12→15 72; 16–17 81; 18–19 90; 20–2[2…] 90; →e 72
-125A: o.10–o.11[a]	1 20; 2 22½; 3–5 24; 6–7 30; 8→15 28; 16→20 30; 21–22 […]; 25→e 20	@b 96; […]→11 66; 12→15 72; 16–17 81; 18–19 90; 20–22 93; 23–24 90; →e 72
Text 8: o.7'	24	36(+)

a. AD III -125A: o.10 … ŠE.IM 1 3(b) 2 *qa* 2 3(b) 4½ *qa* 3 4 5 4(b) 6 7 5(b) TA 8 EN 15 4(b) 4 *qa* TA 16 EN 20 5(b) 21 22 […] (o.11) [TA] 25 EN TIL ITU 3(b) 2 *qa* ZÚ AŠ SAG ITU 2(p) 4(b) [TA nn] ⸢EN⸣ 11 1(p) 5(b) TA 12 EN 15 2 PI 16 17 2(p) 1(b) 3 *qa* 18 19 2(p) 3(b) 20 21 22 2(p) 3(b) 3 *qa* 23 24 2(p) 4(b) 3 *qa* EN TIL ITU 2 PI

Text 9 and the Astronomical Diary (-125A) give quotes for the same breakdown of days for both barley and dates; the quantities themselves are congruent except for barley on the 2nd (Text 9: 21 qa/shekel; -125A: 22½ qa/shekel) and to the end of the month (Text 9: 18 qa/shekel; -125A: 20 qa/shekel), and for dates at the beginning of the month (-125A gives 96 qa/shekel, which, doubled in Text 9, would read 1(g) 2(b), but the tablet (l. o.3) clearly reads 3(p) x. Note that in all three cases the Diary quotes higher quantities. Also note Text 8 quotes a single monthly price equivalent for barley (24 qa/shekel) congruent with the Diary value for days 3 to 5 (lost in Text 9).

II/186 S.E.	*Dates*
Text 9: o.8–o.9	→9 72; 10→[…] 69; 25–26 72; @e 81
Text 8: o.8'	54

All the preserved quantities of dates in Text 9 when equated to 1 shekel are substantially higher than the single monthly quantity of dates in Text 8 (54 qa/shekel). It is not impossible that this value originally corresponded to one or more of the missing values in the middle of the month in Text 9, although note that emending Text 8 to read 4[!] PI would yield an appropriate price equivalent of 72 qa/shekel.

III/186 S.E.	*Barley*	*Dates*
Text 9: o.10–o.12	[...]; 3–5 39; 6–8 36; 9 39; 10→13 36; [...] 30; 23→e 33	@b 72; [... 17] 72; 18→[...]
Text 8: o.8'	36	72

The quantity of barley for both the 6th to 8th and the 10th to 13th in Text 9 (36 qa/shekel) corresponds to the single monthly price equivalent in Text 8, while the value for dates just prior to the 18th in Text 9 (72 qa/shekel) corresponds to the single monthly equivalent in Text 8.

V/186 S.E.	*Barley*
Text 9: o.15	[...] 30; 12→20 33; →e 36(+)
Text 8: o.9'	33

Among the preserved values for barley in Text 9, the quantity for the 12th to 20th (33 qa/shekel) corresponds to the single monthly price equivalent for in Text 8.

VI/186 S.E.	*Barley*
Text 9: o.17–o.18	[...] 31½; @m 30; 18→2[0?]; [...]→e 28
-125A: r.18'[a]	[...] 30; 26→e 28
Text 8: o.9'	33

a. AD III -125A: r.18' [... IT]U 5(b) TA 26 EN TIL ITU 4(b) 4 *q*[*a*]

Both Text 9 and the Astronomical Diary (-125A) show an overall decrease in the price equivalent of barley throughout the course of the month. The first preserved value in the Diary (30 qa/shekel) is congruent with the value at the middle of the month in Text 9; the quantities to the end of the month in the Diary and Text 9 are also congruent (28 qa/shekel). Text 8 gives a single monthly price equivalent for barley (33 qa/shekel) that is greater than any of the preserved values in Text 9 or the Diary, although that value may have originally agreed with now lost data at or near the beginning of the month in Text 9 and the Diary.

IX/186 S.E.	*Barley*
Text 9: o.24	[...]; 25→e 24
Text 8: o.10'	24

The single preserved value in Text 9 for the 25th through the end of the month (24 qa/shekel) corresponds to the single value for the month for barley in Text 8.

X/186 S.E.	*Barley*
Text 9: o.26	[...]; 5→15 22½; 16→2[0? ...]
Text 8: o.11'	22½

The only preserved value in Text 9 for the 5th to 15th (22½ qa/shekel) corresponds to the single monthly equivalent for barley in Text 8.

XII/186 S.E.	*Barley*
Text 9: o.30–o.31	1–2 24; 3→[...]; pq 36; 23 30; 24–26 18(+); [...]
-124B: r.8'–r.9'[a]	@b 24(+); [@m] 28; @e 30
Text 8: o.12'	30

a. AD III -124B: r.8' … ŠE.IM AŠ SAG ITU 4(b) […] (r.9') [… MURUB$_4$ IT]U 4(b) 4 *qa* AŠ TIL ITU 5(b) Z[Ú …]

The price equivalent for barley on the 1st to 2nd of the month (24 qa/shekel) in Text 9 corresponds to the preserved portion of the equivalent for the beginning of the month in the Astronomical Diary (-124B). The single monthly value for barley in Text 8 (30 qa/shekel) corresponds to the value for the 23rd of the month in Text 9 and for the end of the month in the Diary.

III/187 S.E.	*Barley*
Text 9: r.1'	[...] 51; 13 48; 14→[...]
-124A: o.32'[a]	[...]; 58; [...] 42[?]; @m 45; →e 42
Text 8: o.12'	⌜42⌝

a. AD III -124A: o.32' […] ITU 1(p) 3(b) 4 *qa* [… I]TU 1(p) 1(b)[?] AŠ MURUB$_4$ ITU 1(p) 1(b) 3 *qa* EN TIL ITU 1(p) 1(b) ZÚ.LUM AŠ SAG ITU 1 GUR […]

The two preserved price equivalents for barley in Text 9 for prior to and on the 13th (51 and 48 qa/shekel, respectively) do not correspond specifically to but are within the range of equivalents given in the Astronomical Diary (-124A). The single price equivalent for barley in Text 8 (42 qa/shekel) is restored on the basis of the equivalents in Text 9 and the Diary.

IV/187 S.E.	*Barley*	*Dates*
Text 9: r.2'–r.4'	[...]→[...]; 12→ 15 40; 16→e 48	[...]; [...]→22 156; @e 162
-124A: r.3'[a]	[...] 39	→m 168; →e 162

a. AD III -124A: r.3' [… 1] PI 3 *qa* ZÚ EN MURUB$_4$ ITU 4(p) 4(b) EN TIL ITU 4(p) 3(b)

The single partially restored price equivalent for barley (39 qa/shekel) in the Astronomical Diary (-124A) is slightly less than the first preserved value (40 qa/shekel) for the 12th to 15th in Text 9. The price equivalent for dates at the end of the month (162 qa/shekel) in Text 9 corresponds with the value in the Diary to the end of the month.

V/187 S.E.	*Sesame*
Text 9: r.7'	@b 6; @m 5; @e [...]
-124A: r.17'[a]	→m 5; [...]

a. AD III -124A: r.17' … ŠE.GIŠ.Ì EN MURUB$_4$ ITU 5 *qa* x […]

The price equivalent for sesame (5 qa/shekel) at the middle of the month in Text 9 corresponds to the single preserved value to the middle of the month in the Astronomical Diary (-124A).

VI/187 S.E.	*Barley*	*Dates*
Text 9: r.8'	@b 29½; →m 24; →e 26	[...]; 10–12 90; 13→ 23 108; 24→e 90(+)
-124A: r.33'[a]	[...] 24; 24→e 26	1→[...]

a. AD III -124A: r.33' […] x 4(b) TA 24 EN TIL ITU 4(b)? 2 *qa* ZÚ.LUM TA 1 EN? […]

The values for barley to the middle and to the end of the month (24 and 26 qa/shekel, respectively) in Text 9 are congruent with the last two preserved price equivalents in the Astronomical Diary (-124A).

VIII/187 S.E.	*Barley*	*Dates*
Text 9: r.14'–r.15'	→1818(+);[…]	1–2 90; 3–4 102; 5→ [...]; [...] 16 120; 17→ 25 108(+); [...]
Text 8: r.1	39	96(+)

There are no significant remaining values for comparison in the fragmentary data.

IX/187 S.E.	*Barley*	*Dates*	*Sesame*
Text 9: r.17'–r.19'	@b 18(+); [...]	[…]m 108; [...]	@b 9½; →e 10
-124B: o.17'[a]	@b 20½; @m 20; @e 20½	@b 105; @m 108; 16→18 72(+); [...]	@b 9½; →e 10

a. AD III -124B: o.17' ŠE.IM AŠ SAG ITU 3(b) 2½ *qa* AŠ MURUB$_4$ ITU 3(b) 2 *qa* AŠ TIL ITU 3(b) 2½ *qa* ZÚ.LUM AŠ SAG ITU 2(p) 5(b) 3 *qa* AŠ MURUB$_4$ ITU 3 PI TA 16 EN 18 2+[nn(p) … (o.18') … S]AG? ITU 1(b) 3½ *qa* EN TIL ITU 1(b) 4 *qa*

Despite the incomplete nature of both Text 9 and the Astronomical Diary, both appear to chart similarly changes in the price equivalences for barley and dates; the data for sesame are identical.

X/187 S.E.	*Barley*	*Dates*	*Sesame*
Text 9: r.19'–r.23'	[…]; 6–7 20; 8→18 […]; →e 16	1–2 117(+); […]; 5-[…]; […](+)9; 11→17 96; 18–20 84; […] 90; @e 90(+)	[….] 9½; 16–25 9¼; →e 8
-124B: r.8'–r.10'[a]	1–2 […]; 4–5 20½; 6–7 20; 8→18 18; […](+)¼; 14$^{?}$–25$^{?}$ 15; →e 16	[…]; 5–7 66; 8–10 75; 11→17 60; 18–20 84; →e 90	→m 9; 10→[…](+)¼; →e 8

a. AD III -124B: r.8' ŠE.IM 1 2 […] 4 5 3(b) 2½ *qa* 6 7 3(b) 2 *qa* TA 8 EN 18 3(b) (r.9') […] 4-$^{?}$-*ú* TA 14$^{?}$ EN 25$^{?}$ 2(b) 3 *qa* EN TIL ITU 2(b)$^{?}$ 4 *qa* ZÚ […] x 5 6 7 1(p) 5(b) 8 9 10 2 PI 3 *qa* TA 11 EN 17 1(p) 4(b) 18 19 20 2(p) 2(b) EN TIL ITU 2(p) 3(b) (r.10') […] … ŠE.GIŠ.Ì EN MURUB$_4$ ITU 1(b) 3$^{?}$ *qa* x TA 10+[x …] *ù* 4-$^{?}$-*ú* EN TIL ITU 1(b) 2 *qa*

The price equivalents for barley in Text 9 and the Astronomical Diary (-124B), on the basis of the surviving data, appear to be charted similarly throughout the month with congruent prices for the 6th to 7th (20 qa/shekel) and to the end of the month (16 qa/shekel).[97] The price equivalents for dates are charted similarly until after the 20th of the month, after which the Diary gives a single value to the end of the month (90 qa/shekel) whereas Text 9 appears to give two values, one prior to the end of the month (90 qa/shekel) and a second at the end of the month (90+ qa/shekel). There is a significant discrepancy in the price equivalent of dates for the 11th to 17th, 96 qa/shekel in Text 9 versus 60 qa/shekel in the diary—emending the diary to read 2$^{!}$(p) 4(b) would eliminate the divergent and discrepant figure—nonetheless both give congruent prices for the following 18th to 20th (84 qa/shekel). Sesame price equivalences appear to have been charted similarly in Text 9 and the Diary, showing a slight discrepancy in the value to the middle of the month (Text 9: 9½ qa/shekel, -124B: 9 qa/shekel), but with congruent values at the end of the month (8 qa/shekel).

XI/187 S.E.	*Barley*	*Dates*
Text 9: r.23'–r.25'	15½	[…]10 90; 11 96; 12 81; 13→22 84; 23 78; 24 72; […](+)9½; →e 66
Text 8: r.2	15	81

97 Hunger's reading TA 14$^{?}$ (see previous note) is impossible in light of the preceding TA 8 EN 18 (confirmed by Text 9) and requires collation.

The single monthly value for barley in Text 9 (15½ qa/shekel) is close to the single preserved value for barley in Text 8 (15 qa/shekel). The price equivalent for dates for the 12th of the month (81 qa/shekel) in Text 9 is congruent with the single monthly value in Text 8.

COMMENTS

Text 9 is found on the moderately well preserved remains of a comparatively large tablet comprising three joined fragments. The ductus is small but clear. Much of the upper edge and small portions of both the left edge (near ll. o.28–o.30) and right edge (near ll. o.7–o.10) are preserved. The entire lower edge along with perhaps the last four lines of the tablet obverse is lost. The text presents price equivalents per 2 shekels of silver for just three commodities: barley, dates, and sesame.[98] The data cover two full years, 186 – 187 S.E., and are charted on a nearly day-by-day basis, especially for barley and dates. Uniquely within this corpus, portions of a docket summarizing the tablet's contents, not unlike those commonly found among the Astronomical Diaries, are found in the last line of the reverse continuing onto the upper edge, and on the left edge.

Among the Astronomical Diaries providing comparable data with Text 9, two, AD III -125A and AD III -124B, chart the monthly breakdown of price changes for each commodity in virtually the same way, although there are occasional differences in specific price equivalents as noted above. On the other hand, AD III -125B and AD III -124A do not break down the monthly variations in the same way; nonetheless specific price equivalents, especially at the end of the month, are congruent.

Within the present corpus only Text 8 provides parallel data with Text 9 for barley and dates during 186 to 187 S.E. Where the single monthly values offered in Text 8 can be compared directly with the multiplicity of more closely monitored price equivalence fluctuations in Text 9, no clear pattern emerges. This strongly suggests that the single monthly values in Text 8 were not recorded at the same date each month. Nonetheless, when taken together, the data in Texts 8 and 9 for the price equivalent for dates for the period of 186 – 187 S.E., despite minor monthly fluctuations, show on the large scale a relatively steady rise from an average low of 77 qa/shekel in the first four months of 186 S.E. to a peak of 162 qa/shekel in IV/187 S.E., then falling back to a low of just 60 qa/shekel in XII/ 187 S.E. In general, the price equivalents for barley, dates and sesame during 186 – 187 S.E. are quite low. In fact the scribe of the astronomical diary for I/186 S.E. noted after having given the standard market quotations: "That month ... garlic, leek and all ... crops were expensive."[99]

---

98 Texts 17 and perhaps 16 are similarly restricted to just these three commodities.

99 AD III -125A: o.12; for a summary of the market quotations for this period, see conveniently Slotsky 1997, 143–44.

The period of interest to the scribe, 186 – 187 S.E., is coincident with the first two years of the brief reign of the Parthian king Artabanus I (ca. 128/27 – ca. 124/3 BCE) who would lose his life in battle against Scythian nomads in the east. Nonetheless, at the beginning of his reign, Artabanus was able to restore Parthian power in Babylonia following the brief seizure of the region, including Babylon itself, by Hyspaosines, a local dynast operating from the kingdom of Characene (Mesene) located in the former Sealands near the head of the Persian Gulf.[100] Hyspaosines was apparently a former Seleucid governor who was able to declare his independence following the death, about 183 S.E. (129/8 BCE), of Antiochus VII, the last Seleucid king to attempt seriously to reconquer Babylonia from the Parthians (see further Comments to Texts 6–8).[101] The Astronomical Diaries for the same period refer repeatedly to plundering by Arabs[102] that severely restricted travel to Borsippa and beyond and generally created panic; in IV/187 S.E., Arab marauders reportedly "broke a hole into the wall of Babylon" (-124A: r.5').

SUMMARY

(barley, dates, and sesame qa per 1 shekel silver)

Year	*Month*	*Barley*		*Dates*		*Sesame*
[186]	I	1	20	@b	54(+)	27
		2	21	[	]	
		3–[5	]	12→15	72	
		[6–]7	30	16–17	81	
		8→15	28	18–19	90	
		16→20	30	20–2[2	]	
		21[	]	[23–24]	99	
		[2]4	22½	→e	72	
		25→e	18			
	II	1	18(+)	→9	72	21¼
		[ ]	20	10→[	]	

[100] For the proposed location of the kingdom's major cities of Charax and Furat, see Hansman 1967; for a recent monograph on the subject of this kingdom, see Schuol 2000.

[101] See conveniently Habicht 1989, 369–73; Boiy 2004, 166–76.

[102] I/186 S.E. (AD III -125A: o.21); VI/186 S.E. (-125A: r.20'); I/187 S.E. (-124A: o.8'–o.9'); IV/187 (-124A: r.5'–r.7'); IX/124 S.E. (-124B: o.21'); II/188 S.E. (-123A: o.5', cf. -123C: 12').

Year	*Month*	*Barley*		*Dates*		*Sesame*	
		8→10	18	[...24]	69		
		11→e	[21]	25–26	72		
				@e	81		
		new:					
		[ ](+)12					
		[ ]15	36				
		16–17	45				
		18	36				
		19→22	33				
		[	]				
		26→e	40				
	[III		]	@b	72	[	]
		3–5	39	[	]		
		6–8	36	[...17]	72		
		9	39	18→[e	]		
		10→13	36				
		[ ]	30				
		23→e	33				
	[IV		]		66	[	]
		[ ]	33	@e	72(+)		
	[V	]	30	[	]	@b	3
		12→20	33			@m	5
		→e	36(+)			→e	[ ]
	[VI	]	31½		72		3½(+)
		@m	30				
		18–2[0?	]				
		[ ]e	28				
	[VII]			@b	72	[	]
		5→10	22½	(new)@m	108(+)	[ ]11	3½
		11→22	[ ]			12→e	3
		[	]				
	VIII	[	]	[@]b	108		3½
				→m	96		
				@m	[ ]		

Year	*Month*	*Barley*		*Dates*		*Sesame*	
				[ ]→e	78		
	IX	[	]	@b	[ ]	[	]
		25→e	24	[ ]→22	102		
				23→e	90(+)		
	[X		]	@b	96		3¾
		5→15	22½	7→12	90		
		16→2[0	]	[13	]		
		[	]	[	]		
				26→e	123		
	[XI		]	[	]	[	]
				@m	138		
				@e	126		
	XII	1–2	24	[	]	[	]
		3→	[ ]	[ ]→10	120		
		pq	36	11–13	132(+)		
		23	30	[	]		
		24–26	18(+)				
		[	]				
	[...]						
[187	III	]	51	[	]	[	]
		13	48			[@]e	4
		14→[	]				
	V	→[	]	[	]	@b	4
		12→15	40	[ ]→22	156	[	]
		16→e	48	@e	162		
	V	@b	37!	@b	150	@b	6
		14→24	[ ]	[	]	@m	5
		[	]	28–30	135	@e	[ ]
		27–28	33				
		29–30	30				
	[VI]	@b	29½	[	]	[	]
		→m	24	10–12	90	20→23	9
		→e	26	13→23	108	24→27	10
				24→e	90(+)	28–29	9
	VII	[ ]	28½	[	]	[	]

Year	*Month*	*Barley*		*Dates*		*Sesame*	
		12→19	24	12→20	114	[ ]	4
		20→25	22½	(new)@b	[ ]		
		[	]	23→26	132		
				→e	114(+)		
	VIII	→18	18(+)	1–2	90	[	]
		[	]	3–4	102		
				5→[ ]	[ ]		
				[ ]16	120		
				17→25	108(+)		
				[	]		
	IX	@b	18(+)	[	]	@b	9½
		[	]	[@]m	108	→e	10
				[16→	]		
	X	[	]	1–2	117(+)	[ ]	9½
		6–7	20	[	]	16→25	9¼
		8→18	[ ]	5-[7	]	→e	8
		[	]	[8–10	](+)9		
		→e	16	11→17	96		
				18–20	84		
				[ ]	90		
				@e	90(+)		
	XI		15½	[ ]10	90	1–2	8¼
				11	96	3→15	7½
				12	81	16→[ ]	7
				13→22	84	→e	6¾
				23	78		
				24	72		
				[	](+)9½		
				→e	66		
	XII	→10	15	@b	66	1–3	6½
		11–13	16	6–9	60	4→15	6¼
		[14–1]6	17	10–12	62	16→[ ]	
		17–18	18	13–15	54(+)	[	] 7½
		19	21	[ ]e	75	28–29	8
		20	24				

Year	Month	Barley	Dates	Sesame
		21→25 26		
		26→[ ]		

	Barley	Dates	Sesame
High:	51	162	27
Low:	15	60	3

TEXT 10

BM 55535 (82–7–4,118)
Date: 194$^?$ – 195$^?$ S.E. (118/7$^?$ – 117/6$^?$ BCE)
Dimensions: 6.9 x 6.1 x 2.5
Commodity: dates
Equivalence: ?
Unpublished Sachs transliteration (BM 55535)
Photo: Plate XIV

obv.

o.1 [MU.1 ME 1,]⸢3⸣4.KÁM
o.2 [ITU.DU$_6$ Z]Ú.LUM AŠ SAG ITU [ ]
o.3 [MURU]B$_4$ ITU 1 GUR 1(p) 1(b) EN TIL IT[U]
o.4 [1] GUR 1(p) 2(b) ITU.APIN <ZÚ.LUM> 1 GUR 2(p) ⸢2(b)⸣
o.5 [IT]U.GAN <ZÚ.LUM> AŠ SAG ITU 1 GUR ⸢1(p)⸣ 4(b) AŠ MUR[UB$_4$ ITU]
o.6 ⸢1⸣ GUR 3 PI AŠ TIL ⸢ITU⸣ 1 GUR 2(p) 2(b)
o.7 ITU.AB ZÚ.LUM AŠ SAG ITU
o.8 1 GUR 2(p) 2(b) AŠ MURUB$_4$ ITU 1 GUR$^!$ 1(p) 4(b)
o.9 EN TIL ITU 1 GUR 1 PI ITU.ZÍZ
o.10 ZÚ.LUM AŠ SAG ITU 1 GUR 1(p) ⸢4(+)(b)⸣
o.11 [A]Š MURUB$_4$ ITU 1 GUR 1(p) 2(b) AŠ TIL I[TU]
o.12 [1] GUR 1(p) 1(b) ITU.ŠE ZÚ.LUM E[N]
o.13 [*(traces)*]

(remainder lost)

rev.

r.1' [1] ⸢GUR 4(b) x⸣ [ ] ⸢EN⸣ [TIL ITU]

---

r.2' ⸢MU.1 ME⸣ 1,35.KÁM ITU.DU$_6$ Z[Ú.LUM]
r.3' EN MURUB$_4$ ITU 2 GU[R] EN TIL I[TU]
r.4' ITU.APIN ZÚ.LUM EN MU[RUB$_4$ ITU]
r.5' E[N] TIL ITU [2] ⸢GUR⸣ [1] ⸢PI⸣ [ ]
r.6' [ITU.GA]N Z[Ú.LUM]

(remainder lost)

o. 5'

o. 10'

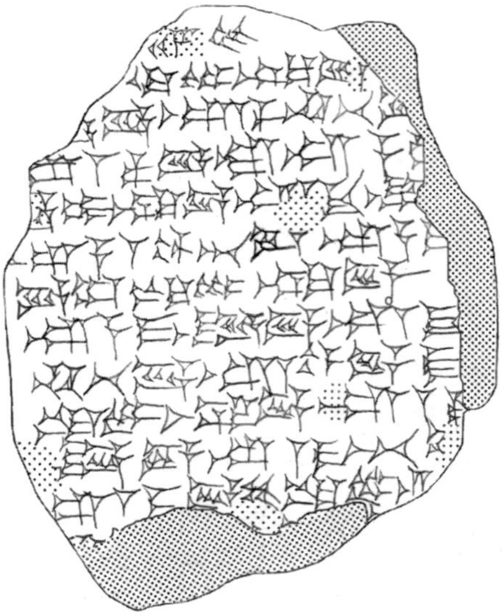

° sic, for GUR

BM 55535 obverse

r. 5'

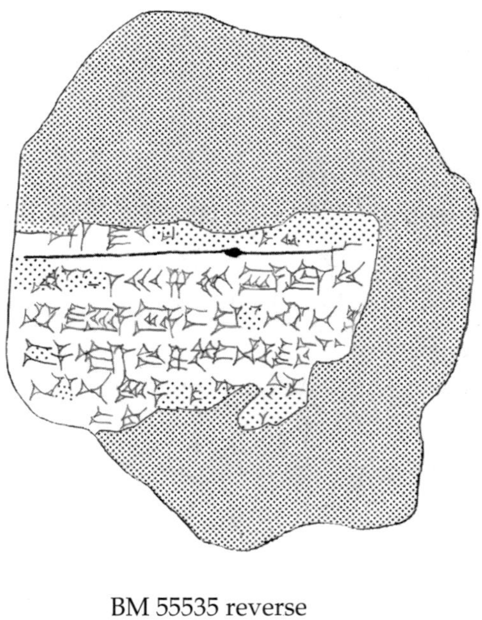

BM 55535 reverse

TRANSLATION

o.1 [Year 19]4.
o.2 [Month VII: d]ates at the beginning of the month [...]
o.3 [... middl]e of the month 1 kur 1 pān 1 sūt, to the end of the mon[th]
o.4 [1] kur 1 pān 2 sūt. Month VIII: <dates> 1 kur 2 pān 2 sūt.
o.5 [Mon]th IX: <dates> at the beginning of the month 1 kur 1 pān 4 sūt, in the mid[dle of the month]
o.6 1 kur 3 pān, at the end of the month 1 kur 2 pān 2 sūt.
o.7 Month X: dates at the beginning of the month
o.8 1 kur 2 pān 2 sūt, in the middle of the month 1 kur$^{!}$ 1 pān 4 sūt,
o.9 to the end of the month 1 kur 1 pān. Month XI:
o.10 dates at the beginning of the month 1 kur 1 pān 4(+) sūt,
o.11 [i]n the middle of the month 1 kur 1 pān 2 sūt, at the end of the mo[nth]
o.12 [1] kur 1 pān 1 sūt. Month XII: dates t[o ...]
o.13 [...]
(*remainder lost*)
r.1' (month XII_2) (dates) [1] kur 4 sūt ... [...], to [the end of the month ...]

---

r.2' Year 195. Month VII: d[ates ...]
r.3' to the middle of the month 2 ku[r], to the end of the mo[nth ...].
r.4' Month VIII: dates to the mid[dle of the month ...],
r.5' t[o] the end of the month [2] kur [1] pān [...].
r.6' [Month I]X: d[ates ...]
(*remainder lost*)

NOTES

o.1 On the restoration of the date, see Comments, below.

o.8 The reading 1 GUR$^{!}$ 1(p) 4(b) rather than 1 GUR 4(b), first entertained by Sachs, is adopted here; note the excessive spacing between the two vertical wedges of the ostensible GUR-sign and compare similar writings in ll. o.3, o.5, o.9, o.10, o.11; the emendation also obviously makes for a more orderly sequence of quantities throughout the period covered.

r.1' The restoration [TIL ITU] is suggested by the traces in Sachs' copy.

r.2' For the possible need to emend the date, see Comments, below.

r.5' The restorations of the numerals are suggested by the traces in Sachs' copy.

COMPARANDA

(Dates qa per 1 shekel silver)

VIII/194 S.E.	*Dates*
Text 10: o.4	264
-117A: 6'[a]	[...]; 18→24 171; 25→e 168(+)

a. AD III -117A: 6' [...] TA 18 EN 24 4(p) 4(b) 3 *qa* TA 25 EN TIL ITU 4(p) 4(b)[?] [...]

The single quoted price equivalent in Text 10 (264 qa) is at complete variance with the one certain Astronomical Diary value from the 18th to the 24th (171 qa/ shekel) (see Comments, below).

XI/194 S.E.	*Dates*
Text 10: o.9–o.12	@b 240/6; @m 228; @e 222
-117B: r.3'[a]	→m 171; [...]

a. AD III -117B: r.3' [...] ZÚ.LUM EN MURUB$_4$ ITU 4(p) 4(b) 3 [*qa* ...]

The three quoted equivalences in Text 10 at the beginning, middle, and end of the month (240/246 qa, 228 qa, and 222 qa, respectively) are at complete variance with the single preserved value in the Diary to the middle of the month (171 qa/shekel) (see Comments, below).

Although no further direct comparisons between Text 10 and the Diaries are available, the quantities quoted in the Diary for month XII and in Text 10 for XII$_2$ continue in their respective divergent trends:

XII/194 S.E.	-117B: r.18'[103][...] 6 162; →e 171	
XII$_2$/194 S.E.	Text 10: r.1'	[...] 210(+); →e [...]

COMMENTS

Text 10 is found on a small tablet with portions of the upper, left, and right edges preserved; the lower edge, a very few lines near the bottom of the obverse and much of the surface of the reverse are lost. The text records the price equivalences, for an undetermined amount of silver (see below) for a single commodity, dates, for the latter halves, beginning in month VII, of the years 194

103 AD III -117B:r18' [...] 6 4(p) 3(b) EN TIL ITU 4(p) 4(b) 3 *qa*.

(date partially restored) and 195 S.E. (see below).[104] Dates are typically harvested by or in month VIII. From one to three quotations are offered for any given month. Presumably the data for intercalary month XII_2/194 S.E. would have been contained in the now missing lines at the top of the tablet's reverse.

There is a complete lack of congruence between the price equivalents in Text 10 and the two preserved quotations from the Diaries for 194 S.E., regardless of any assumed silver equivalence evidenced elsewhere in this corpus (1 shekel, 2 shekels, 1 mina). Whereas minor occasional divergences between the commodity quantities quoted within the study corpus and the Astronomical Diaries are to be noted throughout, the differences here are puzzling, being large and systematic. This presupposes, of course, that the writing and reading of the date in r.2' (⸢MU.1 ME⸣ 1,35.KÁM) and the consequent restoration of the date in o.1 ([MU.1 ME 1,]⸢3⸣4) are correct.[105] One solution might be to emend the reading of r.2' to ⸢MU.1 ME⸣ {1,}35.KÁM, i.e., 13$^!$5 S.E., and accordingly restore o.1 to read [MU.1 ME]⸢3⸣4 S.E.[106]; the missing lines at the top of the tablet's reverse would now be assigned to intercalary month XII_2/134 S.E.[107] Unfortunately there are no data in any preserved dated Astronomical Diaries for these years against which to test directly this hypothesis, although the data for Text 10 do comfortably bridge the quantities of dates per one shekel of silver available during XII/133 S.E. (180, 162, and 168 qa/shekel at the beginning, in the middle, and to the end of the month, respectively)[108] and VIII/138 S.E. (300 qa/shekel).[109] Nonetheless in the absence of any further evidence, all emendations remain speculative.

---

104 Perhaps the tablets summarizing the data for the first half of each year were unavailable to the present scribe or perhaps the scribe was only interested in examining the price equivalents for dates from the harvest through the end of the calendar year. Also note Text 8, which provides equivalence data for just the last half of year (months VI_2–XII) 189 S.E., but data for all months for years 184–188 and 190 S.E.; and Text 3, which omits data for months X–XII_2/47 S.E.

105 Sachs, in his unpublished transliteration of the tablet, expressed some reservations in his reading of the numerals in o.1, drawing out the signs: [ ] 26.KÁM (N.B. collation with the tablet clearly favors reading the digit as "4" rather than "6"); however Sachs did not hesitate in his reading of the date in r. 2': MU.1 ME 1,35.KÁM.

106 Note the transposition of a vertical wedge within the writing of the date in Text 8: r.3, where the scribe wrote MU.2 ME 28.KÁM for the intended MU.1 ME 1,28.KÁM. See also the Notes, above, where it is suggested that in l. 8 the scribe omitted a vertical wedge in his writing there of 1 GUR$^!$ 1(p). The scribe also omitted the writing of ZÚ.LUM following the month name in ll. o.4 (month VIII) and o.5 (month IX).

107 Parker and Dubberstein 1956, 40.

108 AD II -178C: r.15' … ZÚ AŠ <SAG> ITU 1 GUR AŠ MUR[UB$_4$ ITU 4(p)] 3(b) EN <TIL> ITU 4(p) 4(b).

109 AD II -173B: o.4' … ZÚ.LUM 1 GUR 3(p) 2(b).

SUMMARY

(dates qa per nn shekel silver)

Year	*Month*	*Dates*	
[19$^{?}$]4	[VII]	@b	[ ]
		[ ]m	222
		→e	228
	VIII		264
	IX	@b	240
		@m	288
		@e	264
	X	@b	264
		@m	240
		→e	216
	XI	@b	240/6
		@m	228
		@e	222
	XII	→[	]
	[XII$_2$		]
		[ ]	210(+)
		→e	[ ]
195$^{?}$	VII	[	]
		→m	360
		→e	[ ]
	VIII	→m	[ ]
		→e	[396]
	IX	[	]
[...]			

High: [396]
Low: 216

TEXT 11

BM 35710 (Sp III 229)
Date: 11/XII/208 – II/209 S.E. (13 March – May/June 103 BCE)
Dimensions: 4.9 x 6.5 x 2.1
Commodity: barley
Equivalence: 1 shekel silver
Unpublished Sachs transliteration (BM 35710)
Photo: Plate XIV

obv.

1 ⸢ITU.ŠE⸣ ŠE.⸢IM⸣ TA 11 EN ⸢15⸣

2 1(p) 3(b) 3 *qa* TA 16 EN 19

3 1(p) 3(b) 1 *qa* 4-ʾ-*ú* TA 20

4 EN 26 1(p) 3(b) 2 ⸢*qa* 4-ʾ-*ú*⸣

5 EN TIL ITU 1(p) 3(b) 4 *qa* [4]-⸢ʾ-*ú*⸣

6 MU.2 ME 9.KÁM *na-da*[*n*] *šá* ITU.BAR

7 ŠE.IM TA 1 EN 23

lo.e.

8 1(p) 4(b) TA 24 EN TIL I[TU]

9 1(p) 4(b) 3 *qa*

rev.

10 ITU.GU$_4$ ŠE.⸢IM⸣ 1(p) 4(b) NU.D[Ù].MEŠ

11 1(p) 4(b) 4½ *qa*

12 *šá a-na* 1 GÍN [K]Ù.BABBAR

13 *šá* AŠ KUR SUM

14 (*erasure*)

TRANSLATION

1 Month XII: barley from the 11th to the 15th
2 1 pān 3 sūt 3 qa, from the 16th to the 19th
3 1 pān 3 sūt 1½ qa, from the 20th
4 to the 26th 1 pān 3 sūt 2½ qa,
5 to the end of the month 1 pān 3 sūt 4½ qa.
6 Year 209. Delive[ry] for month I:
7 barley from the 1st to the 23rd
8 1 pān 4 sūt, from the 24th to the end of the mo[nth]
9 1 pān 4 sūt 3 qa.
10 Month II: barley 1 pān 4 sūt, poor quality
11 1 pān 4 sūt 4½ qa.
12–13 That which was sold in the land for 1 shekel of [s]ilver.
14 (*erasure*)

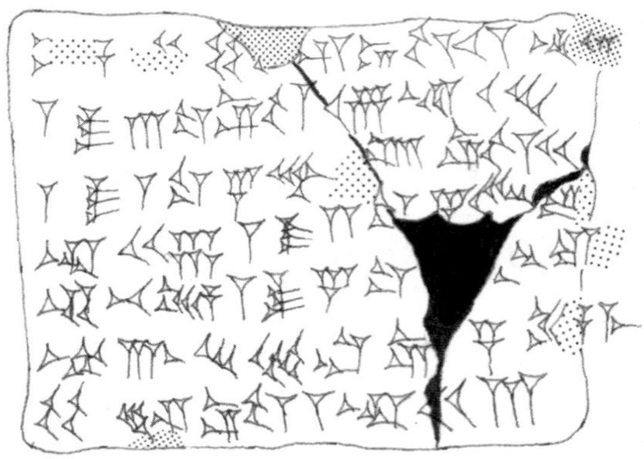

BM 35710 obverse

BM 35710 lower edge

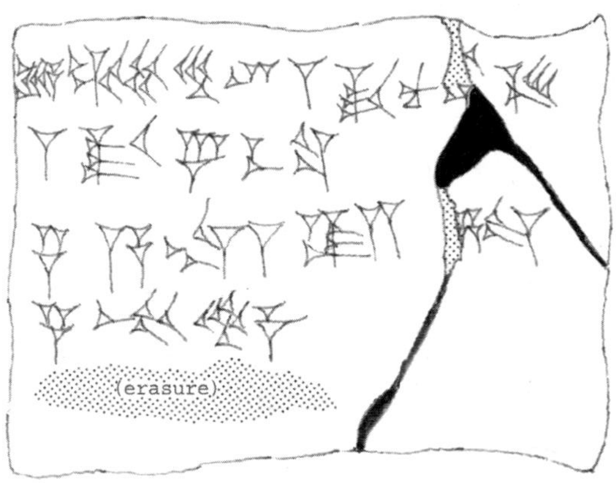

BM 35710 reverse

COMMENTS

Text 11 is found on a nearly complete roughly made tablet composed of three joined fragments; a small triangular-shaped portion is missing right of center and there is only minor surface damage. Unlike the majority of tablets in this corpus—where their shapes can be determined—this tablet is wider than long and closely resembles in its proportions typical Late Babylonian archival tablets.[110] The scribe wrote with a large heavy hand in a vulgar cursive script: the signs are widely spaced with their intended horizontal wedges often on the diagonal. There is evidence of an erasure in the space beneath the signs on the left half of the last line on the reverse.

Text 11 records the price equivalent per 1 shekel of silver of a single commodity, barley, over just a three month period, from 11/XII/208 through II/209 S.E. (13 March to May/June 103 BCE), in the middle of the reign of Mithradates II (124/3 to 88/7 BCE).[111] The quotations, the most precise in the corpus, often given to the nearest ¼ qa, are for different groups of days in the month and the end of the month. No corresponding data are preserved among the Astronomical Diaries. The barley harvest in Babylonia took place in the spring, usually in months I and II, although "new" (GIBIL.MEŠ) barley might still be available in month III.[112] The scribe of Text 11 appears to have been monitoring the quantities of barley available in the month prior to (month XII) and the two months of the harvest season. Not surprisingly, after reaching a low point just after the middle of month XII, the quantities available rose steadily, with less day to day volatility, to a high point late in month I, plateauing in month II.

SUMMARY

(barley qa per 1 shekel silver)

Year	*Month*	*Barley*	
208	XII	11→15	57
		16→19	55¼
		20→26	56¼
		27→e	58¼

110 See also Text 13.

111 For the sources for the history of Babylonia during the reign of this king, see Boiy 2004, 180–84.

112 Slotsky 1997, 25–26. The apparent variability for the month of the harvest likely has more to do with the practice of periodic intercalation causing the calendar to drift back and forth against the more fixed rhythms' of nature that would have determined and delimited the actual time of the harvest.

Year	*Month*	*Barley*	
209	I	1→23	60
		24→e	63
	II		60
		pq	64½

High:	63/64½
Low:	55¼

TEXT 12

BM 33023 (78–10–15,4) + BM 33027 (78–10–15,8) (+) BM 46161 (81–7–6,622)
Dimensions: 6.0 x 9.8 x 3.2
Date: n.d. (Arsacid?)
Commodities: barley, dates, mustard, cress, sesame, wool
Equivalence: 2 shekels silver
Photo: Plate s XV–XVI

obv.

1' [ ] x x x [ ]

2' [nn] PI AŠ ⸢MURUB$_4$ ITU⸣ 1 GUR 1(p) [ ]
3' [ ] 3(p) 2(b) NU.DÙ.MEŠ 5 GUR *k*[*às*]
4' [ ] x [2(p)] ⸢4(b)⸣ EN TIL ITU 2(p) 3(b) ŠE.GIŠ.⸢Ì⸣ [ ]
5' [ ] 2 GUR 1(p) 2(b) AŠ MURUB$_4$ ITU 1 GUR 4(p) 4(b) ⸢GIBIL⸣.M[EŠ]
6' [ ] ⸢ITU⸣ 1 GUR 4 PI AŠ MURUB$_4$ ITU 2 GUR 4(b) AŠ TIL [ITU]
7' [nn] ⸢*qa*⸣ AŠ MURUB$_4$ ITU 1(p) 2(b) AŠ TIL ITU 1(p) 2(b) 4 *qa* S[ÍG]
8' [ ] ⸢TIL⸣ ITU 2 GUR 1(p) 4(b) NU.⸢DÙ⸣.MEŠ 2 G[UR]
9' [nn G]UR 1 PI *saḫ-le*$_{10}$ 2(p) 5(b) 2(+) [*qa*]
10' [ ] x [ ]
11' [ ](+)2 GUR ⸢1(p) 3(b)⸣ [ ]
12' [A]Š SAG ITU 1(p) 2(b) [ ]
13' [nn] GUR ⸢4(+)(p)⸣ [ ]
14' [ ]
15' [ ]
16' [nn] ⸢GUR 2(p)⸣ [ ]

lo.e.

17' AŠ MURUB$_4$ ITU 6 GUR AŠ TI[L I]TU ⸢nn(g)⸣ [ ]
18' SÍG.ḪÁ 5 MA.NA DU$_6$ ŠE.BAR AŠ S[AG ITU]
19' AŠ MURUB$_4$ ITU 4 GUR 2(p) 3(b) TA [ ]

rev.

20' *saḫ-*⸢*le*$_{10}$⸣ 3(p) 1(b) 2 *qa* ŠE.GIŠ.Ì [ ]

21' EN MURUB$_4$ ITU 1 GUR 2(p) 3(b) EN TIL IT[U]

22' *saḫ-le*$_{10}$ EN MURUB$_4$ <ITU> 2(p) 1(b) 2 *qa* EN T[IL ITU]

23' NU.DÙ.MEŠ 1 GUR 3(p) 2(b) ZÚ AŠ S[AG ITU]

24' ⸢ŠE⸣.GIŠ.Ì EN ⸢MURUB$_4$ ITU⸣ x [ ]

25' [ ] x [ ] x x x x [ ]

26' [ ] ⸢3(b)⸣ 2 *qa* SÍG.ḪÁ 4½ M[A.NA *(traces)*]

27' [ ] ⸢5⸣ GUR 1(p) 4(b) AŠ MURUB$_4$ ITU [nn GUR nn] PI AŠ TIL ITU 6 GUR 28 29 4 GUR [ ]

28' [nn] *qa* ŠE.GIŠ.Ì 1(p) 2(b) 4 *qa* [SÍG.ḪÁ nn] MA.NA ŠE ŠE.BAR 1 GUR 2(p) 5(b) ZÚ EN MURUB$_4$ I[TU]

29' [ ] *saḫ-le*$_{10}$ 2(p) 1(b) 2 *qa* Š[E.GIŠ].⸢Ì EN⸣ MURUB$_4$ ITU 1(p) 2(b) EN TIL ITU 1(p) 1(b) 3 *qa* SÍG.ḪÁ 4½ [MA.NA]

30' [MU.nn]⸢(+)1⸣.KÁM BAR ŠE.BAR AŠ SAG [IT]U 1 GUR 2(p) 5(b) AŠ MU[RUB$_4$ ITU] 1 [G]UR 3 PI NU.DÙ.MEŠ 2 GUR 20 21 [ ]

31' [ ] 25 26 1 GUR ⸢nn(p)⸣ 2(b) 27 28 29 [ ] ⸢x ZÚ⸣ AŠ SAG ITU 5 GUR 1 PI x [ ]

32' [ ] 2(p) 1(b) 28 2⸢9 4⸣ GUR 4 PI ⸢*kàs*⸣ [ ] ⸢*saḫ-le*$_{10}$⸣ 2(p) 1(b) 2 *qa* ŠE.GIŠ.⸢Ì⸣ [ ]

33' [ ] ⸢SÍG.ḪÁ⸣ AŠ TIL ITU 6 MA.NA GU$_4$ [ŠE.BAR] 4 PI ZÚ 5 G[UR]

34' [S]ÍG.ḪÁ 5 MA.NA [*(traces)*]

35' [ ] x x x x [ ]

(remainder lost)

le.e.

1 AŠ S[AG ITU]

2 AŠ M[URUB$_4$ ITU]

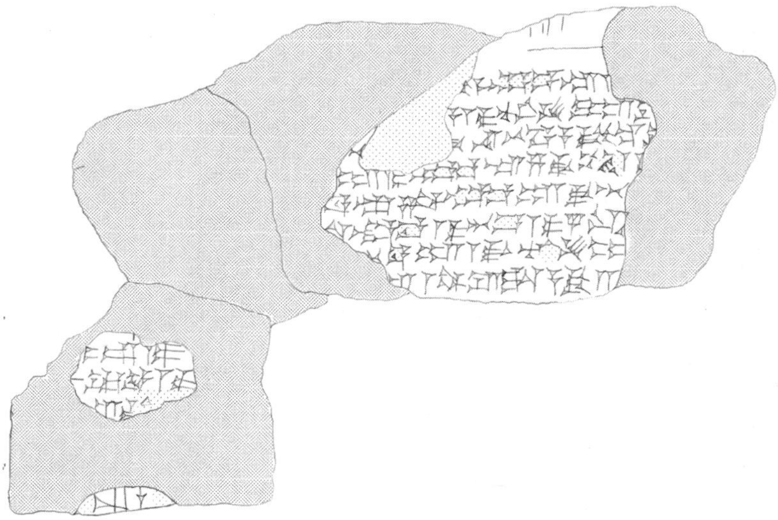

BM 33023 + BM 33027 obverse

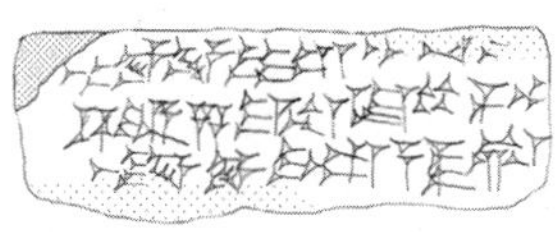

BM 33023 + BM 33027 lower edge

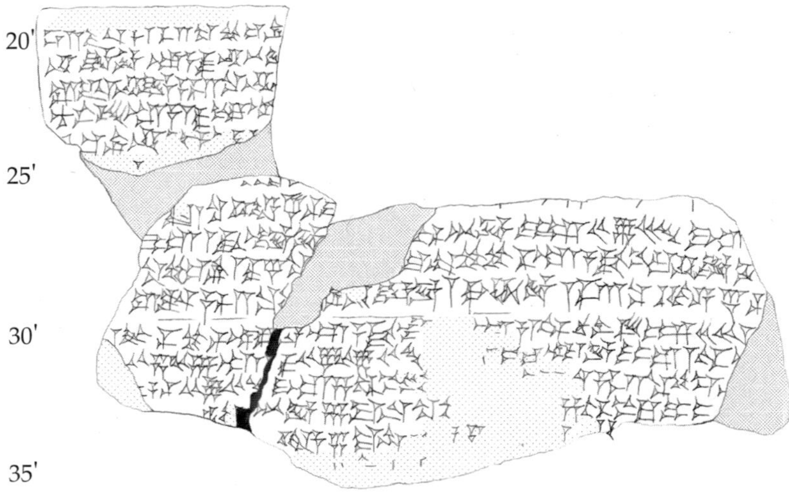

BM 33023 + BM 33027 reverse

TRANSLATION

1' [(year $y_{1'}$) (month $m_{1'}$) …] … […].

2' [(year $y_{2'}$) (month I) (barley) … nn] pān, in the middle of the month 1 kur 1 pān […]

3' [(dates) …] 3 pān 2 sūt, poor quality 5 kur; mu[stard …]

4' […] … [(cress) … 2 pān] 4 sūt, to the middle of the month 2 pān 3 sūt; sesame […]

5' [… (month II) (barley)] 2 kur 1 pān 2 sūt, in the middle of the month, 1 kur 4 pān 4 sūt, new […]

6' […] of the month 1 kur 4 pān, in the middle of the month 2 kur 4 sūt, at the end of [the month …]

7' [(sesame) … nn] qa, in the middle of the month 1 pān 2 sūt, at the end of the month 1 pān 2 sūt 4 qa; w[ool …]

8' [(month III) (barley) …] the end of the month 2 kur 1 pān 4 sūt, poor quality 2 k[ur …]

9' [(mustard) … nn k]ur 1 pān; cress 2 pān 5 sūt 2(+) [qa …]

10' […] … […]

11' [(month IV) (barley) …](+)2 kur 1 pān 3 sūt […]

12' [... (sesame) a]t the beginning of the month 1 pān 2 sūt [...]
13' [(month V) (?) ... nn] kur 4(+) sūt [...]
14' [...]
15' [...]
16' [(month VI$_{(II)}$) (?) ... nn k]ur 2 pâ[n ...],
17' (dates) in the middle of the month 6 kur, at the en[d of the m]onth ... [...];
18' wool 5 mina. Month VII: barley at the be[ginning of the month ...],
19' in the middle of the month 4 kur 2 pān 3 sūt, from [...];
20' cress 3 pān 1 sūt 2 qa; sesame [...]
21' (month VIII) (barley) to the middle of the month 1 kur 2 pān 3 sūt, to the end of the mon[th ...];
22' cress to the middle <of the month> 2 pān 1 sūt 2 qa, to the e[nd of the month ...],
23' (month IX) (barley) poor quality 1 kur 3 pān 2 sūt; dates at the be[ginning of the month ...];
24' sesame to the middle of the month ... [...]
25' [...] ... [...] ... [...]
26' [... (month X) (sesame)] 3 sūt 2 qa; wool 4½ m[ina ...]
27' [... (month XI) (dates)] 5 kur 1 pān 4 sūt, in the middle of the month [nn kur nn] pān, at the end of the month 6 kur, the 28th (and) 29th 4 kur [...]
28' [... (cress) ... nn] qa; sesame 1 pān 2 sūt 4 qa; [wool nn] mina. Month XII: barley 1 kur 2 pān 5 sūt; dates until the middle of the m[onth ...]
29' [...]; cress 2 pān 1 sūt 2 qa; s[esa]me to the middle of the month 1 pān 2 sūt, to the end of the month 1 pān 1 sūt 3 qa; wool 4½ [mina].

30' [Year nn]+1 (= $y_{3'}$). Month I: barley at the beginning of the [mon]th 1 kur 2 pān 5 sūt, in the mi[ddle of the month] 1 [k]ur 3 pān, poor quality 2 kur, the 20th, 21st [...]
31' [...] the 25th (and) 26th 1 kur nn pān 2 sūt; the 27th, 28th (and) 29th [...] ... ; dates at the beginning of the month 5 kur 1 pān ... [...]
32' [...] 2 pān 1 sūt, the 28th (and) 29th 4 kur 4 pān; mustard [...]; cress 2 pān 1 sūt 2 qa; sesame [...]
33' [...]; wool at the end of the month 6 mina. Month II: [barley ...] 4 pān; dates 5 k[ur ...]
34' [...; w]ool 5 mina ... [...]
35' [...] ... [...]
(remainder lost)

Le.E.
1 at the be[ginning of the month ...],
2 in the mi[ddle of the month ...].

COMMENTS

Text 12 is inscribed on two previously joined fragments (33023 + 33027) plus one newly identified fragment (46161) of similar script, fabric, and curvature that does not physically join to the others[113]; together they form a small part of the lower left half of a larger tablet. Small portions of the left and lower edges are preserved on 46161. The text, written continuously from the obverse onto the lower edge and thence onto the reverse and left edge, gives the price equivalents for all six standard staple commodities—a statement of the equivalence rate is not preserved, but is assumed to be per 2 shekels of silver.[114] Data may be identified for portions of three presumably consecutive years: the end of year $y_{1'}$ above the ruled line drawn beneath l. 1'; year $y_{2'}$ beginning beneath this line and continuing onto the reverse, ending with month XII on ll. 28'–29'; and year $y_{3'}$ beginning on l. 30' beneath a second ruled line. The only preserved indication of a date is found near the beginning of l. 30', which shows [MU… .] 𒁹 .KÁM: the single vertical wedge must be part of a numeral ending with the digit 1, ⸢2⸣, or ⸢3⸣.[115] Data in the Astronomical Diaries for the period of circa 169 – 171 S.E., although admittedly spotty, alone show price equivalents of similar orders of magnitude (see Table 11: Astronomical Diary Commodity Price Equivalents for 169 – 171 S.E.), with the data for year $y_{2'}$ in Text 12 offering some similarities to that of 171 S.E., however the data do not correlate with anywhere near sufficient precision to make identification certain (see Summary: Text 12).

TABLE 11
ASTRONOMICAL DIARY COMMODITY PRICE EQUIVALENTS FOR 169 – 171 S.E.

Year	*Mo.*	*Barley*	*Dates*	*Mustard*	*Cress*	*Sesame*	*Wool*
169 S.E. (AD -142A)	VIII	114	@b [			]	2½
170 S.E. (AD-141C)	II	@b 150 @m 180 @e [ ]	[				]
	III	[ ] 192 →e 207	[				]

[113] Jonathan Taylor, British Museum, personal communication, 30 Jan. 2006.

[114] Note the otherwise unprecedentedly large quantities of dates quoted throughout.

[115] Although DIŠ can certainly represent the numeral 60, years 60 and [1]60 are excluded here as they would be expected to be written as (1 ME.)1+*šu* (see e.g., Text 1: o.16', o.17', r.17').

Year	*Mo.*	*Barley*	*Dates*	*Mustard*	*Cress*	*Sesame*	*Wool*
171 S.E. (AD -140 A,B,C,D)	I	@b 150 →m 156 →e 132	@b 468 [ ]	[	](+)16	24	2½
	IV	@b 168 @m [ ]	[		]+3	25	2½
	VII	@b 102 →m 108	@b 396 [ ] 432 new: 504	270	37+nn	[	]+1
	IX	→m 117 →e 120	432	516	40	26	2½
	X	@b 120 @m 121½ @e 123 pq 126	@b 432 @m 468 @e 450 var.: →m 450 →e468(+)	516	40	→m 26 →e 7	2½
	XI	114(+)	[ ] 396(+) →e 360(+)				

(barley, dates, mustard, cress, and sesame qa per 1 shekel silver; wool mina per 1 shekel silver)

SUMMARY

(barley, dates, mustard, cress, and sesame qa per 1 shekel silver; wool mina per 1 shekel silver)

Year	*Mo.*	*Barley*	*Dates*	*Mustard*	*Cress*	*Sesame*	*Wool*
[...]							
[$y_{1'}$	$m_{1'}$						]
[$y_{2'}$	I	]+18 @m 108(+)	[ ]+60 pq 450	[	] 48 →e 45	[	]
	[II	] 204 @m 174 new: [ ] 162 @m 192 @e [ ]	[			@m 24 @e 26	]
	[III	[ ]e 210 pq 180(+)		](+)108	52(+)	[	]
	[IV	] 204	[		]	@b 24	[ ]
	[V						]
	[VI		@m 540 @e [ ]			]	2½

Year	*Mo.*	*Barley*	*Dates*	*Mustard*	*Cress*	*Sesame*	*Wool*
	VII	@b [	@m 405	]	58	[	]
	[VIII]	→m 135 →e [ ]	[	]	→m 58 →e [	[	]]
	[IX	] pq 150	@b[		]	→m [	]
	[X					]+10	2¼
	[XI		] 480 @m [ ] @e 540 28–29 360(+)	[	]	26	[ ]
	XII	141	→m [	]	40	→m 24 →e 22½	2¼
[$y_{3'}$]	I	@b 141 @m 144 pq 180 20–21 [ ] [ ] 25–26 114(+) 27–29 [ ]	@b 468 [ ] [ ](+)39 [ ] 28–29 432	[ ]	40	[ ]	@e 3
	II	[ ]72(+)	450(+)[			]	2½
	III	[					]
	[…]						

High:	210	540	-	58	26	3
Low:	135	405	-	40	22½	2¼

TEXT 13

BM 36960 (80–6–17,701)
Dimensions: 4.0 x 5.0 x 2.3
Date: n.d. (Seleucid?)
Commodities: barley, dates
Equivalence: 2(?) shekels silver
Publ.: Wiseman, *Sachs Mem. Vol.*, 370.
Photo: Plate XVII

obv.

o.1' ⌜ZÚ⌝ [*(traces)*]
o.2' AŠ MURUB$_4$ ITU 2(g) 2 PI AŠ TIL I[TU]
o.3' ZÚ 1(g) 1(p) 4(b) NE ŠE 2(g) [ ]
o.4' KIN ŠE.BAR 2(g) 3(p) 2(b) ZÚ 1(g) ⌜2(+)(p)⌝ [ ]
o.5' 1(g) 3(p) 2(b) DU$_6$ ŠE 2(g) 2(p) ⌜2(b)⌝ [ ]

rev.

r.1 APIN ŠE AŠ SAG I[TU]
r.2 ZÚ 1(g) 1(p) 3(b) GAN ⌜ŠE⌝ [ ]
r.3 AŠ TIL ITU 1(g) 2(p) 3(b) AB ŠE x [ ]
r.4 2(g) 3(p) 2(b) ZÚ 1(g) 2(p) 3(b) ZÍZ ŠE [ ]
r.5 2(g) 3(p) 4(b) AŠ TIL ITU! 2(g) 4(p) Z[Ú]
r.6 ŠE ŠE 1(g) 4(p) 2(b) AŠ MURU[B$_4$ ITU]
r.7 2(g) 1(b) [ ]
(*remainder lost*)

TRANSLATION

o.1' (month III) dates [...],
o.2' (month IV) (barley) in the middle of the month 2 kur 2 pān, at the end of the mo[nth ...];
o.3' dates 1 kur 1 pān 4 sūt. Month V: barley 2 kur [...].
o.4' Month VI: barley 2 kur 3 pān 2 sūt; dates 1 kur 2(+) pān [...],
o.5' (at the end? of the month) 1 kur 3 pān 2 sūt. Month VII: barley 2 kur 2 pān 2 sūt [...].
r.1 Month VIII: barley at the beginning of the mo[nth ...];
r.2 dates 1 kur 1 pān 3 sūt. Month IX: barley [...],
r.3 (dates) at the end of the month 1 kur 2 pān 3 sūt. Month X: barley ... [...]
r.4 2 kur 3 pān 2 sūt; dates 1 kur 2 pān 3 sūt. Month XI: barley [...]
r.5 2 kur 3 pān 4 sūt, at the end of the month 2 kur 4 pān; d[ates ...].
r.6 Month XII: barley 1 kur 4 pān 2 sūt, in the midd[le of the month ...]
r.7 2 kur 1 sūt [...]
(*remainder lost*)

o. 5'

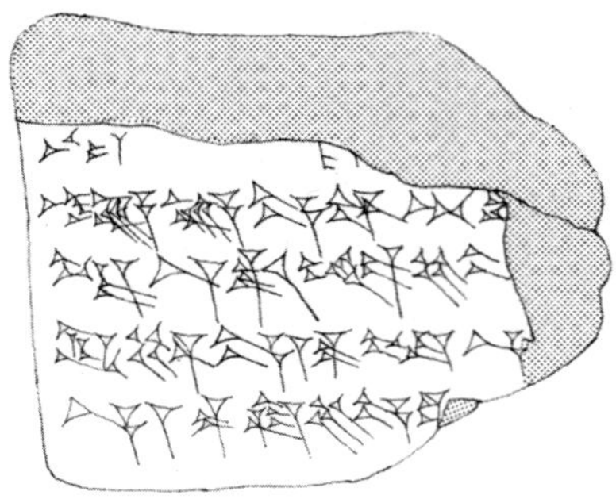

BM 36960 obverse

r. 5'

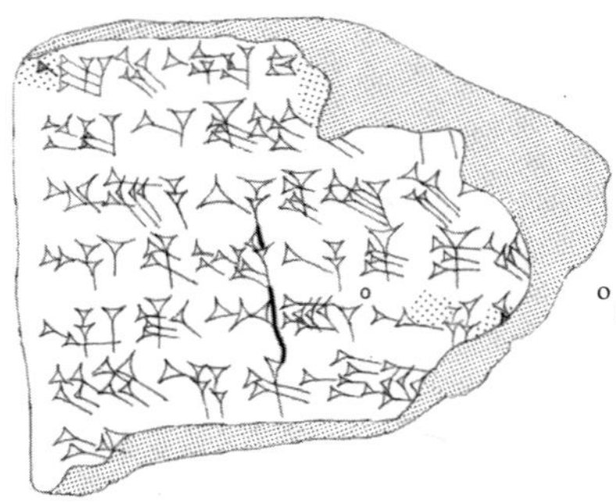

° sic

BM 36960 reverse

COMMENTS

Text 13 is written on a single tablet fragment that retains portions of the original left and lower edges. Unlike the majority of tablets in this corpus, among those whose shapes can be determined, this tablet appears originally to have been wider than long, similar in size and proportion to typical Late Babylonian archival tablets.[116] The strongly diagonal tablet cursive is not unlike that of other early Seleucid tablets in the corpus, e.g., Texts 3 and 4. The preserved portion of this text records from one to three price equivalents per month during an undetermined year at an unspecified rate, for two commodities, barley[117] and dates.[118] The tablet may have originally contained just one full year's worth of data with months I to VII written on the obverse and VIII to XII/XII_2 on the reverse—this suggests that the tablet is missing perhaps just two lines from the upper edge. Comparisons with price equivalents in published Astronomical Diaries suggest that the equivalence rate used in this text is per two shekels of silver. At that rate, the data are similar to, but do not correspond exactly with, price equivalents quoted in Astronomical Diaries dated to 65 to 66 S.E.[119] (see Table 12: Astronomical Diary Price Equivalents for Barley and Dates During 65 – 66 S.E.).

TABLE 12
ASTRONOMICAL DIARY PRICE EQUIVALENTS FOR BARLEY AND DATES DURING 65 – 66 S.E.

AD II	*Date (S.E.)*	*Barley*	*Dates*
-246: 10	I/65	225	126
-246: r.17'	VI/65	210	120
-245A: r.3'	V/66	[ ]	135
-245A: r.15'	VI/66	258	135

(barley and dates qa per 1 shekel silver)

116 See also Text 12.

117 Abbreviated ŠE in all but one case where it is written ŠE.BAR (l. o.4'); although this latter writing is not particularly unusual among the tablets in this corpus (see Table 2: Writings for Commodities on Dated Price Tablets Arranged Chronologically), its use in the Astronomical Diaries appears to be restricted to two brief periods following suspensions of barley sales (Slotsky 1997, 27).

118 Written ZÚ throughout.

119 See also Text 16 Comments where it is suggested that that tablet may cover the period VI/64–VI/66 S.E. However, neither the present tablet nor Text 16 is sufficiently complete to offer significant comparisons.

SUMMARY

(barley and dates qa per 1 shekel silver)

Year	*Month*	*Barley*	*Dates*
[...]			
[$y_{1'}$	III	]	[ ]
	[IV	] @m 216 @e [ ]	120
	V	180(+)	[ ]
	VI	240	126(+) [ ]200
	VII	222(+)	[ ]
	VIII	@b [ ] [ ]	117
	IX	[	] @e 135
	X	[ ] [ ] 240	135
	XI	[ ] 246 @e 252	[ ]
	XII	168 @m [ ] [ ] 183(+)	[ ]
[...]			

	Barley	Dates
High:	252	200
Low:	168	117

TEXT 14

BM 36989 (80–6–17,733)
Dimensions: 4.4 x 6.0 x 2.2
Date: n.d. (Seleucid?)
Commodities: [barley], dates
Equivalence: ?
Publ.: Wiseman, *Sachs Mem. Vol.*, 371
Photo: Plate XVII

obv.

o.1'	[ ] x ⸢3 *qa*	ZÚ⸣.[LUM]
o.2'	[nn] *qa*	ZÚ.LUM x [ ]
o.3'	[ ]	ZÚ.LUM KI.L[AM KUD$^{?}$-*is*$^{?}$]
o.4'	[ ]	ZÚ.LUM {x} 1(p) 1(b) 3 *qa*
o.5'	[ ] ⸢1(+)(p)⸣ 1(b) 3 *qa*	ZÚ.LUM 1(p) 1(b) 3 *qa*
o.6'	[ ] ⸢3⸣ *qa*	ZÚ.LUM 1(p) 1(b) 3 *qa*
o.7'	[ ] ⸢4(b)⸣ 3 *qa*	ZÚ.LUM 1(p) 1(b) 3 *qa*
o.8'	[ ] ⸢4(b)⸣	ZÚ.LUM 1(p) 1(b) 3 *qa*
o.9'	[	ZÚ].L[UM]

(*remainder lost*)

rev.

r.1'	[ ] ⸢3(p)⸣ 4(b)	⸢ZÚ.LUM⸣ [ ](+)1 *qa*
r.2'	[ ] ⸢3(p)⸣ 1(b)	ZÚ.LUM 2(p) 4(b) [ ]
r.3'	[ ]	ZÚ.LUM 2(p) 4(b) [ ]
r.4'	[ ]	ZÚ.LUM 2(p) 3(+)(b) [ ]
r.5'	[	ZÚ].LUM 2(p) 3(+)(b) [ ]
r.6'	[	ZÚ.LU]M 2(p) 3(+)(b) [ ]

(*remainder lost*)

o. 5'

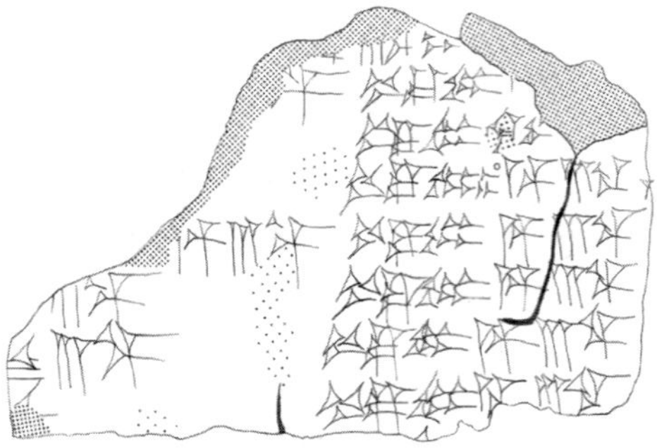

° sic, scribal plus

BM 36989 obverse

r. 5'

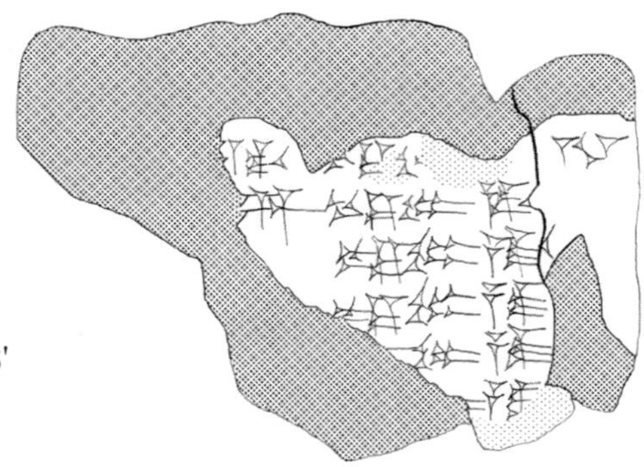

BM 36989 reverse

TRANSLATION

o.1' [(year $y_{1'}$) (month $m_{1'}$) (barley) ...] x 3 qa; da[tes ...]
o.2' (month $m_{2'}$) (barley)[... nn] qa; dates ... [...]
o.3' [(month $m_{3'}$) (barley) ...]; dates—sal[e *was cut off*(?)].
o.4' [(month $m_{4'}$) (barley) ...]; dates {...} 1 pān 1 sūt 3 qa.
o.5' [(month $m_{5'}$) (barley) ...](+)1 pān 1 sūt 3 qa; dates 1 pān 1 sūt 3 qa.
o.6' [(month $m_{6'}$) (barley) ...] 3 qa; dates 1 pān 1 sūt 3 qa.
o.7' [(month $m_{7'}$) (barley) ...] 4 sūt 3 qa; dates 1 pān 1 sūt 3 qa.
o.8' [(month $m_{8'}$) (barley) ...] 4 sūt; dates 1 pān 1 sūt 3 qa.
o.9' [(month $m_{9'}$) ... ; da]t[es ...]
(*remainder lost*)
r.1' [(year $y_{2'}$) (month $m_{1''}$) (barley) ...] 3 pān 4 sūt; dates [... nn](+)1 qa.
r.2' [(month $m_{2''}$) (barley) ...] 3 pān 1 sūt; dates 2 pān 4 sūt [...].
r.3' [(month $m_{3''}$) (barley) ...]; dates 2 pān 4 sūt [...].
r.4' [(month $m_{4''}$) (barley) ...]; dates 2 pān 3(+) sūt [...].
r.5' [(month $m_{5''}$) (barley) ...; da]tes 2 pān 3(+) sūt [...].
r.6' [(month $m_{6''}$) (barley) ...; date]s 2 pān 3(+) sūt [...].
(*remainder lost*)

NOTES

o.3' For the restoration of the end of the line, see the Comments below.

o.4' A small vertical wedge was placed on the right edge of the tablet at the end of the line.

COMMENTS

Text 14 is found on a small fragment of the right half of a tablet with portions of only the right edge preserved. The text appears originally to have contained price equivalents, at an unspecified rate, for just two commodities, the second of which are dates; as the order of the presentation of the commodities in both the study corpus and in the Astronomical Diaries is quite fixed, it seems certain that the fragmentary data preceding that of dates is for barley. Data for nine presumably consecutive months are preserved on the obverse and for six months on the reverse.

The quantities of dates in the price equivalence data of Text 14, when assumed to be at the rate of one shekel of silver, fit quite well within the trends evident between 52 and 60 S.E. in the Diaries and Text 3A (see Table 13: Price Equivalents for Dates duṛing 260 – 247 BCE/52 – 64 S.E.)

TABLE 13
PRICE EQUIVALENTS FOR DATES
DURING 260 – 247 BCE/52 – 64 S.E.

260 BCE	AD -259	X/52 S.E.	114
258 BCE	AD -257A	I/54	82½ @e 84
		II/54	124
257 BCE	AD -256	III/55	51
256 BCE		XI/55	51 @e 45
	AD -255A	I/56	45
		II/56	45
		VI/56	60
		VI_2/56	72
255 BCE	AD -254	IX/57	(+)60
254 BCE	Text 3A	I/58	60
		III/58	36(+)
		IV/58	36(+)
	AD -253	VII/58	cut off
252 BCE	AD -251	VII/60	108
249 BCE	AD -249B	XI/62	120
		XII/62	(+)33
248 BCE	AD -247B	VII/64	@e 120
247 BCE	AD -247C	X/64	135
	AD -247B	XII_2/64	114 @m [ ]

(dates qa per 1 shekel silver)

It is possible that the conjectured suspension of the sale of dates here in Text 14: o.3' is to be equated with the one known for VII/58 S.E. (Slotsky 1997, 14–16). This is the second of just two certain occurrences in the Astronomical Diaries where the sale of dates was suspended at the market in Babylon (Slotsky 1997, 30–31)[120]; in the other, earlier (325 BCE), case the sale of all commodities was cut off until the 5th day of month II, year 12 Alexander III.[121] Identifying the data

120 AD I -324B: o.12'–o.13' (II/12 Alexander III); AD II -253B_1: o.4' (VII/58 S.E.); also note AD III –82A: r.17' [...] ⸢x⸣ *a tú* KUD-*a*, "[...] ... were cut off."

121 AD I -324B: o.12' ... K]I.LAM ŠE-*e u* KI.LAM *mim-ma gab-bi* (o.13') EN U_4.5 AŠ SILA.ME E^{ki} TAR-*is*.

in $m_{3'}/y_{1'}$ (o.3') with VII/58 S.E. implies (assuming the months are in fact sequentially ordered) that the data in $m_{5'}/y_{1'}$ (o.5') be assigned to IX/58 S.E. However, the quantity of barley in Text 14—⌜(+)1(p)⌝ 1(b) 3 *qa*—were it restored to 3(p) 1(b) 3 *qa* = 117 qa, is similar to but not exactly the same as the comparable Diary datum—3(p) = 108 qa.[122] Similarly, $m_{1'}/y_{1'}$ (Text 14: o.1') would most likely represent IV/58 S.E., but again, the data for barley in $m_{1'}/y_{1'}$—x+⌜3 *qa*⌝—cannot be restored to the precise value for that month of 2 PI = 72 qa in Text 3A: o.6. The differences between the quantities quoted in Text 12 and -253 and Text 3A may be insignificant if the values selected were not taken on the same day of the month (cf. Text 8 Comparanda, passim). Unfortunately without further comparative material it remains entirely possible that the suspension possibly referred to here in Text 14 represents a third, previously unknown, suspension of the sale of dates.

Nonetheless, if (1) the restoration in line o.3' ZÚ.LUM KI.L[AM KUD?-*is*?] "dates—sa[le *was cut off*(?)]" and (2) the suggestion that this suspension of the sale of dates in Babylon is the very one referred to in AD II -253[123] in VII/58 S.E. are accepted, new light might then be shed upon the events surrounding that suspension. VII/58 S.E. is significant on two accounts: (1) month VII (and VIII) is the typical time of the date harvest in Babylonia when supplies of fresh dates would be expected to arrive in the market (Slotsky 1997, 29–31); and (2) 58 S.E. (254/3 BCE) is quite near the end of the so-called Second Syrian War (260 – 253? BCE).[124] Although "practically nothing of the details or chronology of this war" is known it is generally accepted that the hostilities were the result of Ptolemy II's attempt to take advantage of the circumstances following the death of Antiochus I in 261 BCE and the accession of his son Antiochus II, coregent since 266 BCE.[125] What is known for certain is that at the conclusion of hostilities, Antiochus repudiated his wife Laodike in order to marry Ptolemy's daughter Berenike.[126] A fragmentary historical anecdote preserved in an Astronomical

---

122 AD II -253B_2:3' [... ITU B]I KI.LAM ŠE.IM 3 PI Z[Ú ... .

123 AD II -253B_1: o.4' ... Z]Ú AŠ *kar-ri* E[ki] TAR-*is* (similary AD II -253A_1: o.8–o.9).

124 For the summer of 253 BCE as the *terminus ante quem* for the peace treaty, see Heinen 1984, 419, n. 17, citing D.J. Crawford, J. Quaegebeur, and W. Clarysse, *Studies on Ptolomaic Memphis*. Studia Hellenistica 24. Louvain, 1980, 83–89.

125 See conveniently Heinen 1984, 418–19; Boiy 2004, 145–49. The precise circumstances regarding the murder or execution of Seleucus (cf. Justin, Prologue 26), coregent with his father Antiochus I since the latter's accession, and his replacement by his younger brother Antiochus (II) is complicated by a recently published cuneiform archival tablet from Babylon that refers to the date 5/V/46 S.E., Antiochus and Seleucus and Antiochus, kings (Stolper Records of Deposit, 46ff., 15: 4'–5').

126 The Third Syrian (Laodikean) War (246 – 241 BCE) would erupt as a result of the rival claims to the Seleucid throne by these two women and their supporters on behalf of their respective sons following the death of Antiochus II. For details and sources, see Heinen 1984, 420–21; Boiy 2004, 149–53; see further the Comments to Text. 4.

Diary for VI_2/56 S.E. (Sept./Oct. 256 BCE) might well be taken to be a reference to a battle in that war in the vicinity of Babylon: "[That$^?$] mo[nth$^?$ ...] entered [Babylon$^?$.] The people of the land [...] in ... in battle in the di[strict$^?$ of Eri]du opposite E-sang[il ...]."[127] The presence of a foreign army in the Babylonian heartland may well have had broad scale adverse effects on the local economy.

It has previously been shown that since the end of the Wars of the Successors (305 BCE) through the reign of Antiochus II (246 BCE) date prices were relatively stable and quite high (Slotsky 1997, 58–59); the anecdotal data available specifically for the years of the Second Syrian War show that the quantities of dates available were consistently at or near their lowest point in the sixty years prior to their complete removal from the market in VII/58 S.E. (see Table 13: Price Equivalents for Dates during 260–247 BCE/52–64 S.E., above). Only after the war does the price equivalent of dates significantly increase, but note that there is a gap of two full years in the data set in the Diaries following the cut off. In the light of the data in Text 14, subject to the assumptions already stipulated, it would appear that immediately following the resumption of the sale of dates that some sort of price controls were in place holding their price equivalent fixed for at least the five following months at a mere 45 qa/shekel, while in the following year price equivalents appear to have been held steady over a similar period of time at just over twice the fixed value of the previous year. In the case of barley, price equivalents in the months (II – V) preceding the cut off of dates remained fixed at 72 qa per shekel silver (Text 3A: o.3–o.6). This streak of unvarying equivalents may have been due to the harvest which usually comes in during months I to II, or perhaps there may have been some sort of price controls in place for barley during the war. Note that immediately afterwards barley price equivalents, despite their fragmentary nature, appear to vary much more freely.[128] The data in the Astronomical Diaries, which only begin again two full years after the suspension, suggests that whatever price controls might have been in place had by now been removed.

127 AD II -255A: r.14' ... I[TU$^?$ BI$^?$ x x] (r.15') [... E$^?$]^{ki} KU_4-*ub* ^{lú}UN.MEŠ KUR AŠ *i-nu-tú* AŠ MÈ AŠ KI-*t*[*ì eri*]-*du*$_{10}$$^{?ki}$ AŠ$^?$ *tar-ṣu* É.SAG.G[ÍL x x x].

128 On the expectation for market prices to "move with a great deal of randomness and ... var[y] over time," see Temin 2002, 59.

SUMMARY

(barley and dates qa per nn shekel silver)

Year	*Month*	*Barley*	*Dates*
	[...]		
[$y_{1'}$	$m_{1'}$	](+)3	[ ]
	[$m_{2'}$	]	[ ]
	[$m_{3'}$	]	[cut off$^{?}$]
	[$m_{4'}$	]	45
	[$m_{5'}$	](+)45	45
	[$m_{6'}$	](+)3	45
	[$m_{7'}$	](+)27	45
	[$m_{8'}$	](+)24	45
	[$m_{9'}$	]	[ ]
	[...]		
[$y_{2'}$	$m_{1''}$	] 132	[ ](+)1
	[$m_{2''}$	] 114	96
	[$m_{3''}$	]	96
	[$m_{4''}$	]	90(+)
	[$m_{5''}$	]	90(+)
	[$m_{6''}$	]	90(+)
	[...]		

High:	132	96
Low:	114	45

TEXT 15

BM 37034 (80–6–17,778)
Dimensions: 6.6 x 5.4 x 3.7
Date: n.d. (Seleucid?)
Commodities: [… dates$^{?}$], mustard, cress, sesame, wool
Equivalence: 1 shekel silver
Publ.: Wiseman, *Sachs Mem. Vol.*, 372 [BM 37034]
Photo: Plate XVII

obv.

o.1' [ ] x
o.2' [*a-na* 1 GÍN] ⸢KÙ.BABBAR⸣
o.3' [ ] ⸢4(b)⸣ *saḫ-le*$_{10}$ 1(p) 4(b)
o.4' [*a-na* 1 GÍ]N KÙ.BABBAR
o.5' [ ] x *saḫ-le*$_{10}$ 1(p) 4(b)
o.6' [*a-na* 1] GÍN KÙ.BABBAR
o.7' [ ] 4(p) 1(b) *saḫ-le*$_{10}$ 1(p) 4(b)
o.8' [*a-na* 1] GÍN KÙ.BABBAR
o.9' [ ] *saḫ-le*$_{10}$ 1(p) 4(b)
o.10' [*a-na* 1] GÍN KÙ.BABBAR
o.11' [ ] ⸢*saḫ-le*$_{10}$ 1(p)⸣ 4(b)
o.12' [*a-na* 1 GÍN KÙ.BABBA]R
o.13' [ ] x x
(*remainder lost*)

rev.

r.1' [*saḫ-l*]*e*$_{10}$ 1(p) 4(b)
r.2' [ ]
r.3' [Š]E.GIŠ.Ì 1(p) 3(b) SÍG.⸢ḪÁ 3⸣ MA.NA *a-na* 1 GÍN
r.4' [ ] ŠE.GIŠ 1(p) 2(b) SÍG.⸢ḪÁ⸣ [3$^{?}$ M]A.NA *a-na* 1 GÍN KÙ.BABBAR
r.5' [ ] x ŠE.GIŠ 1(p) 2(b) SÍG.ḪÁ ⸢3⸣ [MA].NA *a-na* 1 GÍN
r.6' [ ] 4(p) 2(b) 3 *qa kàs* 1(g) 2(p) 3(b) *saḫ-le*$_{10}$
r.7' [*a-na* 1 GÍN KÙ].BABBAR
r.8' [nn] ⸢GUR⸣ 2 PI ⸢*kàs* 1(+) PI
(*remainder lost*)

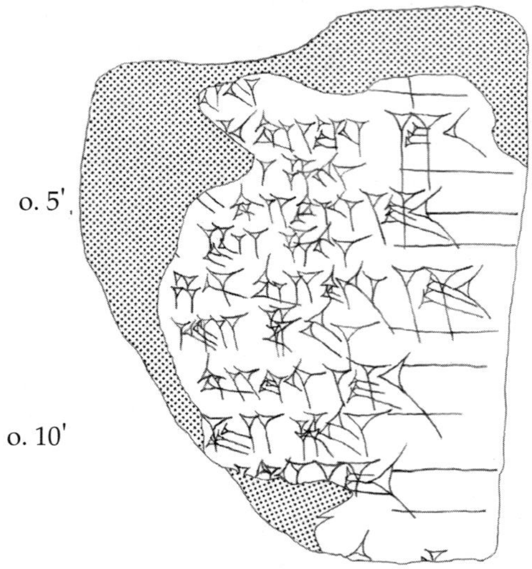

BM 37034 obverse

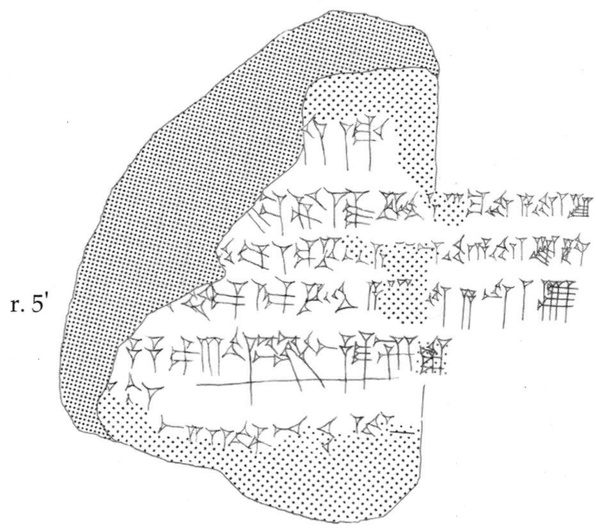

BM 37034 reverse

TRANSLATION

o.1' [(year $y_{1'}$) (month $m_{1'}$) …] …

o.2' [… for 1 shekel of] silver.

o.3' [(month $m_{2'}$) …] 4 sūt; cress 1 pān 4 sūt

o.4' [… for 1 shek]el of silver.

o.5' [(month $m_{3'}$) …] …; cress 1 pān 4 sūt

o.6' [… for 1] shekel of silver.

o.7' [(month $m_{4'}$) …] 4 pān 1 sūt; cress 1 pān 4 sūt

o.8' [… for 1] shekel of silver.

o.9' [(month $m_{5'}$) …]; cress 1 pān 4 sūt

o.10' [… for 1] shekel of silver.

o.11' [(month $m_{6'}$) …]; cress 1 pān 4 sūt

o.12' [… for 1 shekel of silve]r.

o.13' [(month $m_{7'}$) …] …

(*remainder lost*)

r.1' [(year $y_{1''}$) (month $m_{1''}$)…; cres]s 1 pān 4 sūt

r.2' […]

r.3' [(month $m_{2''}$) …; s]esame 1 pān 3 sūt; wool 3 mina for 1 shekel.

r.4' [(month $m_{3''}$) …]; sesame 1 pān 2 sūt; wool [$3^{?}$ m]ina for 1 shekel of silver.

r.5' [(month $m_{4''}$) …] …; sesame 1 pān 2 sūt; wool 3 [mi]na for 1 shekel.

r.6' [(month $m_{5''}$) …(dates) …] 4 pān 2 sūt 3 qa; mustard 1 kur 2 pān 3 sūt; cress

r.7' [… for 1 shekel of si]lver.

r.8' [(month $m_{6''}$) … (dates) nn] kur 2 pān; mustard (nn+)1 pān

(*remainder lost*)

COMMENTS

Text 15 is written on two sides of a fragment of the right half of a tablet. The script displays some cursive diagonal tendencies. An indeterminate number of lines are missing from the top and bottom; a portion of the right edge is preserved with three lines of the text on the reverse extending across it. The full text appears to have originally given monthly price equivalents per one shekel of silver for all six commodities. Mustard, cress, sesame, and wool are variously specified in the fragmentary text and it may be fairly assumed that the data preceding mustard in r.6' and r.8' are in fact for dates; in light of the missing left half of the tablet and the corpus at large, it may be further assumed that each months quotations in fact began with barley. On the obverse, each month's data appear to have occupied two consecutive lines of the tablet and ended with a repetition of the statement of the price equivalent of 1 shekel of silver; whenever a line did not reach the tablet's right edge the scribe impressed a horizontal line in the remaining space. On the tablet reverse the scribe appears to have found himself becoming short of space and cramped his data for at least three consecutive months within individual lines, each continuing well onto the thick right edge. No indication of the date of the tablet is preserved and comparisons with the extant data in the Astronomical Diaries do not provide any compelling parallels; the relatively high equivalents for dates speak for the period after 100 S.E. while the moderate equivalents for wool are suggestive of the period prior to 150 S.E.[129]

SUMMARY

(barley, dates, mustard, cress, and sesame qa per 1 shekel silver; wool mina per 1 shekel silver)

Year	*Month*	*Barley*	*Dates*	*Mustard*	*Cress*	*Sesame*	*Wool*
	[. . .]						
[$y_{1'}$	$m_{1'}$						]
	[$m_{2'}$			]+24	60	[	]
	[$m_{3'}$			]	60	[	]
	[$m_{4'}$			] 150(+)	60	[	]
	[$m_{5'}$			]	60	[	]
	[$m_{6'}$			]	60	[	]
	[$m_{7'}$						]
	[. . .]						
[$y_{1''}$	$m_{1''}$			]	60	[	]
	[$m_{2''}$				]	54	3
	[$m_{3''}$				]	48	[3$^?$]
	[$m_{4''}$				]	48	3
	[$m_{5''}$	]	159	(+)270	[		]
	[$m_{6''}$	]	252(+)[	]+36[			]
	[. . .]						

	Barley	Dates	Mustard	Cress	Sesame	Wool
High:	-	-	-	60	54	3
Low:	-	-	-	60	48	3

129 See conveniently, Slotsky 1997, 138–41.

TEXT 16

BM 37054 (80–6–17,798) + BM 40100 (81–2–1,65)
Dimensions: 10.8 x 4.6 x 2.8
Date: n.d. (Seleucid?)
Commodities: [... dates[?]], sesame
Equivalence: 1(?) shekel silver
Publ.: Wiseman, *Sachs Mem. Vol.*, 372 [BM 37054]
Photo: Plate XVIII
Unpublished Sachs transliteration (BM 40100)

obv.

1	[	ŠE.GIŠ].˹Ì˺ 1(p) 1(b)	
2	[	ŠE.G]IŠ.Ì 1(p) 1(b)	
3	[	ŠE].GIŠ 1(p) 1(b)	
4	[	ŠE].GIŠ 1PI	
5	[	ŠE.GI]Š 1 PI	
6	[	ŠE.GI]Š 1 PI	
7		ŠE.GI]Š 5(b) 3 *qa*	
8	[	] x ————————————	
9	[	ŠE.GIŠ] ˹5(b) 3 *qa*	*(erasure)*
10	[	] x ŠE.GIŠ 5(b)	*(erasure)*
11	[	ŠE.GI]Š 5(b)	*(erasure)*
12	[	ŠE.GI]Š 1(p) 1(b)	*(erasure)*
13	[	] TIL ITU 4 PI ŠE.GIŠ.Ì 1 PI	*(erasure)*
14	[	ŠE.G]IŠ 1(p) 1(b) 3 *qa*	
15	[	] ˹2(p)˺ 2(b) EN TIL ITU 2(p) 4(b) 3 *qa*	
16	[	ŠE.GIŠ] ˹1(p)˺ 1(b)	
17	[	ŠE.GIŠ] 1PI	*(erasure)*
18	[	2(p)] ˹4(b)˺ EN TIL ITU 2(p) 3(b)	
19	[	ŠE.G]IŠ 1 PI	
20	[	E]N TIL ITU 2(p) 1(b) ŠE.GIŠ 1 PI	
21	[	2(p) 3(b)] ŠE.GIŠ 1 PI	
22	[	] ŠE.GIŠ 1(p) 1(b)	

rev.

23	[	] ŠE.GIŠ 1(p) 1(b)	
24	[	Š]E.GIŠ 1(p) 1(b)	
25	[	TI]L ITU 2(p) 4(b) ŠE.GIŠ 1(p) 1(b)	
26	[	ŠE].GIŠ 1(p) 1(b)	

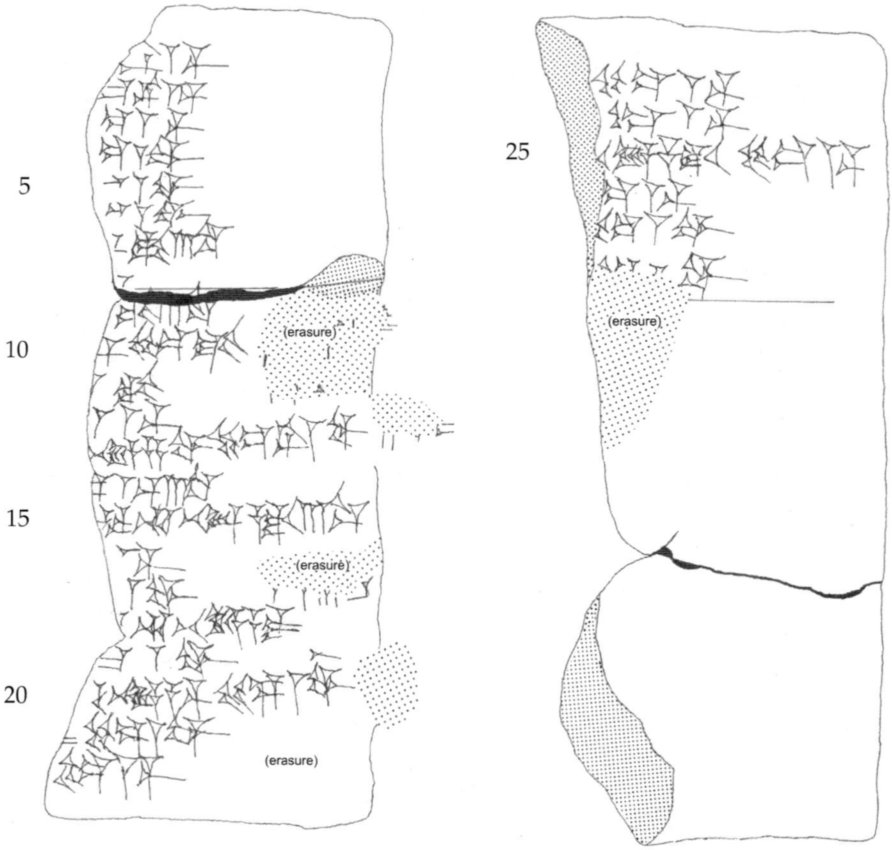

BM 37054 + BM 40100 obverse (left) and reverse (right)

27 [Š]E.GIŠ 1 PI
28 [ ] ⸢ŠE.GIŠ 1⸣ PI
[ ]

(erasure)

TRANSLATION

1 [(year $y_{1'}$) (month $m_{1'}$) … ; sesam]e 1 pān 1 sūt.
2 [(month $m_{2'}$) … ; se]same 1 pān 1 sūt.
3 [(month $m_{3'}$) …; se]same 1 pān 1 sūt.
4 [(month $m_{4'}$) …; se]same 1pān.
5 [(month $m_{5'}$) …; sesa]me 1 pān.
6 [(month $m_{6'}$) …; sesa]me 1 pān.
7 [(month $m_{7'}$) …; sesam]e 5 sūt 3 qa.
8 […] …

---

9 [(year $y_{2'}$) (month $m_{1'}$) …; sesame] 5 sūt 3 qa.
10 [(month $m_{2''}$) …] …; sesame 5 sūt.
11 [(month $m_{3''}$) …; sesa]me 5 sūt.
12 [(month $m_{4''}$) …; sesa]me 1 pān 1 sūt.
13 [(month $m_{5''}$) … (dates?) …] the end of the month 4 pān; sesame 1 pān.
14 [(month $m_{6''}$) …; ses]ame 1 pān 1 sūt 3 qa.
15 [(month $m_{7''}$) … (dates?)] 2 pān 2 sūt, to the end of the month 2 pān 4 sūt 3 qa;
16 […; sesame] 1 pān 1 sūt.
17 [(month $m_{8''}$) …; sesame] 1 pān.
18 [(month $m_{9''}$) … (dates?) 2 pān] 4 sūt, to the end of the month 2 pān 3 sūt;
19 [… sesa]me 1 pān.
20 [(month $m_{10''}$) … (dates?) t]o the end of the month 2 pān 1 sūt; sesame 1 pān.
21 [(month $m_{11''}$)… (dates?) 2 pān 3 sūt]; sesame 1pān.
22 [(month $m_{12''}$)…]; sesame 1 pān 1 sūt.
23 [(year $y_{3'}$) (month $m_{1'''}$) …]; sesame 1 pān 1 sūt.
24 [(month $m_{2'''}$) …; s]esame 1 pān 1 sūt.
25 [(month $m_{3'''}$) … (dates?) … the en]d of the month 2 pān 4 sūt; sesame 1 pān 1 sūt.
26 [(month $m_{4'''}$) …; se]same 1 pān 1 sūt.
27 [(month $m_{5'''}$) …; s]esame 1 pān.
28 [(month $m_{6'''}$) …]; sesame 1 pān.

NOTES

13 Two or three signs underlie the erasure at the end of the line on the right edge.

18 The restoration 2(p)] ⌜4(b)⌝ is suggested by Sachs' transliteration.

21 The restoration 2(p) 3(b)] is suggested by Sachs' transliteration.

COMMENTS

The two joined fragments bearing Text 16 form the right half of a tablet otherwise preserved fully from top to bottom. The text contains price equivalents, at an unstated rate, for at least two commodities: the first, name not preserved, for which at least two quantities were originally given, one prior to the end of the month, the second to the end of the month[130]; and the second, sesame,[131] for which a single monthly quantity is given. Note the obvious absence of any price equivalent for wool which might otherwise be expected to follow in the empty space after sesame on each line. Also note that sesame only occurs on tablets giving price equivalents for all six staple commodities or just barley, dates, and sesame (Texts 9, 17), thus the unnamed commodity is likely to be dates.

The tablet obverse is divided by a ruled line into an upper portion containing seven months worth of data, and a lower portion containing twelve months of data. On the tablet reverse there are six months of data occupying the upper third of the tablet above a ruled line. The lower two-thirds of the preserved portion of the tablet is uninscribed and shows areas of extensive erasure. The distribution of the data suggests that the tablet originally contained price equivalents for the latter half of a year containing an intercalary month, the following full year, and the first or latter half of the next year after that.[132]

Comparisons with the Astronomical Diaries suggest that this text might cover the periods VI – XII_2/64, I – XII/65, and I – VI/66 S.E. at the equivalency rate of 1 shekel of silver.[133] Note the price equivalent for sesame for both $m_{4'}$/$y_{1'}$ (l. 4) and X/64 S.E.[134] is 36 qa/shekel, and for $m_{5'''}$/$y_{3'}$ (l. 27) and V/66

---

130 EN TIL ITU: ll. 15, 18, 20; cf. ll. 13, 15, 25.

131 Written ŠE.GIŠ (passim); also note ŠE.GIŠ.Ì (ll. 1, 2, 13).

132 Compare Text 9 which apparently gave monthly price equivalents for the full years between 184 and 190 S.E., except for 189 S.E., which contains data for just the latter half of the year (months VI_2–XII); and Text 10 which gives data only for the latter halves of two consecutive years, $194^?$–$195^?$ S.E. In Text 3 the scribe appears to have accidentally omitted month X–XII_2/47 S.E. Also note Text 12 which gives just three consecutive months data for XII/208–II/209 S.E.

133 Note that reports of the death of Antiochus II reached Babylon in V/66 S.E. (Sachs and Wiseman *Iraq* 16 pl. LIII: o.12–13; cf. AD II -245B:LoE 1).

134 AD II -247C: o.7' … I]TU BI KI.LAM ŠE.IM 4(p) 1(b) ZÚ.LUM 3(p) 4(b) 3 *qa kàs* 3 GUR *saḫ-le*$_{10}$ 2(p) 5(b) ŠE.GIŠ 1 PI (o.8') SÍG.ḪÁ 5 MA.NA.

S.E.[135] is 36 qa/shekel. Also compare the sesame equivalents for $m_{5''}/y_{2'}$ (l. 13) (36 qa/shekel) with V/65 S.E.[136] (42 qa/shekel)—note that the quantity in Text 16 is followed by an erasure while the Diary quantity is qualified as "in the middle of the month." Also note $m_{1'''}/y_{3'}$ (l. 23) (42 qa/shekel) and I/66 S.E.[137] (36 qa/shekel), a difference of just 1 sūt. None of the preserved values for what is presumed to be dates can be directly compared with Diary data—nonetheless the Diary's quantity for dates for VI/65 S.E.[138] (120 qa/shekel) fits quite nicely between the declining quantities for $m_{5''}/y_{2'}$ (l. 13) (144 qa/shekel) and $m_{7''}/y_{2'}$ (l. 15) (84 and 99 qa/shekel).[139]

SUMMARY

(Barley and dates qa per 1 shekel silver)

Year	*Month*	*[... Dates?]*	*Sesame*
[$y_{1'}$	$m_{1'}$	]	42
	[$m_{2'}$	]	42
	[$m_{3'}$	]	42
	[$m_{4'}$	]	36
	[$m_{5'}$	]	36
	[$m_{6'}$	]	36
	[$m_{7'}$	]	33
[$y_{2'}$	$m_{1''}$	]	33
	[$m_{2''}$	]	30
	[$m_{3''}$	]	30
	[$m_{4''}$	]	42
	[$m_{5''}$	]	36
		[ ]e 144	
	[$m_{6''}$	]	45
	[$m_{7''}$	] 84	42

135 AD II -245A: r.3' … ZÚ.LUM] 3(p) 4(b) 3 *qa kàs* 2(g) 1 PI *saḫ* 2(p) 4(b) ŠE.GIŠ 1 PI SÍ[G …

136 AD II -246: r.5' AŠ MURUB$_4$ ITU 1(p) 1(b) SÍG 4 MA.NA … .

137 AD II -245A: o.10 […] *saḫ*! 2 PI ŠE.GIŠ 1 PI SÍG 5 MA.[NA … .

138 AD II -246: r.16' … ITU BI KI.LAM [ŠE.IM] (r.17') 1(g) 5(b) ZÚ 3(p) 3(b) *kàs* 3 GUR *saḫ-le*$_{10}$ 2(p) 4(b) ŠE.GIŠ [… SÍG.ḪÁ nn] MA.NA *a-na* 1 GÍN KÙ.⌜BABBAR⌝ *ép-šu* … .

139 See also Text 13 Comments where it is suggested that that tablet may date to circa 65–66 S.E. However, neither the present tablet nor Text 13 is sufficiently complete to offer significant comparisons.

Year	*Month*	[... *Dates*?]	*Sesame*
		→e 99	
	[$m_{8''}$	]	36
	[$m_{9''}$	96]	36
		→e 90	
	[$m_{10''}$	]	36
		→e 78	
	[$m_{11''}$	90]	36
	[$m_{12''}$	]	42
[$y_{3'}$	$m_{1'''}$	]	42
	[$m_{2'''}$	]	42
	[$m_{3'''}$	]	42
		[ ]e 96	
	[$m_{4'''}$	]	42
	[$m_{5'''}$	]	36
	[$m_{6'''}$	]	36

High:		144	45
Low:		78	30

TEXT 17

BM 46138 (81–7–6,593)
Dimensions: 3.3 x 5.4 x 2.3
Date: n.d. (Arsacid?)
Commodities: barley, dates, sesame
Equivalence: ?
Photo: Plate XIX

obv.

o.1' [ ] x SUMUN ⸢2(+)(p) 5(b) 3 *qa* ZÚ.LUM⸣ [1] ⸢GUR 3(+)(p) 3(+)(b)⸣
o.2' [ ] ⸢5(b)⸣ 3 *qa* ŠE.GIŠ 2(b) 4½ *qa* AŠ TIL ITU 2(b) 3 *qa*
o.3' [ITU.NE ŠE.IM] x ZÚ 1 GUR 3(p) 4(b) 3 *qa* AŠ MURUB$_4$ <ITU> ⸢1 GUR nn(p)⸣ 2(b)
o.4' [ ] ⸢2(b)⸣ 1½ *qa* AŠ TIL ITU 2(b) 3 *qa* [ITU.KIN ŠE].IM
o.5' [ ] ⸢ŠE.GIŠ⸣ 2(b) 3 *qa* ITU.DU$_6$ ŠE.I[M] ⸢1$^?$ GUR 2(p)⸣ 5(b)
o.6' [nn GU]R 3(p) 2(b) GIBIL.MEŠ 1 GUR 4(p) x [ ]
o.7' [IT]U 2 GUR 2(b) AŠ TIL <ITU> 2 G[UR]
o.8' [ ] ⸢4(b)⸣ 3 *qa* Z[Ú]
o.9' [ ] x x [ ]
(*remainder lost*)

rev.

r.1' [ ] x x x x [ ]
r.2' [ ] ⸢x ITU 3(p)⸣ 2(b) ZÚ.LUM 1 GUR 5(b)
r.3' [ ] 3(p) 2(b) AŠ MURUB$_4$ ITU 3(p) 3(b) 3 *qa* EN TIL ITU
r.4' [ ] ⸢EN⸣ TIL ITU 1 GUR 5(b) ŠE.GIŠ 3(b) 2 *qa*
r.5' [ ] x 3 *qa* ZÚ.LUM <AŠ> SAG ITU
r.6' [ ] x x x x 2(b) 2 ⸢*qa*⸣
r.7' [nn] *qa* Z[Ú]
(*remainder lost*)

o. 5'

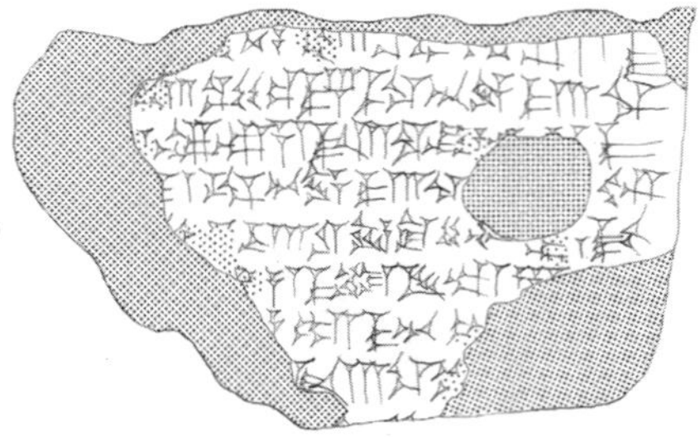

BM 46138 obverse

r. 5'

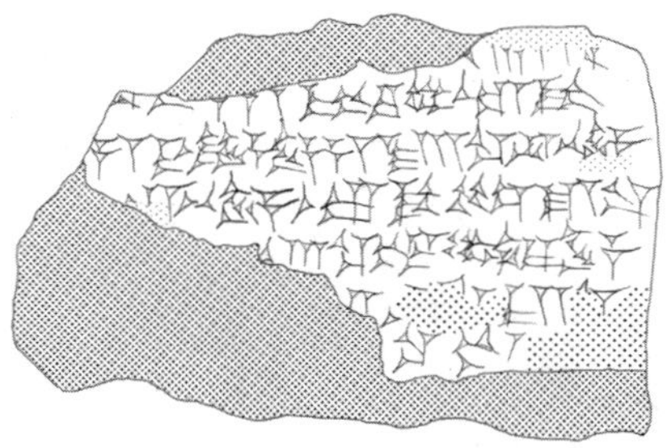

BM 46138 reverse

TRANSLATION

o.1' [(year $y_{1'}$) (month IV) ...] (barley) ... , old 2(+) pān 5 sūt 3 qa; dates [1] kur 3(+) pān 3(+) sūt
o.2' [...] 5 sūt 3 qa; sesame 2 sūt 4½ qa, at the end of the month 2 sūt 3 qa.
o.3' [Month V: barley ...] ...; dates 1 kur 3 pān 4 sūt 3 qa, in the middle of <the month> 1 kur nn pān 2 sūt
o.4' [... (sesame)] 2 sūt 1½ qa, at the end of the month 2 sūt 3 qa. [Month VI: bar]ley
o.5' [...]; sesame 2 sūt 3 qa. Month VII: barl[ey] 1? kur 2 pān 5 sūt
o.6' [... (dates) nn ku]r 3 pān 2 sūt, new 1 kur 4 pān ... [...]
o.7' [(month VIII) (dates) ... of the mon]th 2 kur 2 sūt, at the end of <the month> 2 k[ur ...]
o.8' [(month IX) (barley) ...] 4 sūt 3 qa; da[tes ...]
o.9' [...] ... [...]
(*remainder lost*)
r.1' [...] ... [...]
r.2' [(year $y_{1''}$) (month $m_{1'}$) (barley) ...] ... of the month 3 pān 2 sūt; dates 1 kur 5 sūt
r.3' [(month $m_{2'}$) (barley) ...] 3 pān 2 sūt, in the middle of the month 3 pān 3 sūt 3 qa, to the end of the month
r.4' [... (dates)] to the end of the month 1 kur 5 sūt; sesame 3 sūt 2 qa
r.5' [(month $m_{3'}$) (barley) ...] ... 3 qa; dates <at> the beginning of the month
r.6' [...] ... 2 sūt 2 qa
r.7' [(month $m_{4'}$) (barley) ... nn] qa; da[tes ...]
(*remainder lost*)

COMMENTS

Text 17 is found on a small fragment of a tablet that includes a portion of the right edge. The text appears to be restricted to just three commodities, barley, dates, and sesame[140]; Texts 9 and perhaps 16 are similarly restricted to the same three commodities. No chronological indicators remain in Text 17 except for a single preserved month name—DU_6 (o.5': month VII). The script is quite close to that seen in several other Arsacid-period commodity price lists in this corpus, including Texts 6, 7, and 10, for all of which the price equivalent is at the rate of two shekels; however price fluctuations in the Arsacid period are such that the extant price equivalents here in Text 17 could be at the rate of either one or two shekels with too little evidence preserved to recommend either.[141]

---

140 Note in ll. o.4' and o.5' that the data proceeds directly from sesame to barley at the beginning of the next month, confirming that wool was not included among this tablet's commodities; the magnitude of the quantity (210 qa) of the commodity preceding sesame in l. r.4' almost certainly precludes cress from identification; and barley always precedes dates throughout the study corpus and the Astronomical Diaries.

141 See conveniently Slotsky 1997, 142–46.

SUMMARY

(barley, dates, and sesame qa per nn shekel silver)

Year	*Month*	*Barley*		*Dates*		*Sesame*	
[...]							
[$y_{1'}$	IV]	old	105(+)	[ ]	306(+)		16½
				[	]+33	@e	15
	[V	]			315		13½
				@m	228(+)	@e	15
	[VI			]			15
	VII	[ ]	282$^?$	[ ]	300(+)		
				new	322(+)		
	[VIII		]		372	[	]
				@e	360(+)		
	[IX		]+27	[	]	[	]
[...]							
[$y_{1''}$	$m_{1'}$	]	120		210		
	[$m_{2'}$	]	120	[	]		20
		@m	129	→e	210		
		→e	[ ]				
	[$m_{3'}$		]+27	@b	[		]
	[$m_{4'}$						]
[...]							

	Barley	Dates	Sesame
High:	282$^?$	372	20
Low:	120	210	13½

SELECTED BIBLIOGRAPHY

Aaboe, A.

1991 "Babylonian Mathematics, Astrology, and Astronomy." In John Boardman, I.E.S. Edwards, N.G.L. Hammond, E. Sollberger, and C.B.F. Walker, eds., *The Cambridge Ancient History*. III/2. Second Edition. *The Assyrian and Babylonian Empires and Other States of the Near East, from the Eighth to the Sixth Centuries* B.C. Cambridge, New York, Port Chester, Melbourne, Sydney: Cambridge University Press, 276–92.

Andreau, J., P. Briant, and R. Descat

1997 *Économie antique: Prix et formation des prix dans les économies antiques*. Entretiens d'archéologie et d'histoire, Saint-Bertrand-de-Comminges 3. Saint-Bertrand-de-Comminges Musée archéologique départmental de Saint-Bertrand-de-Comminges.

Aperghis, G.G.

2004 *The Seleukid Royal Economy: The Finances and Financial Administration of the Seleukid Empire*. Cambridge: Cambridge University Press.

Beaulieu, P.-A., and J.P. Britton

1994 "Rituals for an Eclipse Possibility in the 8th Year of Cyrus," *Journal of Cuneiform Studies* 46: 73–86.

Boiy, T.

2004 *Late Achaemenid and Hellenistic Babylon*. Orientalia Lovaniensia Analecta 136. Leuven: Peters.

Briant, P.

2002 *From Cyrus to Alexander: A History of the Persian Empire*. Translated by Peter T. Daniels. Winona Lake, Ind.: Eisenbrauns.

Brinkman, A.J.

1984 *Prelude to Empire: Babylonian Society and Politics, 747–626 B.C.* Occasional Publications of the Babylonian Fund 7. Philadelphia: The Babylonian Fund, University Museum, 1984.

Britton, J., and C. Walker

1996 "Astronomy and Astrology in Mesopotamia." In C. Walker, ed., *Astronomy before the Telescope. With a foreword by Patrick Moore.* London: British Museum Press, 42–67.

Brown, D.

2002 "The Level of the Euphrates." In C. Wunsch, ed., *Mining the Archives: Festschrift for Christopher Walker on the Occasion of his 60th Birthday.* Babylonische Archive 1. Dresden: Islet, 37–56.

2003 "The Scientific Revolution of 700 BC." In A.A. MacDonald, M.W. Twomey, and G.J. Reinink, eds., *Learned Antiquity: Scholarship and Society in the Near-East, the Greco-Roman world, and the Early Medieval West*. Leuven, Paris, and Dudley, Mass.: Peters, 1–12.

Burstein, S.M.

1978 *The* Babyloniaca *of Berossos*. Sources from the Ancient Near East 1/5. Malibu, Calif.: Undena Publications, 143–81.

Cavigneaux, A.

1989 "Le nom akkadien du grain," *Nouvelles Assyriologiques Brèves et Utilitaires*: 33 [52].

Dandamayev, M.A.

1988 "Wages and Prices in Babylonia in the 6th and 5th Centuries B.C." *Altorientalische Forschungen* 15: 53–58.

de Breucker, G.

2003 "Berossos and the Mesopotamian Temples as Centers of Knowledge during the Hellenistic Period." In A. A. MacDonald, Michael W. Twomey, and G. J. Reinink, eds. *Learned Antiquity: Scholarship and Society in the Near East, the Greco-Roman World, and the Early Medieval West*. Groningen: Peters, 13–23.

Del Monte G.F.

1997 *Testi dalla Babilonia Ellenistica I: Test Cronografici*. Studi Ellenistici 9. Pisa and Rome: Istituti Editoriali e Poligrafici Internazionali.

Depuydt, L.

1995 "'More Valuable than all Gold': Ptolemy's Royal Canon and Babylonian Chronology." *Journal of Cuneiform Studies* 47: 97–117.

Dubberstein, W.

1939 "Comparative Prices in Later Babylonia (625–400 B.C.)." *American Journal of Semitic Languages and Literatures* 56: 20–43.

Geller, M.J.

1991 "New Information on Antiochus IV from Babylonian Astronomical Diaries," *Bulletin of the School of Oriental and African Studies* 54: 1–4.

1997 "The Last Wedge," *Zeitschrift für Assyriologie* 87: 43–95.

2000 Review of Slotsky 1997, *Orientalistische Literaturzeitung* 95: 409–12.

2008 "Graeco-Babylonian *Utukku Lemnūtu*," *Nouvelles Assyriologiques Brèves et Utilitaires*: 43–44 [33].

George, A.R.

1993 *House Most High: The Temples of Ancient Mesopotamia*. Mesopotamian Civilizations 5. Winona Lake, Ind.: Eisenbrauns.

Glassner, J.-J.

2004 *Mesopotamian Chronicles*. B.R. Foster, ed. Writings from the Ancient World 19. Atlanta: Society of Biblical Literature.

Golenko, V.K.

1995 "Notes on the Coinage and Currency of the Early Seleucid State," *Mesopotamia* 30: 51–215.

Grainger, J.D.

1999 "Prices in Hellenistic Babylonia," *Journal of the Economic and Social History of the Orient* 42: 303–25.

Habicht, C.

1989 "The Seleucids and their Rivals." In A.E. Astin, F.W. Walbank, M.W. Frederiksen, and R.M. Ogilvie, eds., *The Cambridge Ancient History. Vol. VIII: Rome and the Mediterranean to 133 B.C.* Second Edition. Cambridge: Cambridge University Press, 324–87.

Hallo, W.W.

1984/85 "The Concept of Eras from Nabonassar to Seleucus," *Ancient Studies in Memory of Elias Bickerman. The Journal of Ancient Near East Society* 16–17: 143–51.

1988 "The Nabonassar Era and other Epochs in Mesopotamian Chronology and Chronography." In E. Leichty, M. de J. Ellis, and P. Gerardi, eds., *A Scientific Humanist: Studies in Memory of Abraham Sachs*. Occasional Publications of the Samuel Noah Kramer Fund 9. Philadelphia: University Museum, 175–99.

Hansman, J.F.

1967 "Charax and the Karkheh," In E. Yarshater, ed., *Encyclopedia Iranica* 7. London and Boston: Routledge & Kegan Paul, 21–58.

Heinen, H.

1984 "The Syrian-Egyptian Wars and the New Kingdoms of Asia Minor." In F.W. Walbank, A.E. Astin, M.W. Frederiksen, and R.M. Ogilvie, eds., *The Cambridge Ancient History. Vol. VII, Part 1: The Hellenistic World.* Second Edition. Cambridge: Cambridge University Press, 412–45.

Hunger, H.

1976 "Astrologische Wettervorhersagen," *Zeitschrift für Assyriologie* 66: 234–60.

Hunger, H., and D. Pingree

1999 *Astral Sciences in Mesopotamia*. Leiden, Boston, Köln: Brill.

Hunger, H., and R.J. van der Spek

2006 "An Astronomical Diary Concerning Artaxerxes II (year 42 = 363–2 BC): Military Operations in Babylonia," *Arta* 2006.002. http://www.achemenet.com/ressources/enligne/arta/pdf/2006.002-Hunger-Spek.pdf

Joannès, F.

2000 "Une chronique judiciaire d'époque hellénistique et le châtiment des sacrileges à Babylone." In J. Marzahn and H. Neumann, eds., *Assyriologica et Semitica: Festschrift für Joachim Oelsner anläßlich seines 65. Geburtstages am 18. Februar 1997*. Alter Orient und Altes Testament 252. Münster: Ugarit-Verlag, 193–211.

Leichty, E.

1986 *Catalogue of the Babylonian Tablets in the British Museum, vol. VI: Tablets from Sippar 1.* Introduction by J. E. Reade. London: British Museum Publications.

Lieberman, S.

1990 "Canonical and Official Cuneiform Texts: Towards an Understanding of Assurbanipal's Personal Tablet Collection." In T. Abusch, J. Huehnergard, and P. Steinkeller, eds., *Lingering Over Words: Studies in Ancient Near Eastern Literature in Honor of William L. Moran*. Atlanta, Georgia: Scholars Press, 305–36.

Linssen, M.J.H.

2004 *The Cults of Uruk and Babylon: The Ritual Texts as Evidence for Hellenistic Cult Practices*. Cuneiform Monographs 25. Leiden and Boston: Brill-Styx.

Livingstone, A.

1997 "The Akkadian Word for Barley: A Note from the Schoolroom," *Journal of Semitic Studies* 42: 1–5.

Meisner, B.

1936 *Warenpreise in Babylonien*. Berlin: Verlag Der Akademie Der Wissenschaften.

Müller, G.G.W.

1995/96 "Die Teuerung in Babylon im 6.Jh. v. Chr." *Archiv für Orientforschung* 42/43: 163–75.

1999/2000 "Kurse, Preise, Wasserstände." *Archiv für Orientforschung* 46/47: 192–98.

Neugebauer, O.

1975 *A History of Ancient Mathematical Astronomy*. Three volumes. Berlin, Heidelberg, New York: Springer-Verlag.

Neugebauer, O., and A. Sachs

1967 "Some Atypical Astronomical Cuneiform Texts. I." *Journal of Cuneiform Studies* 21: 183–214.

1969 "Some Atypical Astronomical Cuneiform Texts. II." *Journal of Cuneiform Studies* 22: 92–111.

Oelsner, J.

2000 "Von Iqīša und einige anderen spägeborenen babyloniern." In S. Graziani, ed. *Studi sul vicino oriente ontico dedicate all memoria di Luigi Cagni II*. Istituto Universitario Orientale. Dipartimento di Studi Asiatic, Series Minor 61. Napoli: Istituto Universitario Orientale, 797–814.

Oppenheim, A.L.

1977 *Ancient Mesopotamia: Portrait of a Dead Civilization*. Revised Edition Completed by Erica Reiner. Chicago and London: University of Chicago Press.

Parker, R.A., and W.H. Dubberstein

1956 *Babylonian Chronology 626 B.C.–A.D. 75*. Brown University Studies 19. Providence: Brown University Press.

Parpola, S.

1983 "Excursus: The Substitute King Ritual." In S. Parpola, ed., *Letters from Assyrian Scholars to the Kings Esarhaddon and Assurbanipal. Part II: Commentary and Appendices*. Alter Orient und Altes Testament 5/2. Kevelaer: Butzon and Bercker, xxii–xxxii.

1993 *Letters from Assyrian and Babylonian Scholars*. State Archives of Assyria 10. Helsinki: Helsinki University Press.

Powell, M.A., Jr.

1979 "Ancient Mesopotamian Weight Metrology: Methods, Problems and Perspectives." In M.A. Powell and R.H. Sack, eds., *Studies in Honor of*

Tom B. Jones. Alter Orient und Altes Testament 203. Kevelaer: Butzon and Bercker, 71–109.

1984 "Late Babylonian Surface Mensuration. A Contribution to the History of Babylonian Agriculture and Arithmetic." *Archiv für Orientforschung* 31: 32–66.

1990 "Identification and Interpretation of Long Term Price Fluctuations in Babylonia: More on the History of Money in Mesopotamia." *Altorientalische Forschungen* 17: 76–99.

1996 "Money in Mesopotamia." *Journal of the Economic and Social History of the Orient* 39: 224–42.

Reade, J.E.

1986 "Introduction. Rassam's Babylonian Collection: The Excavation and the Archives." In E. Leichty, *Catalogue of the Babylonian Tablets in the British Museum, vol. VI: Tablets from Sippar 1*. London: British Museum Publications, xiii–xxxvi.

Rochberg, F.

2004 *The Heavenly Writing: Divination, Horoscopy, and Astronomy in Mesopotamian Culture*. Cambridge, United Kingdom: Cambridge University Press.

Rochberg-Halton, F.

1987 "The Assumed 29th *ahû* Tablet of *Enūma Anu Enlil*." In F. Rochberg-Halton, ed., *Language, Literature, and History: Philological and Historical Studies Presented to Erica Reiner*, American Oriental Series 63. New Haven: American Oriental Society, 327–50.

1990 "Astrology, Astronomy, and the Birth of Scientific Inquiry," *Bulletin of the Canadian Society for Mesopotamian Studies* 19: 25–33.

1991 "The Babylonian Astronomical Diaries" (Review of Sachs and Hunger 1988). *Journal of the American Oriental Society* 111: 323–32.

Sachs, A.J.

1948 "A Classification of Babylonian Astronomical Tablets of the Seleucid Period." *Journal of Cuneiform Studies* 2: 271–90.

Sachs, A.J., and H. Hunger

1988 *Astronomical Diaries and Related Texts from Babylonia. I: Diaries from 652 B.C. to 262 B.C.* Österreichische Akademie der Wissenschaften. Philosophisch-Historische Klasse, Denkenschriften 185. Wien: Österreichischen Akademie der Wissenschaften.

1989 *Astronomical Diaries and Related Texts from Babylonia. II: Diaries from 261 B.C. to 165 B.C.* Österreichische Akademie der Wissenschaften. Philosophisch-Historische Klasse, Denkenschriften 210. Wien: Österreichische Akademie der Wissenschaften.

1996 *Astronomical Diaries and Related Texts from Babylonia. III: Diaries from 164 B.C. to 61 B.C.* Österreichische Akademie der Wissenschaften. Philosophisch-Historische Klasse, Denkenschriften 247. Wien: Österreichische Akademie der Wissenschaften.

Schippmann, K.

1987a "The Arsacids. ii. The Arsacid Dynasty." In E. Yarshater, ed., *Encyclopedia Iranica* 2. London and Boston: Routledge & Kegan Paul, 525–36.

1987b "Artabanus." In E. Yarshater, ed., *Encyclopedia Iranica* 2. London and Boston: Routledge & Kegan Paul, 647–50.

Schuol, M.

2000 *Die Charakene: Ein mesopotamisches Königreich in hellenistisch-parthischer Zeit.* Oriens et Occidens 1. Stuttgart: Franz Steiner Verlag.

Slotsky, A.L.

1993 "The Bourse of Babylon: An analysis of the market quotations in the astronomical diaries of Babylonia." Ph.D. dissertation, Yale University.

1997 *The Bourse of Babylon: Market quotations in the Astronomical Diaries of Babylonia.* Bethesda, Md.: CDL Press.

Steele, J.M.

2003 "Planetary Latitudes in Babylonian Mathematical Astronomy." *Journal for the History of Astronomy* 34: 269–89.

Swerdlow, N.M.

1998 *The Babylonian Theory of the Planets.* Princeton: Princeton University Press.

Temin, P.

2002 "Price Behavior in Ancient Babylonia." *Explorations in Economic History* 39: 46–60.

van der Spek, R.J.

1993 "The Astronomical Diaries as a Source for Achaemenid and Seleucid History," *Bibliotheca Orientalis* 50: 91–101.

1997/98 "New Evidence from The Babylonian Astronomical Diaries Concerning Seleucid and Arsacid History," *Archiv für Orientforschung* 44/45: 167–75.

1998a "Cuneiform Documents on Parthian History: The Raimesu Archive. Materials for the Study of the Standard of Living." In J. Wiesehöfer, ed., *Das Partherreich und seine Zeugnisse: Beiträge des internationalen Colloquiums, Eutin (27. –30. Juni 1996).* Historia Einzelschriften 122. Stuttgart: Franz Steiner Verlag, 205–58.

1998b "The Chronology of the Wars of Artaxerxes II in the Babylonian Astronomical Diaries." In M. Brosius and A. Kuhrt, eds., *Studies in Persian History: Essays in Memory of David M. Lewis*. Achaemenid History 11. Leiden: Nederlands Instituut voor het Nabije Oosten 11, 239–56.

2000 "The Effect of War on the Prices of Barley and Agricultural Land in Hellenistic Babylonia," In J. Andreau, P. Briant, and R. Descat, eds., *La Guerre dans les economies antiques*. Entretiens d'archéologie et d'histoire, Saint-Bertrand-de-Comminges 5. Saint-Bertrand-de-Comminges Musée archéologique départmental de Saint-Bertrand-de-Comminges, 293–313.

2004 "Commodity Prices in Babylon 384–61 BC." *International Institute of Social History*. http://www.iisg.nl/hpw/babylon.php

van der Spek, R.J., and C.A. Mandemakers

2003 "Sense and Nonsense in the Statistical Approach of Babylonian Prices." *Bibliotheca Orientalis* 60: 521–34.

van der Waerden, B.L.

1952/53 "History of the Zodiac," *Archiv für Orientforschung* 16: 216–30.

van Driel, G.

1992 "Weather: Between the Natural and Unnatural in First Millennium Cuneiform Inscriptions." In D.J.W. Meijer, ed., *Natural Phenomena: Their Meaning, Depiction and Description in the Ancient Near East*. Amsterdam: Royal Netherlands Academy of Arts and Sciences, 39–52.

Vanstiphout, H.

1989 "The Akkadian Word for Grain and Lahar and Asnan, ll. 189–190," *Nouvelles Assyriologiques Brèves et Utilitaires*: 72–73 [98].

Vargyas, P.

1997 "Les Prix des Denréés Alimentaires de Première Nécessité en Babylonie à l'Époque Achéménide et Hellénistique." In J. Andreau, P. Briant, and R. Descat, eds., *Économie antique: Prix et formation des prix dans les économies antiques*. Entretiens d'archéologie et d'histoire, Saint-Bertrand-de-Comminges 3. Saint-Bertrand-de-Comminges Musée archéologique départmental de Saint-Bertrand-de-Comminges, 335–54.

2000 "Silver and Money in Achaemenid and Hellenistic Babylonia." In J. Marzahn and H. Neumann, eds., *Assyriologica et Semitica: Festschrift für Joachim Oelsner anläßlich seines 65. Geburtstages am 18. Februar 1997*. Alter Orient und Altes Testament 252. Münster: Ugarit-Verlag, 513–21.

2001 *A History of Babylonian Prices in the First Millennium BC, Vol. 1: Prices of the Basic Commodities*. Heidelberg: Heidelberger Orientverlag.

Wallenfels, R.

2001 "Fourth-Century Babylonian Sealed Archival Texts." In W.W. Hallo and I. J. Winter, eds., *Seals and Seal Impressions: Proceedings of the XLVe. Rencontre Assyriologique International Part II Yale University*. Bethesda, Md: CDL Press, 215–38.

Weisberg, D.B.

1967 "Appendix: The Treatment of Final Consonants in Neo-Babylonian." *Guild Structure and Political Allegiance in Early Mesopotamia*. Yale Near Eastern Researches 1. New Haven and London: Yale University Press, 106–11.

Westenholz, A.

2007 "The Graeco-Babylonaica Once Again," *Zeitschrift für Assyriologie* 97: 262–313.

Weszeli, M.

2001 Review of Slotsky 1997. *Journal of the American Oriental Society* 121: 493–94.

Wiseman, D.J.

1988 "A Note on Some Prices in Late Babylonian Astronomical Diaries." In E. Leichty, M. de J. Ellis, and P. Gerardi, eds., *A Scientific Humanist: Studies in Memory of Abraham Sachs*. Occasional Publications of the Samuel Noah Kramer Fund 9. Philadelphia: University Museum, 363–73.

Zaccagnini, C.

1997 "Prices and Price formation in the Ancient Near East. A Methodological Approach." In J. Andreau, P. Briant, and R. Descat, eds., *Économie antique: Prix et formation des prix dans les économies antiques*. Entretiens d'archéologie et d'histoire, Saint-Bertrand-de-Comminges 3. Saint-Bertrand-de-Comminges Musée archéologique départmental de Saint-Bertrand-de-Comminges, 361–84.

GLOSSARY OF ECONOMIC TERMS

GIBIL = *eššu*; new, fresh

GÍN = *šiqlu*, shekel, measure of weight

GUN = *biltu*, talent, measure of weight, = 60 minas

GUR = *kurru*; kur/gur, measure of capacity, = 180 *qa*

ina labāri = from the old; see *labāru*

ina mālak = on the way, en route; see *mālaku*

innadnu = which (KI.LAM) was paid; from N-stem of *nadānu* = to be paid; *šá i-na*/ AŠ KUR SUM/*innadnu*, "which was paid in the land"

ITU BI KI.LAM x *ana* 1 GÍN KÙ.BABBAR = that month, the equivalency/market rate: x amount of a commodity for one shekel of silver

kasû = GAZI.SAR; mustard?

KI.LAM = *maḫāru*; equivalent, market price, market rate

KÙ.BABBAR = *kaspu*; silver

KUD = *parāsu*; to cut off, suspend

kur = GUR, *kurru*; kur/gur, measure of capacity

labāru = SUMUN; old; *ina labāri*, from the old

mālaku = way, course, passage; *ina mālak*, on the way, en route

manû =MA.NA, mina, measure of weight, ~480 g

nadānu = sale, selling, delivery

NU.DÙ.MEŠ = negative of *babbanētu*; not of good quality

pān = PI, *pānu*, measure of capacity = 36 *qa*

PI = *pān*, measure of capacity = 36 *qa*

qa = SÌLA, *qû*, measure of capacity

saḫlû = ZÀ; cress?

SÍG = *šīpātu*; wool

suluppū = ZÚ, ZÚ.LUM; dates

SUM = *nadānu* = to give over, make a payment, sell

SUMUN = *labāru*; old

sūt = BÁN, *sūtu*, measure of capacity, = 6 *qa*

šá ina KUR SUM/*innadnu* = which (KI.LAM) was paid in the land

šamaššammū = ŠE.GIŠ, ŠE.GIŠ.Ì; sesame?

ŠE = *še'u*/*û*; barley

ŠE.BAR = *še'u*/*û*; barley

ŠE.GIŠ, ŠE.GIŠ.Ì = *šamaššammū*; sesame

ŠE.IM = *še'u*/*û*; barley

šiqlu = GÍN, shekel, measure of weight

še'u = ŠE, ŠE.BAR, ŠE.IM; barley

šīpātu = SÍG; wool

û = barley

ZÀ = *saḫlû*; cress?

ZÚ, ZÚ.LUM = *suluppū*; dates

LATE BABYLONIAN MONTH NAMES

I	Nisān(u)	BAR	March–April
II	Ayyār(u)	GU_4	April–May
III	Simān(u)	SIG	May–June
IV	Dûz(u)	ŠU	June–July
V	Ab(u)	NE	July-August
VI	Ulūl(u)	KIN	August–September
(VI_2	intercalary Ulūl(u)	KIN.2.KÁM)	
VII	Tašrīt(u)	DU_6	September–October
VIII	Araḫsamn(u)	APIN	October–November
IX	Kislīm(u)	GAN	November–December
X	Ṭebēt(u)	AB	December–January
XI	Šabāṭ(u)	ZÍZ	January–February
XII	Adar(u)	ŠE	February–March
(XII_2	intercalary Adar(u)	DIRI.ŠE)	

LATE BABYLONIAN METROLOGY

MEASURES OF DRY CAPACITY:

kur	"kor"	GUR (g)	= 5 *pān*
pān	"bushel"	PI (p)	= 6 *sūt*
sūt	"seah"	BÁN (b)	= 6 *qa*
qa		SILA_3	(≈ 1 liter)

MEASURES OF WEIGHT:

biltu	"talent"	GUN	= 60 *manû*
manû	"mina"	MA.NA	= 60 *šiqlu* (≈ 480 g)
šiqlu	"shekel"	GÍN	

A CHRONOLOGY OF LATE BABYLONIAN KINGS

NEO-BABYLONIAN PERIOD:	
Nabopolassar	625–605 BCE
Nebuchadrezzar II	604–562
Ewil-Marduk	561–560
Neriglissar	559–556
Labasi-Marduk	556
Nabonidus	555–539
PERSIAN PERIOD:	
Cyrus II the Great	538–530
Cambyses II	529–522
Bardiya	522
Nebuchadrezzar III	522
Nebuchadrezzar IV	521
Darius I the Great	521–486
Xerxes I	485–465
Bēl-šimanni	484
Šamaš-eriba	484
Artaxerxes I	464–424
Xerxes II	424
Darius II	423–405
Artaxerxes II Memnon	404–359
Artaxerxes III Ochus	358–338
Arses	337–336
Darius III	335–331

EARLY MACEDONIAN PERIOD:

Alexander III the Great	330–323	
Philip III Arrhidaeus	323–316	
Antigonus Monophthalmus	317–309/8	
Alexander IV	316–306/5	

SELEUCID PERIOD:

Seleucus I Nicator	311–295	1–17 S.E.
Seleucus I and Antiochus	294–281	18–31
Antiochus I Soter and Seleucus	281–267	31–45
Antiochus I and Seleucus and Antiochus	266	46
Antiochus I and Antiochus	266–261	46–51
Antiochus II Theos	261–246	51–66
Seleucus II Callinicus	246–226/5	66–87
Seleucus III Soter	226/5–223/2	87–89
Antiochus III the Great	223/2–210	90–101
Antiochus III and Antiochus	210–192	102–119
Antiochus III	192–189	119–122
Antiochus III and Seleucus	189–187	123–125
Seleucus IV Philopater	187–175	125–137
Antiochus IV Epiphanes	175	137
Antiochus IV and Antiochus	175–170	137–142
Antiochus IV	170–164	142–148
Antiochus V Eupator	164/3–162/1	148–150
Demetrius I Soter	161–151	151–161
Alexander I Balas	150–146	162–166
Demetrius II Nicator	145–141	167–171

ARSACID (PARTHIAN) PERIOD:

Arsaces Mithridates I	141–138/7	171–174/5
Arsaces Phraates II and Rinnu	138/7–131/0	174/5–181/2
Antiochus VII Euergetes (Sidetes)	129	183
Arsaces and Ubulna[…]	128/7	184
Hyspaosines, king of Characene	127	185
Arsaces Artabanus I	127–124/3	185–188
Arsaces Mithridates II	124/3–88/7	188–224

INDEX

SOURCES

CLASSICAL AUTHORS

CUNEIFORM TEXTS

PERSONAL NAMES

PLACE NAMES

TABLET PHOTOGRAPHS

BM 34712 obverse (Text 1)

BM 34712 reverse (Text 1)

PLATE III

BM 36847 (Text 2)

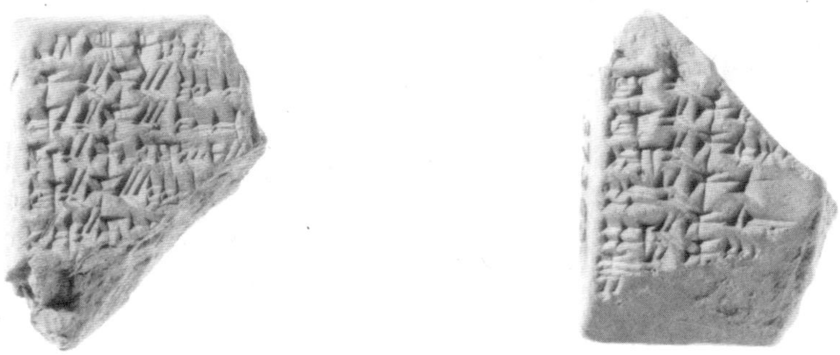

BM 37353 (Text 2)

PLATE IV

BM 32937b (Text 3)

BM 95313 (Text 3A)

BM 36730 (Text 4)

BM 35089 obverse (Text 5)

BM 45724 obverse (Text 5)

BM 34073 + BM 35123 obverse (Text 6)

BM 34073 + BM 35123 reverse (Text 6)

PLATE IX

BM 34598 (Text 7)

BM 33479 + BM 33639 (Text 8)

BM 34686 + BM 35604 obverse (Text 9)

BM 34686 + BM 35604 reverse (Text 9)

PLATE XII

BM 55535 (Text 10)

BM 35710 (Text 11)

BM 33023+BM 33027 (Text 12)

BM 46161 with lower edge (Text 12)

PLATE XV

BM 36960 (Text 13)

BM 36989 (Text 14)

BM 37034 (Text 15)

PLATE XVI

BM 37054 + BM 40100 (Text 16)

BM 46138 (Text 17)